Conversations with Ogotemmêli

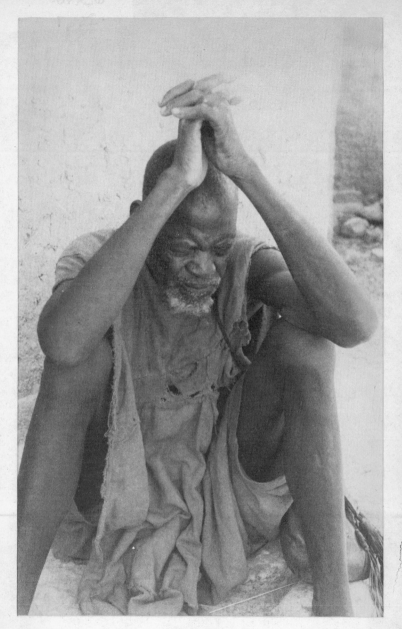

Ogotemmêli

Conversations with Ogotemmêli

AN INTRODUCTION TO DOGON RELIGIOUS IDEAS

by

MARCEL GRIAULE

with an introduction by
GERMAINE DIETERLEN

Published for the
International African Institute
by the
OXFORD UNIVERSITY PRESS
London   Oxford   New York

OXFORD UNIVERSITY PRESS

London   Oxford   New York
Glasgow   Toronto   Melbourne   Wellington
Cape Town   Ibadan   Nairobi   Dar es Salaam   Lusaka   Addis Ababa
Delhi   Bombay   Calcutta   Madras   Karachi   Lahore   Dacca
Kuala Lumpur   Singapore   Hong Kong   Tokyo

gift of Robert N. Minor

Dogon -- African people -- Religion

Nommo -- African deity

© International African Institute 1965
First published by Oxford University Press, London, 1965
First issued as an Oxford University Press paperback, 1970
This printing, 1975
Printed in the United States of America

FOREWORD

In 1948 Marcel Griaule published under the title *Dieu d'Eau: entretiens avec Ogotemmêli* a short book on Dogon religion. Written in an informal style and including no apparatus of scholarship—for it was intended to reach a general audience and to make the character and significance of Dogon religious life more widely known—this book marked a new stage in the intensive studies of Griaule and his colleagues among this people, since it attempted to provide a comprehensive outline of Dogon cosmology as he had recently come to understand it. It was suggested to Professor Griaule that an English translation should be published but he was himself more preoccupied with carrying his Dogon studies further, and indeed subsequent research by himself and his colleagues has greatly elaborated the documentation and in some respects modified interpretations.

Following his deeply regretted death in 1956 the Council of the Institute gave some consideration to the possibility of publishing an English version of some of Professor Griaule's studies. It accordingly welcomed an offer from Professor Robert Redfield, on behalf of the Centre for the Comparative Study of Religion of the University of Chicago, of a grant towards the cost of preparing an English translation of *Dieu d'Eau*. It has not proved easy to obtain such a translation, but we hope that this version will be of value in conveying the personal qualities of Professor Griaule's text and something of the spirit of the original. Our thanks are due to Mr. Ralph Butler who prepared a first version, and to Dr. Audrey I. Richards and Mrs. Beatrice Hooke who undertook its revision.

DARYLL FORDE

CONTENTS

FIGURES

PLATES

INTRODUCTION

PROFESSOR Marcel Griaule directed ethnographic field studies
in Africa for over a quarter of a century. The first took him to
Abyssinia in 1928 and 1929 and was followed by a two-year
mission which traversed the continent from West to East, from
Dakar to Djibouti, 1931–1933. This expedition assembled a
very considerable documentation and enriched the Musée de
l'Homme with collections of several thousand objects. It also
laid the foundations for intensive studies which were to be
carried out later in several areas along its route. From 1935 to
1939 three expeditions followed up these studies, notably in
Mali, Cameroun and Chad. After the interruption of the war,
annual expeditions and sometimes visits twice a year were made
from 1946 to 1956, and were devoted to intensive studies among
the peoples along or close to the Upper Niger in present-day
Mali.[1]

Marcel Griaule participated personally in all these expeditions until January 1956, less than two months before his
deeply regretted death from the malady from which he had
suffered since 1951. In the course of them he took with him a
large number of collaborators trained in his methods and
animated by the enthusiasm and energy which he devoted to his
researches. Many of these colleagues continued studies during
the same period in other areas which he had prospected and so
widened the field of enquiry.

No attempt can be made here to list all the topics and questions with which these expeditions have dealt. Almost all aspects
of human activity have been studied and the members of the

[1] These expeditions were subsidized and sponsored by many official scientific
organizations (institutes, learned societies, foundations, committees), by the
Muséum d'Histoire Naturelle and the Musée de l'Homme, the Centre National
de la Recherche Scientifique, the Ministries of Education, Air and French Overseas Territories, by the Governments of the Overseas Territories, and by private
sources.

field groups have worked variously as ethnographers, linguists, historians of religion, students of art, and archaeologists. They have also advanced the ethnobotany and ethnozoology of the areas studied. Modern techniques have been fully utilized, such as tape recording, cinema and aerial photography, of which extensive use was made. Finally, the Centre National de la Recherche Scientifique of France sponsored the construction and equipping of a laboratory vessel, for which Marcel Griaule had conceived the plans, and placed it under his direction as a base for field studies along the Niger. This boat, which includes living quarters, laboratories and storage space, has been in service since 1955 on the Niger, and provided a mobile base for the continuous study of its populations.

A simple scanning of the publications of Marcel Griaule, which exceed 170 in number, makes clear the range of his studies with regard to both subjects and regions.[2] In them he has recorded original observations, some of which were initial discoveries, concerning social organization, technology, religion, art, games, medicine, and pharmacopoeia relating to many African societies. This rich variety, due in large part to his methods of work, was apparent in his teaching at the Sorbonne.[3] To his personal publications one must also add the considerable number by his collaborators, who took part in the many expeditions.

All this work has brought to the attention of scholars, through the discovery and formulation of its foundations, the full recognition of the remarkable development in all aspects, save only in the technical field, of civilization among African peoples. A consideration of African art, to which Marcel Griaule himself contributed much—an art which has moved and aroused reflections in European peoples, and has also considerably influenced European art—has demonstrated the vigour of African cultures. We are however far from under-

[2] A full list of the works and articles published by Marcel Griaule appeared in Vol. XXVI (1956) of the *Journal de la Société des Africanistes*.
[3] *Méthode de l'ethnographie*, edited by Marcel Griaule, was published by the Presses Universitaires de France in 1957. See also: M. Griaule: 'Introduction méthodologique', *Minotaure*, No. 2, 1933, pp. 7–12; Application de l'aviation à la recherche scientifique', 2nd *Congrès National de l'Aviation Française*, No. 41 bis, 1940, p. 11; 'L'enquête orale en ethnologie', *Revue philosophique*, oct.–déc., 1952, pp. 537–553.

standing all its developments; many years of further patient study will be needed to estimate its range more fully.

It is here that Marcel Griaule's methods of study, due in large measure to his personal temperament and his warm humanity, played so great a part. It was a method that he applied instinctively from the beginning and then developed more systematically during the long period of his field studies. He combined with the most rigorous pursuit of objective and scientific observation of the facts observed, an active participation in the life of the peoples studied, participation which required a prudence that was continually on the alert and the fullest cross-checking of information and impressions in both space and time. While like others he made collections of objects and reported observed facts, he also made the fullest use of discussions and of the analysis of activities conjointly with those who were using the various objects and with the actors in the rituals. The long period of his studies, and the amount of time passed in the field have also been dominant factors, and the persistence with which he returned to the same places (the Dogon studies were undertaken during successive expeditions from 1931 onwards and the Bambara since 1946) are evidence of this.[4]

It became clear in the course of this work that African peoples had, like others, reflected on their own customs, that these customs stemmed from norms which were proper to themselves but which were nevertheless fundamental standards which it was indispensable for the ethnographer to understand. Enquiry, enriched by such an approach, was at the same time complicated by it, for it was by no means easy for minds attached to occidental logic to penetrate systems of thought such as these in which analogies and the power of symbols have the value of facts. Thus for example African techniques, so poor in appearance, like those of agriculture, weaving and smithing, have a rich, hidden content of significance. Religious gestures, whether spectacular or secret, and generally uncomprehended by outsiders, show themselves under analysis to be of an

[4] The funeral of Marcel Griaule was celebrated with full Dogon funeral rites at Sanga on April 7 and May 8, 1956. The Dogon showed in this way the respect, affection and gratitude they felt towards him for his attitude and his acts during all the time he had lived among them.

extreme subtlety in their implications. The smallest everyday object may reveal in its form or decoration a conscious reflection of a complex cosmogony. The observer needs not only finesse but also infinite patience. But the reward for such effort is that these forms and gestures become intelligible and perfectly clear expressions. Thus a checkered coverlet is a text in which the woven designs constitute signs expressed by its makers and known to initiates. A basket for carrying in the harvest represents when upturned the rainbow on which humanity descends from the sky to the earth. Its square base connotes space and the cardinal points. The paintings successively made at different periods of the year on a totemic, sanctuary with materials derived from different cereals are at the same time a writing and form of numeration. The sacrifice of a humble chicken, when accompanied by the necessary and effective ritual gestures, recalls in the thinking of those who have experienced it an understanding that is at once original and coherent of the origins and functioning of the universe.

The Africans with whom we have worked in the region of the Upper Niger have systems of signs which run into thousands, their own systems of astronomy and calendrical measurements, methods of calculation and extensive anatomical and physiological knowledge, as well as a systematic pharmacopœia. The principles underlying their social organization find expression in classifications which embrace many manifestations of nature. And these form a system in which, to take examples, plants, insects, textiles, games and rites are distributed in categories that can be further divided, numerically expressed and related one to another. It is on these same principles that the political and religious authority of chiefs, the family system and juridical rights, reflected notably in kinship and marriages, have been established. Indeed, all the activities of the daily lives of individuals are ultimately based on them.

In African societies which have preserved their traditional organization the number of persons who are trained in this knowledge is quite considerable.[5] This they call 'deep know-

[5] Cf. M. Griaule 'Le savoir des Dogon', *Journal de la Société des Africanistes*, Vol. XXII (1952), pp. 27–42. The author records the different degrees of teaching of this knowledge among the Dogon and gives a figure for the number of initiates of both sexes in the double village of Ogol.

ledge' in contrast with 'simple knowledge' which is regarded as 'only a beginning in the understanding of beliefs and customs' that people who are not fully instructed in the cosmogony possess.[6] There are various reasons for the silence that is generally observed on this subject. To a natural reserve before strangers who, even when sympathetic, remain unconsciously imbued with a feeling of superiority, one must add the present situation of rapid change in African societies through contact with mechanization and the influence of school teaching. But among groups where tradition is still vigorous, this knowledge, which is expressly characterized as esoteric, is only secret in the following sense. It is in fact open to all who show a will to understand so long as, by their social position and moral conduct, they are judged worthy of it. Thus every family head, every priest, every grown-up person responsible for some small fraction of social life can, as part of the social group, acquire knowledge on condition that he has the patience and, as the African phrase has it, 'he comes to sit by the side of the competent elders' over the period and in the state of mind necessary. Then he will receive answers to all his questions, but it will take years. Instruction begun in childhood during assemblies and rituals of the age-sets continues in fact throughout life.

These various aspects of African civilization gradually became clear in the course of intensive studies undertaken among several of the peoples of Mali and Upper Volta over more than a decade. In the case of the Dogon, concerning whom there have already been numerous publications,[7] these studies have made possible the elaboration of a synthesis covering the greater part of their activities.

We should now record the important occurrence during the field expedition of 1947 which led to the writing of this particular study. From 1931 the Dogon had answered questions and commented on observations made during previous field trips on the basis of the interpretation of facts which they call 'la parole de face'; this is the 'simple knowledge' which they give

[6] Cf. G. Dieterlen: *Essai sur la religion bambara*, Paris, Presses Universitaires de France, 1950, p. xvii, note 1.

[7] The writings of Marcel Griaule and his colleagues published before 1946 are concerned with 'simple knowledge'. Cf. 'La savoir des Dogon', p. 27, n. 2.

in the first instance to all enquirers. Publications of information obtained before the studies in 1948 relate to this first level of interpretation.[8]

But the Dogon came to recognize the great perseverance of Marcel Griaule and his team in their enquiries, and that it was becoming increasingly difficult to answer the multiplicity of questions without moving on to a different level. They appreciated our eagerness for an understanding which earlier explanations had certainly not satisfied, and which was clearly more important to us than anything else. Griaule had also shown a constant interest in the daily life of the Dogon, appreciating their efforts to exploit a difficult country where there was a serious lack of water in the dry season, and our relationships, which had thus extended beyond those of ethnographical enquiry, became more and more trusting and affectionate. In the light of all this the Dogon took their own decision, of which we learned only later when they told us themselves. The elders of the lineages of the double village of Ogol and the most important totemic priests of the region of Sanga met together and decided that the more esoteric aspects of their religion should be fully revealed to Professor Griaule. To begin this they chose one of their own best informed members, Ogotemmêli who, as will be seen in the introduction, arranged the first interview. This first exposition lasted exactly the number of days recorded in *Dieu d'Eau*, in which the meandering flow of information is faithfully reported. Although we knew nothing of it at the time, the progress of this instruction by Ogotemmêli was being reported on daily to the council of elders and priests.

The seriousness and importance of providing this exposé of Dogon belief was all the greater because the Dogon elders knew perfectly well that in doing so they were opening the door, not merely to these thirty days of information, but to later and more intensive work which was to extend over months and years. They never withdrew from this decision, and we should like to express here our grateful thanks to them. After Ogotemmêli's death, others carried on the work. And since Professor Griaule's death they have continued with the same patience and eagerness to complete the task they had undertaken. These later

[8] M. Griaule, 'Le savoir des Dogon', p. 27; *ibid*, p. 2.

enquiries have made possible the publication of the many further studies cited in the bibliography and the preparation of a detailed treatise entitled *Le Renard Pâle*, the first part of which is now in the press. And in 1963, as this is written, the investigation still continues.

G. DIETERLEN

PREFACE

IN one of the most remarkable mountain areas in Africa lives a population of peasant-warriors who were one of the last peoples to lose their independence and come under French rule. Many Europeans have regarded the Dogon as savages, if not the most backward race in the whole region. They have been thought to practise human sacrifice and to offer resistance to outside influence all the more effectively because of the natural difficulties of the country they inhabit. Writers have described their fears when embarking on what were thought to be rash expeditions. In the light of these stories, and on account of suspected revolts, often the result of misunderstandings, whole villages have sometimes been laid under an interdict.

The Dogon, in short, were thought to present one of the best examples of primitive savagery, and this view has been shared by some Muslim Africans, who are no better equipped intellectually than Europeans to understand those of their brothers who cling to the traditions of their ancestors. Only those officials who have undertaken the hard task of governing these people have learnt to love them.

The author of this book and his numerous fellow-workers have been associated with the Dogon for some fifteen years, and through their published works these people are today the best-known tribe in the whole of the Western Sudan. *Les Ames des Dogon*, by G. Dieterlen (1941), *Les Devises*, by S. de Ganay (1941), and *Les Masques*, by M. Griaule (1938), have furnished scholars with proof that the life of these Africans was based on complicated but orderly conceptions and on institutional and ritual systems in which there was nothing haphazard or fantastic. Ten years ago these works had already drawn attention to new facts concerning the 'vital force', about which sociologists have been telling us for half a century past. They have shown the primary importance of the notion of the person and his relations with society, with the universe, and with the divine.

Thus Dogon ontology has opened new vistas for ethnologists and placed the problem on a broader basis.

More recently, too, in his notable book *La Philosophie bantoue* (1945) the Rev. Fr. Tempels presented an analysis of conceptions of this kind, and raised the question of whether 'Bantu thought should not be regarded as a system of philosophy'.

As a result of patient and methodical research, pursued for fifteen years from the time when the first steps were taken in the rocky cliffs of Bandiagara, this question can now be answered, so far as the Dogon are concerned: for these people live by a cosmogony, a metaphysic, and a religion which put them on a par with the peoples of antiquity, and which Christian theology might indeed study with profit.

The teaching on these subjects was imparted to the author by a venerable individual, Ogotemmêli, of Lower Ogol. This man, a hunter who had lost his sight by an accident, was able, as a result of his infirmity, to devote long and careful study to these things. Endowed with exceptional intelligence, a physical capacity which was still apparent in spite of his affliction, and a wisdom, the fame of which has spread throughout his country, he had quickly appreciated the interest attaching to the ethnological work of the Europeans, and had been waiting fifteen years for an opportunity to impart his knowledge to them. He was anxious, no doubt, that they should be acquainted with the most important institutions, customs, and rituals of his own people.

In October 1946 he summoned the author to his house, and on thirty-three successive days, in a series of unforgettable conversations, he laid bare the framework of a world system, the knowledge of which will revolutionize all accepted ideas about the mentality of Africans and of primitive peoples in general.

It might be thought that we are here concerned with esoteric teaching; some have even suggested, on a first impression, without waiting for further details, that it was a case of personal speculations of merely secondary interest. These are, moreover, the very people who will devote a lifetime to the presumably personal ideas of Plato or Julian of Halicarnassus.

But although the full range of this teaching is known only to the elders and to certain initiates, it is not esoteric in character, since anyone who reaches old age can acquire it. Moreover, totemic priests of all ages are acquainted with those parts of the doctrine which specially concern them, while the ritual observances attaching to this corpus of beliefs are practised by the whole people.

Obviously the ordinary people do not apprehend the profounder significance of their actions and their prayers; but this is true of all peoples. The Christian dogma of Transubstantiation cannot be called esoteric merely because the man in the street is ignorant of the word and has only vague ideas as to its meaning.

Similar reservations might be made as to the explanatory and representative value of these doctrines and their bearing on African mentality in general. It might be maintained, for example, that what is true of the Dogon is not true of the other peoples of the Western Sudan.

To that contention the author and his colleagues have a convincing reply: the thought of the Bambara is based on an equally systematic and equally rich metaphysic, the fundamental principles of which are comparable to those of the Dogon. The works of Madame G. Dieterlen and Madame de Ganay present evidence that this is so. The same is true of the Bozo fishermen of the Niger, of the Kouroumba farmers of the Niger bend, and of the mysterious iron-workers of these same regions, on which research is only just beginning.

We are not concerned, therefore, in the present instance, with a single unusual system of thought, but rather with the first example of a series which will prove to be a long one.

In his work in this connection the author hopes to attain two objects: on the one hand to present to a non-specialist public, and without the usual scientific apparatus, a work which would customarily be addressed only to experts. On the other hand he is concerned to pay a tribute to the first African in French West Africa who has revealed to the European world a cosmogony as rich as that of Hesiod, poet of a dead world, and a metaphysic that has the advantage of being expressed in a thousand rites and actions in the life of a multitude of living people.

1947

The Ogols

THE sun had risen abruptly from the plain of the Gondo, and was shining down upon the roofs of Lower Ogol. The birds had ceased their song, leaving the sun to take the centre of the stage. In the courtyard of the caravanserai, typical of every camping place in the French Sudan, the last moments of peace were slipping away. Round a forgotten dish of food remaining from the previous day traces of asses' hooves marked the tracks of the night's visitors. Four neat heaps of dung, which might have served as specimens for the Mammals' department of a museum, had not yet at that hour become a centre of attraction for the dung-beetles.

A large sloping rock of pinkish-grey served as a low table in the service-yard in front of the cube-shaped building of cracked earth, which faced away from the rising sun and looked out from all its entrances on the Dolo valley. No mountain broke the view in any direction except to the east, where by going up to one of the roofs it was possible to discern the gentle slope of Ninu rising above the debris of Banani.

We were engulfed in a turbulent sea of sandstone, cleft by narrow sandy valleys and broken by wave-like ridges of rock which reflected the sunlight. The only shelter was provided by folds in the arid landscape, and faces and bodies were scoured by the sand with which the air was laden.

In the shadowy interior of the building, open to every wind since it was without doors or windows, the first stirrings of early morning activity were beginning. Four Europeans under mosquito-nets were exchanging the usual trivial remarks. In the courtyard, now bathed in a subdued pinkish-yellow light, a figure flooded with sunlight appeared between two pillars of the surrounding wall. He paused for a moment to contemplate the scene inside, still arranged for the night. He saw the bowl and

5

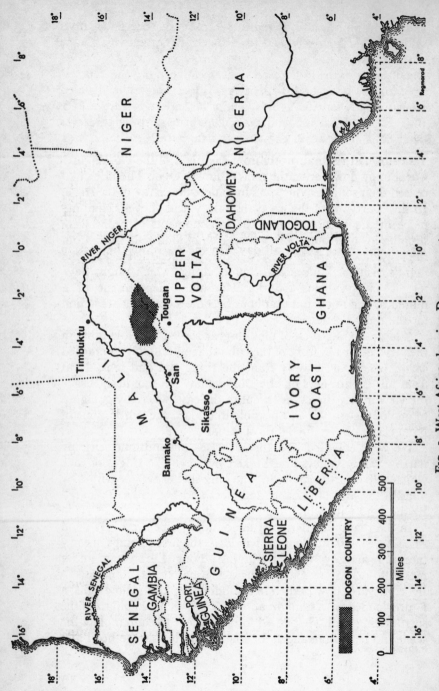

Fig. 1. West Africa showing Dogon country

the ass-droppings and, fallen in the dust, the barrier of mats which should have screened the kitchen. Eventually his glance came to rest on the window of the store-room, and he noticed the disorder of the millet stalks put up to keep out the cats.

Mênyu was a gentle African of Upper Ogol, the devoted servant of the four foreigners, whom he had known for a long time. He stifled an oath and, waving his arms in the wide sleeves of his long white coat, advanced to deal with these calamities.

The action of the day began to take shape. Apurali, the steward, had already exchanged interminable greetings with his colleague. Other Dogon made their appearance, filling the courtyard; woman with their children on their backs needing eye-treatment; a girl with a skull injury; naked babies with bulging stomachs settled themselves to watch the spectacle which was going to last all day. On the walls, on the rock in the centre, on the steps of the house, informants and inter-preters waited in groups till their names were called. The scene was a repetition of what had happened the day before and the day before that, and every day for fifteen years past whenever white men visited the southern ridge of Upper Ogol.

In a corner of the verandah a European was continuing an enquiry, begun the day before, into a mysterious sacrifice which had taken place in a cleft in the Gorge of I. On the pre-vious day he had penetrated into the caves and funnels in the sandstone and, descending by ledges in the rocks, had come to some ruins where the scent of wild animals and bats was strong. An elderly Dogon was giving scraps of information in reply to his questions, reluctantly surrendering the bare bones of the truth, now going back on what he had said before, now proffer-ing lies, smiling or abashed, but resolutely clinging to his mysteries. His brown Phrygian cap hung down over one ear, covering his dark face with its only slightly thick lips, his thin nose and eyes without lashes.

In the north gallery actions were more animated. A young European woman was conducting a choir of four Dogon belonging to different groups, each speaking a dialect of its own; since each possessed a rich vocabulary and a great number of verbs of action, the four speakers soon' became impassioned actors, miming the attitudes they were expressing and shouting examples.

7

The north room was more like a confessional; priests of the cult of the ancestors were speaking in lowered voices to a European woman who was at once patient and persistent.

In the south gallery another white woman was writing down the text of prayers to Komo at the dictation of a bright-eyed Bambara.

'Komo! Killer of fat dead!'

'Shroud of the living!'

All four points of the compass therefore were full of the usual daily sequence of rumour, short-lived outbursts, and slackening of tension.

But now a novelty was approaching in the person of Gana, son of the Hogon, the oldest man, and consequently the religious chief, of Ogol. He was coming towards the building along the embankment a bare handsbreadth wide between two fields of high millet. Between his lips he had a chewing-stick, which he took in his hand when he wished to greet his acquaintances. His baggy breeches and full tunic introduced a touch of brown colour among the cornstalks.

On reaching the rocky slope of Upper Ogol, he proceeded to climb it, following the track worn smooth by thousands of feet. He saluted the building from the outside before entering the courtyard. There he came up to the European and smiled; his ears seemed to draw closer to each other on either side of his narrow skull.

'A hunter wishes to see you.'

'Is he sick?'

When an African asks to see a European, it is usually because he is sick; otherwise he is not particularly interested in meeting a white man.

'No! He wishes to sell you an amulet.'

'What amulet?'

'The amulet you ordered ten years ago in return for the bullets.'

'I have no recollection of that.'

The European bit his lip, realizing suddenly the unusual character of this request. 'Good!' he said and, continuing his conversation with the man who had offered the sacrifice, sent Gana to fetch the amulet.

The latter with his chewing-stick in his mouth made his way

8

back along the path he had come by, leaping down the rocks of Upper Ogol and crossing through the millet, till he was lost to view in the tangle of houses in Lower Ogol. Here he entered a courtyard, and said something in a low voice in front of an open door. A thin hand emerged from the shadows within to hand him a trapeze-shaped piece of leather covered with dried blood.

Gana made his way back along the same path, and appeared before the European.

'And the formula?' said the white man. 'Have you got that?'

'What formula?'

'The formula for its manufacture and use. Go and get it!'

'I know it,' said the man who had offered the sacrifice, speaking when Gana's back was turned, and proceeded at once to repeat it to the European, who wrote it down.

The seventeen-year-old Gana knew well enough what to make of these concerns of his elders and betters. Once again he leapt down the rocks of Upper Ogol, but this time he remained standing stiffly on the track, and with a quick movement took his chewing-stick from his mouth : he had got a thorn in his foot. Then he proceeded on his way limping, and again sought out the courtyard in the labyrinth of narrow streets. Sitting down on the threshold of the African's house he spoke at length, while he removed a splinter from his toe. A slow voice answered him, to which he listened respectfully. Then with a slight sigh he returned to the white man, whom he now found alone on the verandah. To him, after removing his chewing-stick, he repeated the formula, forgetting three verses, which his interlocutor promptly read out to him from his notes. Gana's jaw dropped for a moment in astonishment.

'But who is this old hunter?' the white man asked.

He did not understand. He thought that the European wanted to know the man's device.

'*Vizê!*' he said. '*Vizê karandiang!*'

Which means : 'A man to keep away from! A terrible man!'

9

Ogotemmêli

Lower Ogol, like all Dogon villages, was a collection of houses and granaries all crowded together, flat roofs of clay alternating with cone-shaped roofs of straw. Picking one's way along its narrow streets of light and shade, between the truncated pyramids, prisms, cubes or cylinders of the granaries and houses, the rectangular porticoes, the red or white altars shaped like umbilical hernias, one felt like a dwarf lost in a maze. Everything was mottled by the rains and the heat; the mud-walls were fissured like the skins of pachyderms. Over the walls of the tiny courtyards might be seen, under the floors of the granaries, fowls, yellow dogs, and sometimes great tortoises, symbols of the patriarchs.

At a turn of the street there was a door, shaped with an axe, but, even when new, it could never have fitted the entrance built of earthen pillars with a pediment of wooden blocks. The door was as wide as a man's two shoulders; winter rains had ploughed wave-like furrows in the wood between which the knots looked like open eyes. Drought, clutching hands, and the muzzles of goats had worn it away so that it grated on its hinges and swung back against the wall with a bang like a gong, revealing a squalid courtyard, which belonged to the most remarkable man of the plains and rocks from Oropa to Nimbé, Asakarba and Tintam.

The white man stepped over the scanty midden of an old man with no family. A row of cabins, broken by a low door on the ground floor and a flat panel on the floor above, stood in the middle of the courtyard forming a façade which concealed the main building behind it. In the pediment were ten swallows' nests, and the edge of the roof was adorned by eight cones with flat stone tops. To right and left were six granaries in a row like big dice, two of them facing the neighbouring

11

house, to which they belonged. Of the other four one was empty, another rickety, and the third split across like a half-bitten fruit. Only one of them was in use: it was half full of grain.

Opposite, between the main building and the granaries, a low house, in which there were faint sounds of life, completed the enclosure of the courtyard. On the right in a store-room open to the sky there was a perpetual whirl of down blown about by a light breeze.

The man accompanying the European pronounced the usual words of greeting. Immediately a voice replied clearly and distinctly:

'God brings you! God brings you!'

'Greetings! How is your health?'

Slowly the voice drew nearer. From the shadows of the interior came the sound of hands feeling their way along walls and woodwork. A stick tapped on the floor: there was a sound of hollow earthenware: some tiny chickens made their way out one by one through the cat-hole, thrust out by the great being who was approaching.

At last there appeared a brown tunic, drawn in at the seams and frayed by long use like the standards of the warriors of old. Then a head bent beneath the lintel of the door, and the man stood up to his full height, turning towards the stranger a face that no words can describe.

'Greetings!' he said, 'Greetings to those who are athirst!'

The thick lips spoke the purest Sanga language. So alive were they that one saw nothing else. All the other features seemed to be folded away, particularly as, after the first words, the head had been bent. The cheeks, the cheek-bones, the forehead and the eyelids seemed all to have suffered the same ravages; they were creased by a hundred wrinkles which had caused a painful contortion as of a face exposed to too strong a light or battered by a hail of stones. The eyes were dead.

The two visitors came from outside, and might therefore be supposed to have been working in the heat. Accordingly the old man leaning on his stick greeted them with the words:

'Welcome! Welcome after weariness! Welcome from the sun!'

The longest task of the first day was the choice of a place for the conversations. The space in front of the dwelling-house, even if the aged Ogotemmêli remained indoors, and even if the white man bent his head towards him and spoke in low tones as if in the confessional, was, according to Ogotemmêli, open to the objection that interviews there might excite the eternal curiosity of the women. The minute courtyard on the other side of the building, on the other hand, which was exposed to all the winds from the north, might be watched by children hidden in the ruined granary. There remained the courtyard itself with its wretched dung-heap, its hollow stone, its ashes and its dilapidated wall with a gap in the middle of it just high enough for curious eyes to look through.

Ogotemmêli still hesitated; he had much to say about the inconvenience of the courtyard for the purpose of conversations between men of mature years. The European for his part did not open his mouth except to agree; he even stressed the indiscreet nature of walls and the stupidity of men and, naturally, the unconscionable curiosity of women and their insatiable thirst for novelties. All these precautions interested him: they seemed so out of proportion to the simple sale of an amulet.

In the end Ogotemmêli sat down on the threshold of the lower door of the main façade; doubled up, with his face bent downwards and his hands crossed above his head, his elbows resting on his knees, he waited.

The white man was beginning to realize that the sale of the amulet was only a pretext. There was no reference to it in the subsequent conversations, and the underlying reason for the old man's action never transpired. But from various details it appeared, as time went on, that Ogotemmêli wished to pass on to the foreigner, who had first visited the country fifteen years before, and whom he trusted, the instruction which he himself had received first from his grandfather and later from his father.

But he was waiting. He was perplexed by the result of his own approaches to this man whom he could not see. Not that the man was unknown to him: for fifteen years he had been hearing about groups of Europeans, who came, under this man's guidance, to live rough and to ride about the country studying the customs of the people.

He had even followed their work since the beginning, for he had been closely associated with Ambîbê Babadyé, the great dignitary of the masks and the white men's regular informant, who had only recently died. Many times in the last fifteen years Ambibê had come to Ogotemmêli for information and advice. From what Ambibê had told him, and from the reports of a number of other persons, he had formed a correct idea of the aims and objects of his interlocutor and his unwearying passion for research.

But the situation was unique. How was one to instruct a European? How could one make him understand things and rites and beliefs? Moreover this white man had already found out about the masks, and knew their secret language. He had been all over the country in every direction, and about some of its institutions he knew as much as he knew himself. How then to set about it?

The European relieved him of his embarrassment.

'When your gun exploded in your face, what were you firing at?'

'At a porcupine.'

The white man was trying by an indirect approach to lead the conversation to hunting and the attitude towards the animal world, and so to totemism.

'It was an accident,' said the old man. 'But it was also a last warning. I knew by divination that I was to give up hunting if I wanted to protect my children. Hunting is a work of death, and it attracts death. I have had twenty-one children, and now only five are left.'

All the tragedy of African mortality was in his words, and all the deep questionings of these men about death and their defencelessness in the face of it. They clung to their beliefs, as do all men everywhere, but though beliefs may console and explain, they cannot avert the experience.

It was on this plane of suffering that Ogotemmêli's personality was revealed, in itself and in its relation with supernatural powers. From the age of fifteen he had been initiated in the mysteries of religion by his grandfather. After the latter's death his father had continued the instruction. It seemed that the 'lessons' had gone on for more than twenty years, and that Ogotemmêli's family was not one that took these things lightly.

Ogotemmêli himself, no doubt, had from a very early age shown signs of an eager mind and considerable shrewdness.

Until he lost his sight, he was a mighty hunter who, though one-eyed from childhood as a result of smallpox, would always come back from the chase with a full bag, while the others were still toiling in the gorges. His skill as a hunter was the fruit of his profound knowledge of nature, of animals, of men and of gods. After his accident he learnt still more. Thrown back on his own resources, on his altars and on whatever he was able to hear, he had become one of the most powerful minds on the cliffs.

Indeed his name and his character were famous throughout the plateau and the hills, known (as the saying was) to the youngest boy. People came to his door for advice every day and even by night.

Phrygian caps were even now showing above the walls, and the women were making signs from a distance. It was time to go, and make room for the clients. But contact had now been made, and the conversations thereafter came about by tacit consent, according to a sort of programme and at convenient times.

The First Word
and the Fibre Skirt

OGOTEMMÊLI, seating himself on his threshold, scraped his stiff leather snuff-box, and put a pinch of yellow powder on his tongue.

'Tobacco,' he said, 'makes for right thinking.'

So saying, he set to work to analyse the world system, for it was essential to begin with the dawn of all things. He rejected as a detail of no interest, the popular account of how the fourteen solar systems were formed from flat circular slabs of earth one on top of the other. He was only prepared to speak of the serviceable solar system; he agreed to consider the stars, though they only played a secondary part.

'It is quite true,' he said, 'that in course of time women took down the stars to give them to their children. The children put spindles through them and made then spin like fiery tops to show themselves how the world turned. But that was only a game.'

The stars came from pellets of earth flung out into space by the God Amma, the one God. He had created the sun and the moon by a more complicated process, which was not the first known to man but is the first attested invention of God: the art of pottery. The sun is, in a sense, a pot raised once for all to white heat and surrounded by a spiral of red copper with eight turns. The moon is the same shape, but its copper is white. It was heated only one quarter at a time. Ogotemmêli said he would explain later the movements of these bodies. For the moment he was concerned only to indicate the main lines of the design, and from that to pass to its actors.

He was anxious, however, to give an idea of the size of the sun.

'Some,' he said, 'think it is as large as this encampment, which would mean thirty cubits. But it is really bigger. Its surface area is bigger than the whole of Sanga Canton.'

And after some hesitation he added:

'It is perhaps even bigger than that.'

He refused to linger over the dimensions of the moon, nor did he ever say anything about them. The moon's function was not important, and he would speak of it later. He said however that, while Africans were creatures of light emanating from the fullness of the sun, Europeans were creatures of the moonlight: hence their immature appearance.

He spat out his tobacco as he spoke. Ogotemmêli had nothing against Europeans. He was not even sorry for them. He left them to their destiny in the lands of the north.

The God Amma, it appeared, took a lump of clay, squeezed it in his hand and flung it from him, as he had done with the stars. The clay spread and fell on the north, which is the top, and from there stretched out to the south, which is the bottom, of the world, although the whole movement was horizontal. The earth lies flat, but the north is at the top. It extends east and west with separate members like a foetus in the womb. It is a body, that is to say, a thing with members branching out from a central mass. This body, lying flat, face upwards, in a line from north to south, is feminine. Its sexual organ is an ant-hill, and its clitoris a termite hill. Amma, being lonely and desirous of intercourse with this creature, approached it. That was the occasion of the first breach of the order of the universe.

Ogotemmêli ceased speaking. His hands crossed above his head, he sought to distinguish the different sounds coming from the courtyards and roofs. He had reached the point of the origin of troubles and of the primordial blunder of God.

'If they overheard me, I should be fined an ox!'

At God's approach the termite hill rose up, barring the passage and displaying its masculinity. It was as strong as the organ of the stranger, and intercourse could not take place. But God is all-powerful. He cut down the termite hill, and had intercourse with the excised earth. But the original incident was destined to affect the course of things for ever; from this defective union there was born, instead of the intended twins, a single being, the *Thos aureus* or jackal, symbol of the difficulties of God.

Ogotemmêli's voice sank lower and lower. It was no longer a question of women's ears listening to what he was saying; other, non-material, ear-drums might vibrate to his important discourse. The European and his African assistant, Sergeant Koguem, were leaning towards the old man as if hatching plots of the most alarming nature.

But, when he came to the beneficent acts of God, Ogotemmêli's voice again assumed its normal tone.

God had further intercourse with his earth-wife, and this time without mishaps of any kind, the excision of the offending member having removed the cause of the former disorder. Water, which is the divine seed, was thus able to enter the womb of the earth and the normal reproductive cycle resulted in the birth of twins. Two beings were thus formed. God created them like water. They were green in colour, half human beings and half serpents. From the head to the loins they were human: below that they were serpents. Their red eyes were wide open like human eyes, and their tongues were forked like the tongues of reptiles. Their arms were flexible and without joints. Their bodies were green and sleek all over, shining like the surface of water, and covered with short green hairs, a presage of vegetation and germination.

These spirits, called Nummo, were thus two homogeneous products of God, of divine essence like himself, conceived without untoward incidents and developed normally in the womb of the earth. Their destiny took them to Heaven, where they received the instructions of their father. Not that God had to teach them speech, that indispensable necessity of all beings, as it is of the world-system; the Pair were born perfect and complete; they had eight members, and their number was eight, which is the symbol of speech.

They were also of the essence of God, since they were made of his seed, which is at once the ground, the form, and the substance of the life-force of the world, from which derives the motion and the persistence of created being. This force is water, and the Pair are present in all water: they *are* water, the water of the seas, of coasts, of torrents, of storms, and of the spoonfuls we drink.

Ogotemmêli used the terms 'Water' and 'Nummo' indiscriminately.

'Without Nummo,' he said, 'it was not even possible to create the earth, for the earth was moulded clay and it is from water (that is, from Nummo) that its life is derived.'

'What life is there in the earth?' asked the European.

'The life-force of the earth is water. God moulded the earth with water. Blood too he made out of water. Even in a stone there is this force, for there is moisture in everything.

'But if Nummo is water, it also produces copper. When the sky is overcast, the sun's rays may be seen materializing on the misty horizon. These rays, excreted by the spirits, are of copper and are light. They are water too, because they uphold the earth's moisture as it rises. The Pair excrete light, because they are also light.'

While he was speaking, Ogotemmêli had been searching for something in the dust. He finally collected a number of small stones. With a rapid movement he flung them into the court-yard over the heads of his two interlocutors, who had no time to bend down. The stones fell just where the Hogon's cock had been crowing a few seconds before.

'That cock is a squalling nuisance. He makes all conversation impossible.'

The bird began to crow again on the other side of the wall, so Ogotemmêli sent Koguem to throw a bit of wood at him. When Koguem came back, he asked whether the cock was now outside the limits of the Tabda quarter.

'He is in the Hogon's field,' said Koguem. 'I have set four children to watch him.'

'Good!' said Ogotemmêli with a little laugh. 'Let him make the most of what remains to him of life! They tell me he is to be eaten at the next Feast of Twins.'

He returned to the subject of the Nummo spirits, or (as he more usually put it, in the singular) of Nummo, for this pair of twins, he explained, represented the perfect, the ideal unit.

The Nummo, looking down from Heaven, saw their mother, the earth, naked and speechless, as a consequence no doubt of the original incident in her relations with the God Amma. It was necessary to put an end to this state of disorder. The Nummo accordingly came down to earth, bringing with them fibres pulled from plants already created in the heavenly regions. They took ten bunches of these fibres, corresponding to

19

the number of their ten fingers, and made two strands of them, one for the front and one for behind. To this day masked men still wear these appendages hanging down to their feet in thick tendrils.

But the purpose of this garment was not merely modesty. It manifested on earth the first act in the ordering of the universe and the revelation of the helicoid sign in the form of an undulating broken line.

For the fibres fell in coils, symbol of tornadoes, of the windings of torrents, of eddies and whirlwinds, of the undulating movement of reptiles. They recall also the eight-fold spirals of the sun, which sucks up moisture. They were themselves a channel of moisture, impregnated as they were with the freshness of the celestial plants. They were full of the essence of Nummo: they *were* Nummo in motion, as shown in the undulating line, which can be prolonged to infinity.

When Nummo speaks, what comes from his mouth is a warm vapour which conveys, and itself constitutes, speech. This vapour, like all water, has sound, dies away in a helicoid line. The coiled fringes of the skirt were therefore the chosen vehicle for the words which the Spirit desired to reveal to the earth. He endued his hands with magic power by raising them to his lips while he plaited the skirt, so that the moisture of his words was imparted to the damp plaits, and the spiritual revelation was embodied in the technical instruction.

In these fibres full of water and words, placed over his mother's genitalia, Nummo is thus always present.

Thus clothed, the earth had a language, the first language of this world and the most primitive of all time. Its syntax was elementary, its verbs few, and its vocabulary without elegance. The words were breathed sounds scarcely differentiated from one another, but nevertheless vehicles. Such as it was, this ill-defined speech sufficed for the great works of the beginning of all things.

In the middle of a word Ogotemmêli gave a loud cry in answer to the hunter's halloo which the discreet Akundyo, priest of women dying in childbirth and of stillborn children, had called through the gap in the wall.

Akundyo first spat to one side, his eye riveted on the group of men. He was wearing a red Phrygian cap which covered his ears, with a raised point like a uraeus on the bridge of the nose in the fashion known as 'the wind blows'. His cheek-bones were prominent, and his teeth shone. He uttered a formal salutation to which the old man at once replied and the exchange of courtesies became more and more fulsome.

'God's curse,' exclaimed Ogotemmêli, 'on any in Lower Ogol who love you not!'

With growing emotion Akundyo made shift to out-do the vigour of the imprecation.

'May God's curse rest on me,' said the blind man at last, 'if I love you not!'

The four men breathed again. They exchanged humorous comments on the meagreness of the game in the I valley. Eventually Akundyo took his leave of them, asserting in the slangy French of a native soldier that he was going to 'look for porcupine', an animal much esteemed by these people.

The conversation reverted to the subject of speech. Its function was organization, and therefore it was good; nevertheless from the start it let loose disorder.

This was because the jackal, the deluded and deceitful son of God, desired to possess speech, and laid hands on the fibres in which language was embodied, that is to say, on his mother's skirt. His mother, the earth, resisted this incestuous action. She buried herself in her own womb, that is to say, in the anthill, disguised as an ant. But the jackal followed her. There was, it should be explained, no other woman in the world whom he could desire. The hole which the earth made in the anthill was never deep enough, and in the end she had to admit defeat. This prefigured the even-handed struggles between men and women, which, however, always end in the victory of the male.

The incestuous act was of great consequence. In the first place it endowed the jackal with the gift of speech so that ever afterwards he was able to reveal to diviners the designs of God.

It was also the cause of the flow of menstrual blood, which stained the fibres. The resulting defilement of the earth was incompatible with the reign of God. God rejected that spouse, and decided to create living beings directly. Modelling a womb in damp clay, he placed it on the earth and covered it with a pellet flung out into space from heaven. He made a male organ

21

in the same way and having put it on the ground, he flung out a sphere which stuck to it.

The two lumps forthwith took organic shape; their life began to develop. Members separated from the central core, bodies appeared, and a human pair arose out of the lumps of earth.

At this point the Nummo Pair appeared on the scene for the purpose of further action. The Nummo foresaw that the original rule of twin births was bound to disappear, and that errors might result comparable to those of the jackal, whose birth was single. For it was because of his solitary state that the first son of God acted as he did.

'The jackal was alone from birth,' said Ogotemmêli, 'and because of this he did more things than can be told.'

The Spirit drew two outlines on the ground, one on top of the other, one male and the other female. The man stretched himself out on these two shadows of himself, and took both of them for his own. The same thing was done for the woman. Thus it came about that each human being from the first was endowed with two souls of different sex, or rather with two principles corresponding to two distinct persons. In the man the female soul was located in the prepuce; in the woman the male soul was in the clitoris.

But the foreknowledge of the Nummo no doubt revealed to him the disadvantages of this makeshift. Man's life was not capable of supporting both beings: each person would have to merge himself in the sex for which he appeared to be best fitted.

The Nummo accordingly circumcised the man, thus removing from him all the femininity of his prepuce. The prepuce, however, changed itself into an animal which is 'neither a serpent nor an insect, but is classed with serpents'. This animal is called a *nay*. It is said to be a sort of lizard, black and white like the pall which covers the dead. Its name also means 'four', the female number, and 'Sun', which is a female being. The *nay* symbolized the pain of circumcision and the need for the man to suffer in his sex as the woman does.

The man then had intercourse with the woman, who later bore the first two children of a series of eight, who were to become the ancestors of the Dogon people. In the moment of birth the pain of parturition was concentrated in the woman's clitoris, which was excised by an invisible hand, detached itself and left her, and was changed into the form of a scorpion. The pouch and the sting symbolized the organ: the venom was the water and the blood of the pain.

The European, returning through the millet field, found himself wondering about the significance of all these actions and counteractions, all these sudden jerks in the thought of the myth.

Here, he reflected, is a Creator God spoiling his first creation; restoration is effected by the excision of the earth, and then by the birth of a pair of spirits, inventive beings who construct the world and bring to it the first spoken words; an incestuous act destroys the created order, and jeopardizes the principle of twin-births. Order is restored by the creation of a pair of human beings, and twin-births are replaced by dual souls. (But why, he asked himself, twin-births at all?)

The dual soul is a danger; a man should be male, and a woman female. Circumcision and excision are once again the remedy. (But why the *nay*? Why the scorpion?)

The answers to these questions were to come later, and to take their place in the massive structure of doctrine, which the blind old man was causing to emerge bit by bit from the mists of time.

Over the heads of the European and Koguem the dark millet clusters stood out against the leaden sky. They were passing through a field of heavy ears, stiffly erect and motionless in the breeze. When the crop is backward and thin, the ears are light and move with the slightest breath of wind. Thin crops are therefore full of sound. An abundant crop, on the other hand, is weighed down by the wind and bows itself in silence.

The Second Word
and Weaving

ANYONE entering the courtyard upset its arrangements. It was so cramped that the kites, most cunning of all the acrobats of the air, could not get at the poultry. In a hollow stone there were the remains, or rather, the dregs of some millet-beer, which the poultry, cock, hen and chickens, were glad to drink. So was a yellow and white striped dog with tail erect like an Ethiopian sabre. When the door banged, all these creatures dispersed, leaving the courtyard to the humans.

Ogotemmêli, ensconced in his doorway, proceeded to enumerate the eight original ancestors born of the couple created by God. The four eldest were males: the four others were females. But by a special dispensation, permitted only to them, they were able to fertilize themselves, being dual and bisexual. From them are descended the eight Dogon families.

For humanity was organizing itself in this makeshift condition. The permanent calamity of single births was slightly mitigated by the grant of the dual soul, which the Nummo traced on the ground beside women in childbirth. Dual souls were implanted in the new-born child by holding it by the thighs above the place of the drawings with its hands and feet touching the ground. Later the superfluous soul was eliminated by circumcision, and humanity limped towards its obscure destiny.

But the divine thirst for perfection was not extinguished, and the Nummo Pair, who were gradually taking the place of God their father, had in mind projects of redemption. But, in order to improve human conditions, reforms and instruction had to be carried out on the human level. The Nummo were afraid of the terrifying effect of contact between creatures of flesh and blood on the one hand and purely spiritual beings on the other. There had to be actions that could be understood, taking place within the ambit of the beneficiaries and in their own environment. Men after regeneration must be drawn towards the ideal as a peasant is drawn to rich farmland.

The Nummo accordingly came down to earth, and entered the anthill, that is to say, the sexual part of which they were themselves the issue. Thus, they were able, among other tasks, to defend their mother against possible attempts by their elder, the incestuous jackal. At the same time, by their moist, luminous, and articulate presence, they were purging that body which was for ever defiled in the sight of God, but was nevertheless capable of acquiring in some degree the purity required for the activities of life.

In the anthill the male Nummo took the place of the masculine element, which had been eliminated by the excision of the termite-hill clitoris, while the female Nummo took the place of the female element, and her womb became part of the womb of the earth.

The Pair could then proceed to the work of regeneration, which they intended to carry out in agreement with God and in God's stead.

'Nummo in Amma's place,' said Ogotemmêli, 'was working the work of Amma.'

In those obscure beginnings of the evolution of the world, men had no knowledge of death, and the eight ancestors, offspring of the first human couple, lived on indefinitely. They had eight separate lines of descendants, each of them being self-propagating since each was both male and female.

The four males and the four females were couples in consequence of their lower, i.e. of their sexual, parts. The four males were man and woman, and the four females were woman and man. In the case of the males it was the man, and in the case of the females it was the woman, who played the dominant role. They coupled and became pregnant each in him or herself, and so produced their offspring.

But in the fullness of time an obscure instinct led the eldest of them towards the anthill which had been occupied by the Nummo. He wore on his head as head-dress and to protect him from the sun, the wooden bowl he used for his food. He put his two feet into the opening of the anthill, that is of the earth's womb, and sank in slowly as if for a parturition *a tergo*.

The whole of him thus entered into the earth, and his head itself disappeared. But he left on the ground, as evidence of his passage into that world, the bowl which had caught on the edges of the opening. All that remained on the anthill was the round wooden bowl, still bearing traces of the food and the finger-prints of its vanished owner, symbol of his body and of his human nature, as, in the animal world, is the skin which a reptile has shed.

Liberated from his earthly condition, the ancestor was taken in charge by the regenerating Pair. The male Nummo led him into the depths of the earth, where, in the waters of the womb of his partner he curled himself up like a foetus and shrank to germinal form, and acquired the quality of water, the seed of God and the essence of the two Spirits.

And all this process was the work of the Word. The male with his voice accompanied the female Nummo who was speaking to herself and to her own sex. The spoken Word entered into her and wound itself round her womb in a spiral of eight turns. Just as the helical band of copper round the sun gives to it its daily movement, so the spiral of the Word gave to the womb its regenerative movement.

Thus perfected by water and words, the new Spirit was expelled and went up to Heaven.

All the eight ancestors in succession had to undergo this process of transformation; but, when the turn of the seventh ancestor came, the change was the occasion of a notable occurrence.

The seventh in a series, it must be remembered, represents perfection. Though equal in quality with the others, he is the sum of the feminine element, which is four, and the masculine element, which is three. He is thus the completion of the perfect series, symbol of the total union of male and female, that is to say of unity.

And to this homogeneous whole belongs especially the mastery of words, that is, of language; and the appearance on earth of such a one was bound to be the prelude to revolutionary developments of a beneficent character.

In the earth's womb he became, like the others, water and spirit, and his development, like theirs, followed the rhythm of the words uttered by the two transforming Nummo.

'The words which the female Nummo spoke to herself,' Ogotemmêli explained, 'turned into a spiral and entered into her sexual part. The male Nummo helped her. These are the words which the seventh ancestor learnt inside the womb.'

The others equally possessed the knowledge of these words in virtue of their experiences in the same place; but they had not attained the mastery of them nor was it given to them to develop their use. What the seventh ancestor had received, therefore, was the perfect knowledge of a Word—the second Word to be heard on earth, clearer than the first and not, like the first, reserved for particular recipients, but destined for all mankind. Thus he was able to achieve progress for the world. In particular, he enabled mankind to take precedence over God's wicked son, the jackal. The latter, it is true, still possessed knowledge of the first Word, and could still therefore reveal to diviners certain heavenly purposes; but in the future order of things he was to be merely a laggard in the process of revelation.

The potent second Word developed the powers of its new possessor. Gradually he came to regard his regeneration in the womb of the earth as equivalent to the capture and occupation of that womb, and little by little he took possession of the whole organism, making such use of it as suited him for the purpose of his activities. His lips began to merge with the edges of the anthill, which widened and became a mouth. Pointed teeth made their appearance, seven for each lip, then ten, the number of the fingers, later forty, and finally eighty, that is to say, ten for each ancestor.

These numbers indicated the future rates of increase of the families; the appearance of the teeth was a sign that the time for new instruction was drawing near.

But here again the scruples of the Spirits made themselves felt. It was not directly to men, but to the ant, avatar of the earth and native to the locality, that the seventh ancestor imparted instruction.

At sunrise on the appointed day the seventh ancestor Spirit spat out eighty threads of cotton; these he distributed between his upper teeth which acted as the teeth of a weaver's reed. In this way he made the uneven threads of a warp. He did the same with the lower teeth to make the even threads. By opening and shutting his jaws the Spirit caused the threads of the warp to make the movements required in weaving. His whole face took part in the work, his nose studs serving as the block, while the stud in his lower lip was the shuttle.

As the threads crossed and uncrossed, the two tips of the Spirit's forked tongue pushed the thread of the weft to and fro, and the web took shape from his mouth in the breath of the second revealed Word.

For the Spirit was speaking while the work proceeded. As did the Nummo in the first revelation, he imparted his Word by means of a technical process, so that all men could understand. By so doing he showed the identity of material actions and spiritual forces, or rather the need for their co-operation.

The words that the Spirit uttered filled all the interstices of the stuff: they were woven in the threads, and formed part and parcel of the cloth. They were the cloth, and the cloth was the Word. That is why woven material is called *soy*, which means 'It is the spoken word'. *Soy* also means 'seven', for the Spirit who spoke as he wove was seventh in the series of ancestors.

While the work was going on, the ant came and went on the edge of the opening in the breath of the Spirit, hearing and remembering his words. The new instruction, which she thus received, she passed on to the men who lived in those regions, and who had already followed the transformation of the sex of the earth.

Up to the time of the ancestors' descent into the anthill, men had lived in holes dug in the level soil like the lairs of animals. When their attention was drawn to the bowls which the ancestors had left behind them, they began to notice the shape of the anthill, which they thought much better than their holes. They copied the shape of the anthill accordingly, making passages and rooms as shelters from the rain, and began to store the produce of the crops for food.

They were thus advancing towards a less primitive way of life; and, when they noticed the growth of teeth round the opening, they imitated these too as a means of protection against wild beasts. They moulded great teeth of clay, dried them and set them up round the entrances to their dwellings.

At the moment of the second instruction, therefore, men were living in dens which were already, in some sort, a prefiguration of the place of revelation and of the womb into which each of them in due course would descend to be regenerated. And, moreover, the human anthill, with its occupants and its store-chambers for grain, was a rudimentary image of the system which, much later, was to come down to them from Heaven in the form of a marvellous granary.

These dim outlines of things to come predisposed men to take advice from the ant. The latter, after what it had seen the Spirit do, had laid in a store of cotton-fibres. These it had made into threads and, in the sight of men, drew them between the teeth of the anthill entrance as the Spirit had done. As the warp emerged, the men passed the thread of the weft, throwing it right and left in time to the opening and shutting movements of the jaws, and the resulting web was rolled round a piece of wood, fore-runner of the beam.

The ant at the same time revealed the words it had heard and the man repeated them. Thus there was recreated by human lips the concept of life in motion, of the transposition of forces, of the efficacy of the breath of the Spirit, which the seventh ancestor had created; and thus the interlacing of warp and weft enclosed the same words, the new instruction which became the heritage of mankind and was handed on from generation to generation of weavers to the accompaniment of the clapping of the shuttle and the creaking of the block, which they call the 'creaking of the Word'.

All these operations took place by daylight, for spinning and weaving are work for the daytime. Working at night would mean weaving webs of silence and darkness.

29

FOURTH DAY

The Third Word and
the Granary of Pure Earth

OGOTEMMÊLI had no very clear idea of what happened in
Heaven after the transformation of the eight ancestors into
Nummo. It is true that the eight, after leaving the earth, having
completed their labours, came to the celestial region where the
eldest Pair, who had transformed them, reigned. It is true also
that these elders had precedence of the others, and did not fail
to impose on them at once a form of organization and rules of
life.

But it was never quite clear why this celestial world was
disturbed to the point of disintegration, or why these disorders
led to a reorganization of the terrestrial world, which had
nothing to do with the celestial disputes. What is certain is that
in the end the eight came down to earth again in a vast
apparatus of symbols, in which was included a third and
definitive Word necessary for the working of the modern world.

All that could be gathered from Ogotemmêli, by dint of
patient attention to his words, was the evasive answer:

'Spirits do not fall from Heaven except in anger or because
they are expelled.'

It was obvious that he was conscious of the infinite complexity of the idea of God or the Spirits who took his place, and
was reluctant to explain it. However an outline, slight but
nevertheless adequate, of this obscure period was eventually
obtained.

The Nummo Pair had received the transformed eight in
Heaven. But though they were all of the same essence, the Pair
had the rights of the elder generation in relation to the new-
comers, on whom they imposed an organization with a network
of rules, of which the most onerous was the one which separated

them from one another and forbade them to visit one another.

The fact was that, like human societies in which numbers are a source of trouble, the celestial society would have been heading for disorder, if all its members had gathered together.

Though this rule was their security, the new generation of Nummo, however, proceeded to break it and thereby overthrew their destiny; and this was how it came about.

God had given the eight a collection of eight different grains intended for their food, and for these the first ancestor was responsible. Of the eight, the last was the *Digitaria*, which had been publicly rejected by the first ancestor when it was given to him, on the pretext that it was so small and so difficult to prepare. He even went so far as to swear he would never eat it.

There came, however, a critical period when all the grains were nearly exhausted except the last. The first and second ancestors, who incidentally had already broken the rule about separation, met together to eat this last food. Their action was the crowning breach of order, confirming as it did their first offence by a breach of faith. The two ancestors thereby became unclean—that is to say, of an essence incompatible with life in the celestial world. They resolved to quit that region, where they felt themselves to be strangers, and the six other ancestors threw in their lot with them and made the same decision. Moreover, they proposed to take with them when they left anything that might be of use to the men they were going to rejoin. It was then that the first ancestor, no doubt with the approval and perhaps with the help of God, began to make preparations for his own departure.

He took a woven basket with a circular opening and a square base in which to carry the earth and puddled clay required for the construction of a world-system, of which he was to be one of the counsellors. This basket served as a model for a basket-work structure of considerable size which he built upside down, as it were, with the opening, twenty cubits in diameter, on the ground, the square base, with sides eight cubits long, formed a flat roof, and the height was ten cubits. This framework he covered with puddled clay made of the earth from heaven, and in the thickness of the clay, starting from the centre of each side of the square, he made stairways of ten steps each facing towards one of the cardinal points. At the sixth step of the north staircase he put a door giving access to the interior in which were eight chambers arranged on two floors.

The symbolic significance of this structure was as follows:

The circular base represented the sun.

The square roof represented the sky.

A circle in the centre of the roof represented the moon.

The tread of each step being female and the rise of each step male, the four stairways of ten steps together prefigured the eight tens of families, offspring of the eight ancestors.

Each stairway held one kind of creature, and was associated with a constellation, as follows:

The north stairway, associated with the Pleiades, was for men and fishes;

The south stairway, associated with Orion's Belt, was for domestic animals.

The east stairway, associated with Venus, was for birds.

The west stairway, associated with the so-called 'Long-tailed Star', was for wild animals, vegetables, and insects.

In fact, the picture of the system was not easily or immediately grasped from Ogotemmêli's account of it.

'When the ancestor came down from Heaven,' he said at first, 'he was standing on a square piece of Heaven, not a very big piece, about the size of a sleeping-mat, or perhaps a bit bigger.'

'How could he stand on this piece of Heaven?'

'It was a piece of celestial earth.'

'A thick piece?'

'Yes! As thick as a house. It was ten cubits high with stairs on each side facing the four cardinal points.'

The blind man had raised his head, which was almost always bent towards the ground. How was he to explain these geometrical forms, these steps, these exact measurements? The European had begun by thinking that what was meant was a tall prism flanked by four stairways forming a cross. He kept returning to this conception in order to get it quite clear, while the other, patiently groping in the darkness which enveloped him, sought for fresh details.

At last his ravaged face broke into a kind of smile: he had found what he wanted. Reaching into the inside of his house

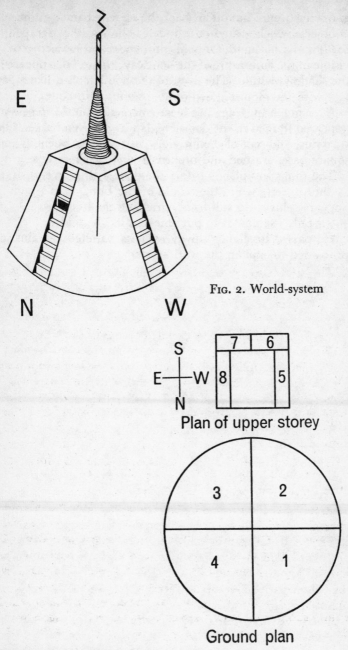

E   S

N   W

Fig. 2. World-system

S
E ─┼─ W
N

7	6
8	5

Plan of upper storey

3	2
4	1

Ground plan

Fig. 3. World-system: plan

and lying almost flat on his back, he searched among a number of objects which grated or sounded hollow as they scraped the earth under his hand. Only his thin knees and his feet were still visible in the embrasure of the doorway; the rest disappeared in the shadows within. The front of the house looked like a great face with the mouth closed on two skinny shin-bones.

After much tugging, an object emerged from the depths and appeared framed in the doorway. It was a woven basket, black with dust and soot of the interior, with a round opening and a square base, crushed and broken, a wretched spectacle.

The thing was placed before the door, losing several strands in the process, while the whole of the blind man's body reappeared, his hand still firmly grasping the basket.

'Its only use now is to put chickens in,' he said.

He passed his hands slowly over its battered remains, and proceeded to explain the world-system.

The Third Word and the Classification of Things

THE basket had been put away, with some embarrassment; returned to the place of mystery behind Ogotemmêli's back, no one ever alluded to it again. The exposure of this ruin to the light of day had been, as it were, a defiance of worldly vanity; but it had served its purpose. All was now clear and the divine geometry was defined. It was possible to make a beginning with the detailed enumeration of the beings posted at the four cardinal points of the structure.

The west stairway was occupied by wild animals. From the top stair to the bottom stair it was given up to antelopes, hyenas, cats (two stairs for these), reptiles and saurians, apes, gazelles, marmots, the lion, and the elephant.

After the sixth step came the trees from the baobab to the *Lannea acida*, and on each of them were the insects commonly found there today.

On the south stairway were the domestic animals, beginning with fowls, then sheep, goats, cattle, horses, dogs and cats.

On the eighth and ninth steps were the chelonians, the giant tortoises, which today in each family take the place of the family heads, while these are absent, and the smaller tortoises, which are slowly done to death in the regional purification sacrifices.

On the tenth step were mice and rats (house and field).

The east stairway was occupied by birds. On the first step were the larger birds of prey and the hornbills; on the second were ostriches and storks; on the third, the small bustards and lapwings; on the fourth, vultures. Then came the smaller birds of prey, and then the herons. On the seventh step were the

35

pigeons; on the eighth, turtle-doves; on the ninth, ducks; and last of all, the great bustards, white and black.

The north stairway was that of men and fish.

This clearly presented complications, for Ogotemmêli had to go through it more than once before he could give a satisfactory account of it.

He certainly thought the men were Bozo, the original inhabitants of the Niger and still regarded by all the peoples of the Niger Bend as the only true fishermen. But their several positions on the different steps embarrassed Ogotemmêli, and it was not until his second reference to the subject at the end of the day that he arrived at a final version, probably after consultation with another elder.

On each of the first two steps stood a male Bozo with a fish attached to his navel and hanging between his legs. This attachment to the navel had a significance for Ogotemmêli which the European could not grasp. The man's navel was nipped between the fins of the fish: that is to say, the fish was quite clear of the man's belly. On the other hand, the name that the Dogon give to the Bozo was thought by Ogotemmêli to indicate that the fish was in process of passing into the body of the man.

This name *sologonon* or *sorogonon*, from which is derived *Sorko*, another name for the Bozo, does in fact mean 'which has not completely passed'. It would apply therefore primarily to the fish, but ultimately to the Bozo himself, the two (i.e. the man and the fish) being twin brothers, as indicated by the umbilical connection.

On each of the next two steps was a Bozo woman, also attached to a fish. On the fifth step was a Bozo woman standing alone.

The five last steps were empty.

A question occurred to the European: 'Only some of the animals and vegetables were on the building; where were the rest?'

'Each of those mentioned was as it were a file-leader. All the others of his kind were behind him. The antelope on the first step of the west stairway is the *walbanu*, the red antelope. After him come the white, the black and the *kâ* antelopes. So too on the first step of the south stairway, where the poultry stand, the guinea-fowl, the partridge and the rock-fowl are behind.'

'How could all these beasts find room on a step one cubit deep and one cubit high?'

The European had calculated that, according to the slope of the walls, the tread of each step must be six-tenths of a cubit deep, but he made no mention of the fact out of politeness, so as not to seem to be examining heavenly matters too closely.

'All this had to be said in words,' said Ogotemmêli, 'but everything on the steps is a symbol, symbolic antelopes, symbolic vultures, symbolic hyenas.' He paused for a moment, and added : 'Any number of symbols could find room on a one-cubit step.'

For the word 'symbol' he used a composite expression, the literal meaning of which is 'word of this (lower) world'.

Ogotemmêli, having described the structure as a granary, now proceeded to explain its design.

'The whole thing,' he said, 'with its stairways is called the "Granary of the Master of Pure Earth". It is divided into eight compartments, four below and four above. The door opens to the north on the sixth stair. It is as it were the mouth, and the granary is the belly, that is the interior, of the world.'

The structure having set the pattern for present-day granaries, the European wished to get a closer view of the arrangement of the system, and whispered to his assistant Koguem that he ought to see one of these constructions.

In point of fact nearly half the circumference of the courtyard was surrounded by granaries, some half a dozen of them in number. But to poke one's head into a granary is to invade the privacy of the family, to pry into its secrets. To scrutinize the foodstuffs, the seeds and ears of grain lying steeped in the darkness, is to measure up present resources and intrude into the provision for future needs.

Koguem put the point to the old man, suggesting a visit to an empty house he had noticed in Dyamini-Kuradondo, a village belonging to another family : but perhaps, he said, they could find a specimen nearer at hand.

Ogotemmêli reflected. Obviously he was considering, in his blindness, possible ruined granaries in the locality. At the end of his list appeared no doubt his own granaries, for he pointed to two of these in the backyard.

The farthest of these was a ruin; it was there that Koguem used to throw stones a dozen times a day at the children who came to listen with ears alert to catch the secrets that were being talked about. The other granary was in good condition, empty but closed. A pair of hoes were needed to open it, for the door was fastened as if in the jaws of a vice. Ogotemmêli waited on his threshold, his hands crossed as always above his head. From time to time Koguem reported on the progress of the work. When the door at length gave way, the European took up a position in the embrasure, from which came the smell of old grain.

The four lower compartments in a Dogon granary are separated by two intersecting partitions, the junction of which forms a cup-like depression in the earth big enough to hold a round jar. This jar, containing grain or valuable objects, is the centre of the whole building. The door opens above these compartments, and is only just wide enough to admit the passage of a man's body.

Above the door is the upper storey comprising four other compartments, two of them in a line along the back wall and the other two along the side walls. They form a sort of ledge round the three sides, leaving the space at the entry free so that if a man crouched on the top of the lower compartments his shoulders would be level with the balcony.

In the celestial granary these compartments had a numbered order. The first was to the right of the entry on the lower floor; the second was the one on the right at the back, and so on round the building. The fifth was on the upper floor on the right, and so on to the eighth, which was to the left on the upper floor.

Each of these compartments contained one of the eight seeds given by God to the eight ancestors in the following order: little millet, white millet, dark millet, female millet, beans, sorrel, rice and *Digitaria*. With each of these seeds were all the varieties of the same species.

But the eight compartments were not merely receptacles for the seeds which were to be introduced to human use. They also represented the eight principal organs of the Spirit of water, which are comparable to the organs of men with the addition of the gizzard, for the Spirit has the speed of birds.

These organs were disposed in the following order: stomach, gizzard, heart, small liver, spleen, intestines, great liver, gall-bladder.

A round jar in the centre symbolized the womb; a second smaller jar closed the first; it contained oil of *Lannea acida*, and represented the foetus. On top of it again was a still smaller jar containing perfume, and on the top of this last was a double cup.

All the eight organs were held in place by the outer walls and the inner partitions which symbolized the skeleton. The four uprights ending in the corners of the square roof were the arms and legs. Thus the granary was like a woman, lying on her back (representing the sun) with her arms and legs raised and supporting the roof (representing the sky). The two legs were on the north side, and the door at the sixth step marked the sexual parts.

The granary and all it contained was therefore a picture of the world-system of the new order, and the way in which this system worked was represented by the functioning of the internal organs. These organs absorbed symbolic nourishment which passed along the usual channels of the digestion and the circulation of the blood. From compartments 1 and 2 (stomach and gizzard) the symbolical food passed into compartment 6 (the intestines) and from there into all the others in the form of blood and lastly breath, ending in the liver and the gall-bladder. The breath is a vapour, a form of water, which maintains and is indeed the principle of life.

As Ogotemmêli spoke, the deserted granary seemed to come to life, and the setting sun lighting up the west beyond the I gorges heightened the illusion. The walls of the building became tinged with rose colour, and cast gleams of light on the sand-stone surfaces and the straw of the dung-heap. On the roof a bunch of purple sorrel stood out like fire. The moment was near when all the western walls of Upper and Lower Ogol would be aflame. All the visible surface of the granary shared in this prodigal display of light, while in the dark interior the wonders of the past came to life again.

Ogotemmêli, his head bowed and his hands on the nape of

his neck, was lost in the past history of the heavens. At last he arrived at the final stratum of symbols which showed the universe compressed within the walls of the primal granary, as a body filled with life and absorbing food.

'What is eaten,' he said, 'is the sunlight. What is excreted is the dark night. The breath of life is the clouds, and the blood is the rain that falls on the world.'

The Third Word
The Descent of the Granary
of Pure Earth and Death

OGOTEMMÊLI had omitted to find a place in his system for the scorpion and the *nay*. He now placed them underneath the granary in the circle symbolizing the sun.

The ancestral constructor had assembled on the flat roof the tools and implements of a forge, for his future task was to teach men the use of iron to enable them to cultivate the land.

The bellows was made out of two vessels of unfired powdered earth and a white sheepskin; the two vessels were joined to one another like two twins, the wide opening being closed by a skin. An earthen duct led from each to the nozzle.

The hammer was in the form of a large iron block with a cone-shaped handle and a square strike. The anvil similarly shaped was fixed in a wooden beam.

The ancestral smith was equipped with an iron bow and spindles for arrows. One of these arrows he aimed at the granary roof at the centre of the circle representing the moon and he wound a long thread of gossamer round the shank to form a bobbin, so that the whole edifice became a gigantic spindle-whorl. Taking a second arrow, he attached the other end of the thread to it, and shot it into the vault of the sky to give it purchase.

A whole constellation of symbols was now to appear. In the first place there was the miraculous granary itself symbolizing the world-system, set in place and classified into categories of creatures. It was the plaited basket, which its constructor had copied, and which was to serve men as a unit of volume. The unit of length was the tread or the rise of the steps in the stairways, or one cubit. The unit of area was provided by the flat roof, whose sides were eight cubits. The two primary geometrical figures were shown in the square of the roof and the circular base, which, in the basket, was in fact the opening. This was the model granary in which men were to store their crops.

As such it was the ideal and ultimate realization of the arrangement of the anthill, which had already served as a model for men in the transformation of their underground dwellings.

It was also the spindle-whorl, the deadhead of the arrow which the smith had shot at the flat roof, and which served as the axis for the winding of the downward thread.

Symbolically it represented the shape of the iron used for ginning cotton, a shuttle, pointed at each end, in outline resembling a smith's hammer.

It was the head of the hammer; and, according to popular belief, it was in his hammer that the smith brought the seeds to men.

It was also the four-sided anvil, which is female, forged in imitation of the hammer, which is male.

It was the webbed hand of the Nummo, of which the hammer was the image; it was the upper half of the Nummo's body, which is also symbolized by the hammer; two opposite surfaces represent his breast and back: the others are his arms.

Lastly, it was the bodily form of the female element of the smith, who, like all beings, was dual.

All was now ready for departure except that there was no fire in the smithy. The ancestor slipped into the workshop of the great Nummo, who are Heaven's smiths, and stole a piece of the sun in the form of live embers and white-hot iron. He seized it by means of a 'robber's stick' the crook of which ended in a slit, open like a mouth. He dropped some of the embers, came back to pick them up, and fled towards the granary; but his agitation was such that he could no longer find the entrances. He made the round of it several times before he found the steps and climbed to the flat roof, where he hid the stolen goods in one of the skins of the bellows, exclaiming: '*Gouyo!*', which is to say, 'Stolen!'

The word is still part of the language, and means 'granary'.

42

It is a reminder that without the fire of the smithy and the iron of hoes there would be no crops to store.

Without losing a moment the smith flung the truncated pyramid along a rainbow. The edifice stood without turning on itself, and the thread unwound in serpentine coils suggesting the movement of water.

With hammer and bow in his hands, the smith stood ready to defend himself against attack from outer space. But the attack, when it came, was unexpected; to the accompaniment of a clap of thunder a brand flung by the female Nummo hit the flat roof. The smith in self-defence snatched one of the skins of the bellows and brandished it above his head—thus making a buckler of it. The skin, inasmuch as it had been in contact with a piece of the sun, had absorbed the essence of the sun, and the celestial fire could not prevail against it. The ancestor thereupon extinguished with water from his leather bottle the burning brand which was setting the edifice on fire. This brand, whose name was *bazu*, was to become the origin of the worship of the female fire.

A second thunderclap followed the first. It came this time from the male Nummo, but was no more effective than its predecessor. The smith extinguished the second brand, named *anakyé*, which was to become the origin of the worship of the male fire.

The granary then pursued its course along the rainbow, but its speed increased owing to the impetus given by the thunder.

The smith meanwhile resumed his position of defence on the roof, but, tired of holding his hammer clasped in his hand, he laid it across his arms raised slightly in front of him. The anvil he carried in a kind of sling made of a long leather strap round his neck hanging down over his shoulders behind. The wooden beam in which the anvil was fixed knocked against his legs.

During his descent the ancestor still possessed the quality of a water spirit, and his body, though preserving its human appearance, owing to its being that of a regenerated man, was equipped with four flexible limbs like serpents after the pattern of the arms of the Great Nummo.

The ground was rapidly approaching. The ancestor was still standing, his arms in front of him and the hammer and anvil hanging across his limbs. The shock of his final impact on the

43

earth when he came to the end of the rainbow, scattered in a cloud of dust the animals, vegetables and men disposed on the steps.

When calm was restored, the smith was still on the roof, standing erect facing towards the north, his tools still in the same position. But in the shock of landing the hammer and the anvil had broken his arms and legs at the level of elbows and knees, which he did not have before. He thus acquired the joints proper to the new human form, which was to spread over the earth and to devote itself to toil.

It was in order to work that his arm was bent, for the flexible limbs were ill-fitted for the labours of forge and field. For hammering red-hot iron or for digging the land the leverage of the forearm was needed.

On making contact with the soil, therefore, the ancestor was ready for his civilizing work. He came down the north stairway, and marked out a square field, ten times eight cubits on each side, oriented in the same way as the flat roof on which he had descended, and on which the unit measurement of land-holdings was to be based.

The field was divided into eighty times eighty squares of one cubit a side, which were distributed among the eight families descended from the ancestors whose destiny it was to remain on earth. Along the median line of the square from north to south eight dwelling-houses were built, in which the earth was mixed with mud taken from the granary. The smithy was set up to the north of this line.

'They put celestial mud in the field,' said Ogotemmêli, 'and thus purified the soil; and later, as the land was gradually cleared, the impurity of the earth receded.'

The blind man always insisted on this matter of the impurity of the soil, the cause of the first disturbance of the order of the world.

'Originally, at the creation, the earth was pure. The lump flung by God was of pure clay. But the offence of the jackal defiled the earth and upset the world-order. That is why the Nummo came down to reorganize it. The earth which came down from Heaven was pure earth, and wherever it was put, it imparted its purity to the spot and to all the ground that was cleared. Wherever cultivation spread, impurity receded.'

44

The renewal of the soil was not the only work to be done. The granary came down full of new foods, intended for the regeneration and renewing of men. But the beginning of these labours was not without other incidents.

The smith, formerly a Nummo, could not by himself carry out his task as guide. Besides, his role was mainly that of a technician, and other forms of instruction were needed as well. Immediately after the smith, the first ancestor, the seven other ancestors descended. The ancestor of the leather-workers and the ancestor of the minstrels followed in order, each with his tools or instruments, and the others after them according to their rank. It was then that the incident occurred which was to determine the course of the reorganization.

The eighth ancestor, breaking the order of precedence, came down before the seventh, the master of Speech. The latter was so greatly incensed that, on reaching the ground, he turned against the others and, in the form of a great serpent, made for the granary to take the seeds from it.

According to another version, he bit the skin of the bellows in order to scatter the seeds which had been put in it. Others say that he came down at the same time as the smith in the form of the granary itself. On the ground he assumed the body of a great serpent, and a quarrel broke out between the two Spirits.

Be that as it may, the smith, in order to rid himself of an adversary and carry out the great purposes of God, advised men to kill the snake and eat its body and give him the head.

'According to others,' said Ogotemmêli, who attached the utmost importance to this turning-point in the history of the world and was concerned to make the attitude of the Spirits quite clear, 'according to others the smith, on his arrival, found the men of the eight families, and set up his smithy in their midst. When he put down the skins of the bellows, the great serpent suddenly appeared and fell upon them, scattering the millet all around. The men, seeing this newcomer and taken aback by its action, killed it. The smith thanked them, gave them the carcase to eat, and kept the head. But all agree as to what happened after the death of the serpent.

'When he had the head, the smith took it to the stone that he

45

used as a seat when hammering the iron; he made a hole, buried it and put the stone on top.'

'Then is the Nummo seventh ancestor in every smithy today?' asked the European.

'Yes,' said the blind man. 'Every smith when at work, is as it were sitting on the serpent's head.'

But there were other intricacies in the story. The Nummo seventh ancestor in the form of a serpent was killed by men, and his head was buried. But it might also be said that he was the granary which came down from Heaven, and that it was broken up and divided into pieces, and that the mud of its walls was spread over the primal field and mixed with the earth of the houses, while the seeds that were in it were buried in the soil at the time of sowing. It can be said that the serpent was killed, destroyed, and buried as serpent, as granary, and as seed.

'And why should this happen to him?'

'Because he was master of Speech.'

'And why did the master of Speech have to die?'

Ogotemmêli did not at once reply. His chin resting on his knees, which were drawn up to his breast, his hands against his cheeks, he looked into the night of his blindness.

'He died about the middle of November,' he said at last.

The European took his leave. The fact that his question had not been answered was none the less promising; he remembered that two days before, when he asked what was in the granary, the old man replied:

'*Wolo!*'

Which being interpreted means 'Nothing!'

The Third Word
and the Regurgitation
of the World-System

In Ogotemmêli's courtyard everyone lived cheek by jowl with the poultry, whose moments of agitation and subsequent quiet were both short-lived; the universal panic aroused by the throwing of a stone or a piece of wood was never followed by more than a few moments of peace. This is because, in African villages, the fowls rarely get enough to eat. Their life is one incessant frenzied search for food, all the more so since the area in which they have to seek it is confined to the courtyards and narrow streets. Their wretchedly low weight makes them an easy prey for kites, and their only safe refuge is in the crowded living areas where the skimming flights or dives of their enemies are impossible.

Ogotemmêli was no sooner seated on his threshold and the European absorbed by the enquiry than the farmyard began to marshal its forces; chickens poked into the calabashes with dregs of beer in them or scratched in the hollow rocks, ready to make for the wall at the slightest shadow passing overhead. Some of them, in the heat of the day, would even roost on the stranger's canvas shoes, so that he no longer dared move a toe.

The chickens with their twittering voices were good company, but the cocks, and especially the Hogon's cock, disturbed the sequence of Ogotemmêli's cosmogonies and interrupted his sentences by their loud cries and flapping movements. Ogotemmêli, looking up from the embrasure of the doorway, cursed them vigorously, voicing the hope that they would meet an early end in the cooking-pot. A moment afterwards he would

47

resume, in slow monotonous tones, the discourse which had been broken off in the middle of the smith's thundering and the mechanism of heaven.

There had been a long week's gap of work in the northern country, between the sixth and seventh days of interviews with Ogotemmêli, and the European was anxious to renew the conversations. He sat down on his usual rock-seat, put his topee on the ground and threw into it the guavas on which he proposed to lunch.

'From the time of the smith's coming,' said Ogotemmêli, 'men had joints. Up till then they had flexible bones which would not bend enough. A flexible arm is no good for work.'

But arms alone, he added, and bare hands were limited in what they could do. Accordingly, in the months which followed, the smith gave men iron in the form of hoes which he helved. The hoe gave man a longer arm.

The introduction of the hoe was inevitably the signal for agricultural labour. Till that time there had only been a few plants on the earth, such as cotton, which was picked for weaving but not cultivated. Similarly, before the descent of the celestial granary there were only a few animals such as the ant, the termite, the jackal, and perhaps also the scorpion and the so-called 'Sun' lizard.

But the use of the hoe to break up the ground and the sowing of seed were not enough to start agriculture on its course. For that abundance of rain was needed.

It was also necessary for men to be organized if all the purposes of God were to be fulfilled.

Eight families, descendants of the eight ancestors, were living on the earth; and the oldest of all these men belonged to the eighth family.

Though all the families were equal in rank, the eighth enjoyed a special privilege.

'Seven,' said Ogotemmêli, 'is the rank of the master of Speech; $1 + 7 = 8$. The eighth rank is that of Speech itself. Speech is separate from the one who teaches it, that is, the seventh ancestor; it is the eighth ancestor. The eighth ancestor is the foundation of the speech which all the other ancestors used and which the seventh taught.'

The oldest man then living, therefore, because he belonged

to the eighth family, was of all living beings on earth the most truly representative of the Word. His name was Lébé.

But men possessed an older Word, the second, which they had learnt from weaving; and this Word had to give place to the third Word. The new Word should have been imparted by the seventh ancestor Nummo, who had been killed by men, and whose head was now lying under the seat in the smithy in the northern section of the primal field.

The oldest man had to die in order to pass into the same world as the seventh ancestor, and so enable the purposes of God to be fulfilled. So he died.

'But not really,' said Ogotemmêli: 'only in appearance. The common people were told that he was dead, just as they had been told that the seventh ancestor had been killed and eaten. But in reality neither of them was dead. The old man could not die, because Death did not appear on the scene till later. The seventh ancestor could not die, because he was a Nummo.'

'Then why deceive the people?' asked the European.

'To make them understand things better,' said the blind man. He proceeded further:

When the old man died they laid him on the ground while they dug a grave, oriented north–south in the field not far from the smithy. In this they buried him lying flat on his back with his head to the north, that is, in the position of the earth, and exactly in its navel, that is, its centre.

The reason why they laid him flat on his back was in order that the purposes of God might be fulfilled, and also because men knew nothing of death or of funerary ceremonies. As time went on, when people died, they were laid in the bottom of graves or in caves with their heads to the north, males on their right sides and females on their left, in the position in which they slept on the platform-bed of the second room. They did not bend their limbs for a few moments, as they were to do later with all their dead, so as to give them temporarily the form of the foetus and so prefigure the regeneration.

The primal field thus contained on the one hand the body of the oldest man, who belonged to the eighth family, which was of the rank of the Word. It also contained, under the smith's stone, the head of the seventh ancestor.

The first sounds of the smithy began to be heard. They

penetrated into the depths of the earth and reached the seventh ancestor, whom men had killed. As the rhythmic sounds of the bellows blowing up the fire and the hammer striking the anvil came down to him, the seventh ancestor Nummo took his spirit form of a human trunk ending in a reptile. Rising up on his tail, with regular movements of his arms held out in front of him, and rhythmic jerks of his body he swam into the first dance movements, which brought him underground to the tomb of the old man.

To the rhythm of the work of the smith he made his way to the north of the body where the skull was, and proceeded to swallow it. He took it into his womb and gave new life to it. Then, always in time to the same sounds, he expelled into the tomb a torrent of water and the transformed being.

On the place where the body had been, this water, symbol of rushing torrents and of stagnant pools, lay in a great sheet, from which issued five rivers flowing in the directions of the head and the limbs.

The water was also the water of parturition. The Nummo's womb had transformed the man's bones into coloured stones, and ejected them into the bottom of the tomb so as to form the outline of a skeleton laid out flat on its back in the place where the body had been, with its head to the north.

'The seventh ancestor,' Ogotemmêli explained, 'swallowed the old man head-first, and brought up the *dougué* stones, putting them in the shape of the stretched-out body. It was like a drawing of a man picked out with stones.'

The outline was also like the outline of a man's soul which the Nummo makes at every birth, and he indicated, by the arrangement of the stones, the order of human society.

'He organized the world,' said Ogotemmêli, 'by vomiting the *dougué* stones in the outline of a man's soul.'

He placed the stones one by one, beginning with the one for the head, and with the eight principal stones, one for each ancestor, he marked the joints of the pelvis, the shoulders, the knees, and the elbows. The right-hand side came first; the stones of the four male ancestors were placed at the joints of the pelvis and shoulders, that is, where the limbs had been attached, while the stones of the four female ancestors were placed at the other four joints.

'The joints,' said Ogotemmêli, 'are the most important part of a man.'

Next came the stones of secondary importance designating the long bones, the vertebral column and the ribs.

All these *dougué* were covenant-stones which the totemic priests were later to wear round their necks. They were pledges of the affection of the eight ancestors, repositories of their life-force, which they desired to put into circulation again in their descendants.

The *dougué* were eight in number like the eight ancestors or the eight sorts of seed. They represented the eight elders at the origin of mankind; and the eight men, the eight seeds and the eight joints are all the same order as the *dougué*.

All the colours of the rainbow, along which the smith had descended, were represented, but not in their natural order: the left leg was almost black, the right leg and left arm were reddish, and the right arm almost white. But only the dominant colour of each member was distinguishable: the skeleton as a whole was multi-coloured.

The colours of the eight principal *dougué*, assigned to the different ancestors according to their rank, recalled either the colours of the organs of the celestial granary or those of the corresponding seeds.

The first stone, chestnut-yellow like the Dogon dress, was the colour of the stomach (compartment 1);

the second, reddish with a white line across it, was the colour of the gizzard (compartment 2);

the third was red like the heart (compartment 3);

the fourth was whitish like female millet (compartment 4);

the fifth was brown like beans (compartment 5);

the sixth was black like crushed sorrel (compartment 6);

the seventh was pink like the liver (compartment 7);

the eighth was green and white like gall (compartment 8).

The Nummo also spat out the dead man's nails in the form of cowries, eight for each hand and each foot. He put them in the place of the hands and feet beginning with the right in the following order:

One cowrie on the second finger and another on the fore-finger, to indicate that the first two ancestors were twins;

51

one cowrie on the thumb, the third ancestor having been born singly;

one on the ring-finger and one on the little finger for the fourth and fifth ancestors, who were also twins;

one in addition on the thumb, forefinger and second finger for the sixth, seventh and eighth ancestors.

The European noted, by the way, that cowries 7 and 8, the

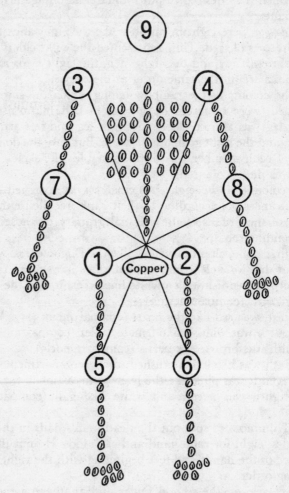

FIG. 4a. Social system of the Third Word

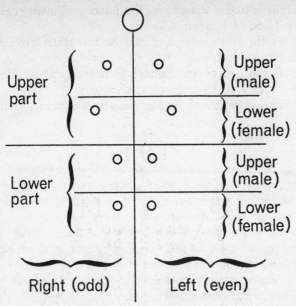

Upper part
{
  ○   ○   } Upper (male)
  ○   ○   } Lower (female)
}

Lower part
{
  ○   ○   } Upper (male)
  ○   ○   } Lower (female)
}

Right (odd)   Left (even)

FIG. 4*b*. Social system of the Third Word

numbers relating to speech, were placed on two fingers (fore-finger and second finger), which among the Dogon 'divide' words.

Ogotemmêli did not offer much explanation on this point. He said, however, that when any suspicion of foul play attached to a death, the dead man's second finger was left outside the shroud and slightly curved, in order to point to and 'catch' the guilty man.

But he reverted to the cowries.

'Later,' he said, 'when trade was invented, cowries were placed in heaps of eight in the order of the fingers. Beyond that number men counted by as many times eight as there were nails on the two hands, that is by eighties. Eight times eighty, or 640, was the limit.'

Between the legs of the outline the Nummo put copper, the product of his digestion and the metal which was later used to make bracelets for ritual purposes.

The arrangement of the eight stones of the joints later came to determine the system of marriages based on the principle of alternation between left and right, upper and lower, odd and even, male and female, as follows:

first family (right thigh, male) with eighth family (left forearm, female);

third family (right arm, male) with sixth family (left leg, female);

fifth family (right leg, female) with fourth family (left arm, male);

seventh family (right forearm, female) with second family (left thigh, male).

The principle of alternation was carried so far that in the case of upper and lower, for example, it was not only between the upper and lower parts of the body but between the upper and lower parts of a limb that unions were authorized. For instance, a thigh (lower part of the body but upper part of a limb) with a forearm (upper part of the body but lower part of a limb). The system of marriages was so arranged that the sum of the numbers representing the rank of the two families was always 9, which is the rank of chieftainship.

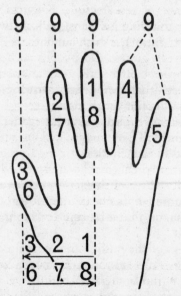

FIG. 5. Numerical value of the fingers

54

As for the stone in the place of the skull, that also had the rank of 9, as it was to be assigned to the chieftainship in each family.

The cowries put in the place of the fingers also indicated the marriage system, the second finger having the rank of 1 and 8, the forefinger that of 2 and 7, and the thumb that of 3 and 6. The idea was to show that the mating of ranks was indicated on a single finger. Mating and marrying meant uniting in one.

The 4 and 5 of the ring and little fingers represented the mating of twins of opposite sexes, that is to say, of two beings forming only one. (Were not the fourth male and fifth female ancestors twins?)

Ogotemmêli's account had not proceeded without interruptions. To begin with, he had had considerable difficulty in his exposition of the joints. As it was impossible for him to make drawings in the dust, he gave concrete form to his calculations by tapping on his thighs or forearms. In addition to this, his discourse was interrupted a score of times by fowls, dogs and inquisitive women. For instance, when he was describing the subterranean dance of resurrection, Koguem hurled himself into the courtyard, waving his arms, puffing and whistling like a snake. He had come back to hand to the European the dilapidated pieces of a guava, which a hen with six chickens had stolen from his topee.

'Poor brutes!' said the European, throwing the fruit to the hen, who made off, taking it for a stone.

'What is happening?' asked the blind man.

Koguem explained; Ogotemmêli, looking up from the doorway, was indignant. Stretching out his hands he asked for the fruit, which he then proceeded to divide into three and distribute between the three of them.

'A hen,' he grumbled, 'is not entitled to eat guava.'

The Third Word and the Work of Redemption

THE millet harvest had long been over. Between the two Ogols, in the Hogon's field, the dry stalks rustled in the slightest breath of wind. The earth had to wait through a whole season of wind and sun before it would be opened up again. Not for a long time would the peasants begin to reckon the crop by its height, anxiously watching its growth in the meantime and assisting it by sacrifices of fowls, by unremitting prayer and complicated precautions. It would be months before the first appearance of the young stalks would be hailed as 'nose tips', or the first sign of the leaves bending to the wind as 'cock's tails', or before the earth, disappearing under a carpet of green growth, would be described as 'hidden mounds' or the expression 'swallow the beasts' would indicate that the stalks were high enough to hide a sheep from view.

The European walked along the raised tracks above the harvested fields in which the baobabs stood out pinkish-green against the rising sun. He knew the names of all those in the Ogol country and the chronological order of their planting for twenty years back. He admired from a distance the eighth on the list, Adama, the largest of them all. Nine men with linked arms would hardly be able to encircle its trunk. Adama was larger than the Gravel baobab, whose seeds were like sand, larger than the Ropy baobab, whose fruit yielded a cream running like cheese, larger too than the Tall one, or gnarled Ancestor, or Small Seeds, High Bosom, Little Bulk or Plac-Plac, whose fragile fruits burst as they fall. Then, as he made his way into the narrow streets and took up his position in Ogotemmêli's courtyard, he cast a glance at the topmost branches, visible above the roofs, of the tree known simply as *the* Baobab without further qualification, the ancestor of all these monster growths.

'The old man whom the seventh Nummo ate,' said Ogotemmêli, 'was called Lébé. The stones which all priests wear round their necks are his bones.' But men had no knowledge of the subterranean resurrections at the time when they occurred. They did not acquire the treasure of the stones immediately after they had been placed there. They did not know what caused the rains which now began to fall and were the signal for the clearing of the field marked out by the smith.

These first rains indeed were for the purpose of purification. The seventh Nummo, a pure spirit, in swallowing the old man, had assimilated defiled human nature and the lapsed second Word. When he vomited to the rhythm of the blows on the anvil, there was ejected, with the pure covenant stones, a liquid which carried away the impurity. This liquid spread out into stagnant pools and flowing rivers, carving out valleys and flooding hollows. It had to be swept away and replaced by water which was pure and beneficent. This was done by the rain, which the Great Nummo in Heaven sent to help the seventh Nummo in his labours.

But this water from Heaven did not merely drive back the flood of the rivers; it also watered the primal field, and thus made it possible for the smith to teach the art of sowing.

It was much later, according to some, that men learnt of the prodigious events which had taken place underground. The land became too small for their needs, and they decided to emigrate *en masse*. Wishing, however, to keep their links with the past, and to have the same soil under their feet, they opened Lébé's grave, intending to take the bones and the earth with them when they went. It was then that they discovered the arrangement of stones thrown up by the seventh Nummo and the Spirit himself in the form of a serpent.

According to others, they made this discovery in the first year of cultivation, when the time came to give the field its first dressing.

Others again say that they buried Lébé and sowed the seed the same day. It was at the harvest that they opened the grave, thinking the old man had risen again like the millet.

In this way, therefore, the spiritual and the material organization went hand in hand. As in the case of the first and second Words, instruction concerning the third Word was embodied in technical processes.

'But why,' said the European, returning to his former question, 'why should the seventh ancestor be killed? And why should he eat Lébé on account of his being a descendant of the eighth ancestor?'

'The seventh Nummo ate Lébé,' replied Ogotemmêli, 'in order that men should believe that the stones were his bones digested and transformed . . . in order that the affair should be an affair of men and not of heaven, so that something of heaven should become part of human nature; it was to make men believe that the aged Lébé, the oldest and most venerable of them all, and he alone, was present in the covenant-stones. It was so that men might understand all the things he had done that the Nummo came down on to the skeleton of a man.'

'You speak of "making" people "believe". Was there then something secret, which they were not to know?'

'If you wanted to explain what happened to someone who knew nothing about it, to an ordinary man, you would say that a Power came down from heaven to eat the old man and change his bones into beneficent stones.'

'But what is the truth?'

'If one wanted to explain it to you, a Nazarene, one would say that someone came down from heaven like a woman with a woman's dress and ornaments, and ate the old man, and that the stones are not his bones but her ornaments.'

'The stones and cowries,' he added, 'were contained in the jar at the meeting point of the partitions in the centre of the granary.'

'But why,' the European insisted, 'was the seventh ancestor killed?'

There was no reply.

'The seventh Nummo,' went on Ogotemmêli as though talking to himself, 'sacrificed himself. He alone could do it, he the master of Speech, which is to say the master of the world. Without him no reorganization was possible. He might say— he did not say it, but he might have said—"What I did, the work that I accomplished and the word that I spoke, is: *ku ma inné déga dâ bébadou*," which means "My head has fallen for man's salvation".'

Lébé was eaten because he was a descendant of the eighth ancestor, of the family of the Word. The Word is the most important thing in the world. In eating Lébé the seventh Nummo, the master of Speech, took all that there was of good in the earlier Word and incorporated it in the stones. All that was impure was cast out with the water and carried away by the rains.

The seventh ancestor, dead only in appearance, ate Lébé, also dead only in appearance. In eating the man he took what was good in him but, for his own part, he gave his life-force to the human flesh of the man, that is to say, to men: for in doing this for the oldest man he did it for all mankind. Thus because the seventh ancestor consumed Lébé, descendant of his brother the eighth ancestor, their respective life-forces were mingled.

'And what of their souls? What happened to them?'

'Their souls were joined together and, though they remain distinct, they are never parted. Every year, at the Great Sacrifice in honour of Lébé, the men who eat the victim representing the ancestor ask that it shall always remain so. They go to the sanctuary and say: "May Nummo and Lébé never cease to be the same good thing they now are! May they never lose this identity!"'

'In short,' said the European, 'it is a case of human and celestial natures indissolubly linked.'

But the European was never greatly interested in his own speculations.

'All the same,' observed Ogotemmêli, 'the new Lébé who emerged from the vomit, the Lébé whom we honour today . . . '

He pulled himself together. It was a difficult thing to explain. Moreover the Hogon's wife had just come into the courtyard and greeted them. She was an old woman with a gentle voice, which broke at certain words because of palpitations of the heart; bending her small round head forward, wide-eyed and open-mouthed, she listened intently to what the European said to her.

'God brings you!' she said. 'Give me a cure for my heart!'

'It is old stuff,' he explained. 'How can one make a new heart out of an old one?'

He repeated this joke to her every time they met, because he knew it made her laugh till she cried.

Ogotemmêli had ceased speaking after the interminable greetings were concluded and remained silent as long as the old woman was moving about in the courtyard until he heard her go.

'One cannot speak of Lébé,' he said, 'before the Hogon's wife.'

The Hogon is in fact the priest of Lébé, the oldest man of the group and the highest religious dignitary.

'Women have ears,' he whispered as if imparting the most sensational confidence.

This scene was repeated a dozen times a day. Now it was the Hogon's wife, now the wife of a totem-priest, now an uncircumcised girl, now a mistrustful old man, now a smith, who wandered into the courtyard, or showed their heads at the gap in the stone wall.

One could not speak of the Lébé in front of the Hogon's wife, of the eight ancestors in front of a priest's wife, of the Nummo in front of a smith or of anything before fools.

'Lébé,' said Ogotemmêli, continuing his discourse, 'was something new in the record of the eight.' He meant by this that eight was in a certain sense the last of the symbolic numbers, and there was nothing beyond it. By 'Lébé' he meant, not the original old man, but the new elemental being resulting from the union of the old man and the Nummo.

'Lébé,' he said, 'is in some sort of ninth Power, as if he had been created by the seventh Nummo ancestor and the descendant of the eighth ancestor.'

He also meant that the descendant of the eighth ancestor was like the eighth ancestor himself. But in the series of Nummo ancestors the seventh and eighth are both female.

'Lébé is a new Word created by two females. This ninth Power is the offspring of an unknown father, like a bastard; it is not known which of the two, the seventh or the eighth played the part of the male.'

But Ogotemmêli was careful to explain that all this was a manner of speaking, and that he was merely trying to explain to the Nazarene the absence of a father. Incidentally the principle of dual beings might explain this creation. Since all beings were dual and bisexual (though with one or the other sex predominating) they were all capable of procreation, subject apparently to the intervention of a third being. In the case therefore of the two Nummo ancestors, the seventh and the eighth, believed to be female but with a non-dominant male element, it was possible that the female element in the one was fertilized by the male element (even though not dominant) in the other.

'Lébé,' concluded Ogotemmêli, 'proceeding as he did from the seventh and the eighth, ranks as 9; and that is the rank of chieftainship. It is indicated by the stone placed in the grave in the position of the skull, and it derives from the transformation of the central jar of the granary. It is at once the skull and the jar containing the eight other stones.'

At this moment Koguem's comrade Allaye brought him a calabash of ten francs' worth of milk, half of which had been paid for by Koguem.

'You drink first,' said Allaye.

Koguem drank in long gulps, his eyes upturned so as not to lose sight for a moment of the other, who watched him narrowly.

'Enough!' cried Allaye, taking back the vessel. 'Enough! I know how much five francs' worth of milk is!'

The Third Word and the Drums

By almost imperceptible signs the fact that it was market day became apparent. The Dogon week has five days, the number of fingers on one hand; market day therefore recurred with a frequency which agreeably disturbed the European's customary reckoning of time. Market day had its own sounds and its silences, its light and its shadows, from the subdued craftiness of the early morning, through the feverish clamour of midday, to the relaxation of the evening. The night before the small fires of the merchants could be seen from Gôna, flickering on the sandstone flats which stretched towards the Kamma country. All the sky-line was ringed with bales of merchandise wrapped in skins, fat asses relieved of their loads, clamour of men chattering or dreaming of gain. At sunrise, men and merchandise, with a thud of unshod feet, would pour into the Ogols.

There was also a notable change in the volume of barking at the approaches to the market; the dogs were clustering round the butchers' yards, attracted by the blood trickling under the doors or through the holes in the walls.

From the third hour of the day the great rock of Dolo was bathed in sunlight and crowded with men. Not a single tree cast the slightest shade on the stones which formed the rough divisions between the pitches of the salesmen. To the west the sun sloped abruptly to the valley with its flat slabs of rock, between which tepid trickles of water made their way. Men and women clung to this outfall as they dragged themselves up to the market-place, brimming with sun, heat and pungent smells and venting its overflowing stench into the hollows below.

Everyone was wearing his best clothes of white or toast-coloured cotton cloth. The men swept along in their full-sleeved tunics cut low at the neck, where the ritual stones hung. Adults wore short breeches fitting tightly round the calf but very full in the seat and billowing to right and left. The older men wore them longer reaching nearer the ground, while those of important persons were of vast size, though none of them approached the dimensions of the garment worn by the untouchable Hogon, who never went outside the village. The width of the seat varied with the status of the wearer.

Young boys were dressed in long white tabard-like garments, some of which were open at the sides exposing the thighs. These were called 'Pick me up, Mum!' because young children in these were easier to pick up and carry.

All the women, their bodies naked and their breasts flabby or firm, wore loin-cloths of four strips, bracelets at the bend of the arm or on the wrist, and necklaces of green or red beads, while their ears were edged with eight metal studs and the lobes were adorned with a red triangular pendant.

Owing to conditions overseas during recent years, there was little evidence of those frilled costumes, ridiculous umbrellas, useless spectacles and other tasteless trade goods which had formerly poured into the country. Distant wars had, for the time being, protected these lands from the invasion of such rubbish.

The market stirred the emotions of all the men and many of the animals from Kamma to Yugo. By midday all were immersed in its busy hum with ears burning and eyes on the watch for modest but exciting purchases.

The hubbub was not confined to the market-place and the tracks which led to it; eddies and incidents reached the very foundations of the houses. The old people, too dignified to satisfy their curiosity by mingling with the crowd, and the Hogon himself, without leaving his rock-dwelling, knew hour by hour every happening, great or small, in Dolo; and Ogotemmêli in ordinary times—that is to say, before his acquaintance with Nazarenes—was at the very centre of the news.

He used in those days to have clients who took advantage of their journey to seek medical attention; and from them he gathered first-hand information as to events in Yènndumman, Mendéli, Ninu and Pêguê. Plain, plateau and scree all discharged their sick and their sportsmen, the latter eager to learn how to be sure of killing a bush-buck. Ogotemmêli gave them all advice or powders, and his reputation continued to spread from street to street and from courtyard to court-yard.

Seeing the Nazarene there, the flood of visitors had retreated into the square of perplexity. Ever since the fourth day of the conversations, which happened to be a market-day, they had avoided the Tabda quarter. But this time a few bold spirits had ventured as far as the gap in the wall, and called their greetings. The unusual presence of the stranger had frightened some and put the others out of countenance.

A *modus vivendi* had had to be found for these exceptional days of crowd and confusion; and the conversation had been resumed in spite of the hubbub. Ogotemmêli was expounding the gift of the third Word and the work of civilization and resurrection in which it was embodied.

The most important of all drums, he said, was the armpit drum. The Nummo made it.

It consists of two hemispherical wooden cups connected through their centres by a slender cylinder. It is like an hour-glass with a very long narrow neck. With this instrument tucked between his left arm and armpit, the drummer, by pressing on the hollow structure of thin wood, can tighten or relax the tension on the skins and so modify the tone.

'The Nummo made it. He made a picture of it with his fingers, as children do today in games with string.'

Holding his hands apart, he passed a thread ten times round each of the four fingers, but not the thumb. He thus had forty loops on each hand, making eighty threads in all, which, he pointed out, was also the number of teeth in each of his jaws. The palms of his hands represented the skins of the drum, and thus to play on the drum was, symbolically, to play on the hands of the Nummo. But what do they represent?

Cupping his two hands behind his ears, Ogotemmêli explained that the spirit had no external ears but only auditory holes.

'His hands serve for ears,' he said; 'to enable him to hear he always holds them on each side of his head. To tap the drum is to tap the Nummo's palms, to tap, that is, his ears.'

Holding before him the web of threads which represented a weft, the Spirit with his tongue interlaced them with a kind of endless chain made of a thin strip of copper. He coiled this in a spiral of eighty turns, and throughout the process he spoke as he had done when teaching the art of weaving. But what he said was new. It was the third Word, which he was revealing to men.

For the technique of making a drum was similar to the technique of weaving; and the bodkin with which the craftsman pierces the edge of the skins to thread the tension-cord through is a symbol of the shuttle and of the Nummo's tongue. Beating the drum is also a form of weaving. The blows of the drumstick make the sound leap from one skin to the other inside the cylinder, as the shuttle and its thread pass from one hand to the other in the warp.

'But why the copper spirals? Ordinary drums do not have these.'

'The drum with the copper winding is easier for the Nummo to hear. It is reserved for the chieftainship of the Aru. Ordinary people do not have it. Moreover it is not played except on rare occasions.

'As for the copper spiral, it is the channel for the sound, which is to say, for the Word. Beating the skin animates the copper and the Word which Nummo took through the interlacing of the tension thread and the metal band. From the copper the sound passes to the drum; it then returns to the copper-strip, and from there reverberates in the ears of the Spirit, which are already alerted because the skins represent them. But the drum was not intended merely to link men with the Nummo. It taught them the new Word, complete and clear, of the new age.'

But the armpit drum was not enough to teach this Word, which had to take many forms to meet the various needs of men. Accordingly the head of each of the eight families made a drum for his own group following the instructions of the seventh Nummo.

For the size of his drum and the tension of the skin the smith of the first family took his bellows as a model. The body of the bellows suggested the idea of the sound-box, and the leather with its fastening served as a pattern for the skin to be beaten.

Thus a drum was made from half a baobab fruit, on which was stretched the skin of a frog or toad. It resembles a woman's breast, and its sound is like that which an infant makes when

FIG. 6. Range of drums and languages

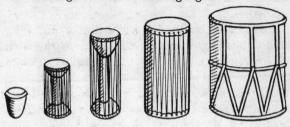

sucking. On this drum the smith beat the first rhythms he had heard on the double skin of the bellows, when he blew up his fire at the time of the subterranean resurrection of the Nummo.

The second family had an armpit drum of smaller size. The third family had the one taught them by the Nummo. The fourth family constructed a cylindrical box recalling the small stature of the first men. The fifth family did the same with a larger block of wood, which gave out a loud sound like the roar of a lion.

The sixth family stretched a skin over the opening of a large spherical calabash in the shape of a woman's belly. Its sound is like the groans of childbirth. The seventh family made a box out of a trunk of different dimensions from that of the fifth family. The eighth family had the largest box. It is like the belly of a cow, and owing to its size gives a fine rolling sound.

Each drum had a sound of its own, and so each family had its own language, which is the reason why there are different languages today.

The first two families, settled in the south, spoke two dialects of *Toro*, not very different from each other; the third family spoke *Mendéli*; the fourth spoke *Sanga*; the fifth another form of *Toro*; the sixth *Bamba*; and the seventh *Iréli*. Lastly the eighth family was given a language which is understood in all parts of the cliff. Just as the eighth drum dominates all the others, so the eighth language is understood everywhere.

It was thus that men were given the third Word, final, complete

and multiform to suit the new age. It was closely associated, like the first and second Words, and even more than they, with material objects.

At this point an odd reflection occurred to the European.

The first imperfect Word was associated with a technical process, simple in character and no doubt the most archaic of all processes, which had produced the most primitive form of clothing made of fibre. The fibre, which was neither knotted nor woven, flowed in a wavy line, and might be said therefore to be of one dimension. The second Word, less restricted than the first, arose from weaving, done on a wide warp crossed by vertical threads forming a surface, that is to say, having two dimensions. The third Word, clear and perfect in character, took shape in a cylinder with a strip of copper winding through it, that is to say, in a three-dimensional figure.

These three technical processes (as he further remarked) all proceeded by following a line, either undulating or zig-zag, and each was characterized by three distinct features: humidity of the fibres, ensuring the freshness necessary for procreation; light for the weaving, that being a daylight process, prohibited at night on pain of blindness; sonority of the drum.

There was also a development, from the material point of view, from trimmed bark to cotton thread, and from thread to leather strips and to a copper band.

Throughout this day's conversation Ogotemmêli had seemed absent-minded. He was no doubt in touch, through invisible channels, with all the commercial and political activities of the district. His thoughts were probably occupied also with certain friends to whom he had entrusted commissions, among them the close friend who was to bring him his tobacco.

His pre-occupation on this last account had been noticeable more than once during the morning's conversation, and allusions to the signal service rendered by tobacco had punctuated his account of the third Word.

By evening, his pre-occupation had grown into a certain perceptible impatience. He had indeed received the tobacco, but he would have liked to prepare it: for the leaves had to be reduced to powder by beating them on a stone and crushing them like grain.

In the end he could no longer restrain his impatience and said he would be fined.

'Fined?'

'Is it not forbidden to beat the ground at night?'

The stranger had indeed forgotten that at night silence must be preserved, in particular no sound of blows on the ground may be heard, or grinding in the hollows of the rock or in mortars.

Tobacco, which clarifies ideas, was well worth an interruption in the cosmogonic narrative.

The European took his leave. He went by a roundabout way through the tangle of narrow lanes, finally arriving in the street which ran through all five quarters of the village. It was the hour of after-market exhaustion, the hour of satiety, of chewing over successful business transactions. In every courtyard digestion was proceeding, digestion of a day of words.

The Word and
the Craft of Weaving

On the previous day the European had not been to Ogotem-mêli's house. He had been anxious to make soundings elsewhere in order to verify and correct what he had learnt. He had been to Ongnonlu, a man of weight in the Dudya quarter, father of the priest-designate of the sanctuary erected at Ogoiné.

The entrance to Ongnonlu's house was through a low room giving on to an open shed, which itself opened on to the dung-heap. All Dogon houses seem to be made for small men. Koguem had to sit first on a rock and later on an umbilical-shaped hen-house in which a broody hen was clucking. Ongnonlu squatted on a piece of wood laid across the dung-heap, which occupied the whole courtyard. The European sat on a tin, the seat of honour. Seventeen sheep and lambs wandered back and forth unceasingly like the waves on a beach. None of them could decide to lead the others along the street to an open place. From time to time the woolly tide blocked a corner holding up the traffic.

Ongnonlu proved to be a first-rate source of information. There were slight reticences when the conversation touched on certain reserved subjects; but on the whole he provided admirable cross-checks on Ogotemmêli's information.

The sheep passed through the narrow space between the European and Koguem, who were seated less than a yard apart. For a moment the ranks of the intruders widened, only to be narrowed again as they passed between two women spinning, till finally after a moment's hesitation they disappeared into the narrow entry of the dwelling-house. But the women and Ongnonlu were so intent on talking to the European, watching him out of the corners of their eyes, and generally getting used to his presence, that they took no notice of the sheep.

Ongnonlu was expounding the mystery of Death, the pomp and circumstance of man, and the invention of materials. Suddenly he pricked up his ears: his dark face, puckered into a pleasant smile, relaxed as he turned towards the back of the courtyard. He leapt up with a shout, pulling on his Phrygian cap (which was slipping) and, followed by the women who dropped the pestles they had in their hands, rushed into the low doorway which opened into the dark interior. A great noise followed, and three clouds of dust poured from the door and the openings in the side-walls. One by one the sheep emerged and stood there shyly, dazzled by the light. Ongnonlu's head appeared above a mass of wool. Spitting and fuming he drove the flock into a blind alley between the wall and the granary, and blocked the opening with a large basket.

The door of the house having now been shut, the actors in this comedy returned, the one to his conversation and the two others to their mortars.

Suddenly one of the women paused—Ongnonlu was at the moment rooted to the spot—and hurried to the door, through which she vanished. New shouts! More dust! The biggest of the rams, which his master had shut up in his haste, burst out, and the rest of the imprisoned animals, smashing the basket, joined him and, charging between the European and Koguem, made straight for the entry to the yard, stopped short, urinated and settled down to sleep.

There was a quarter of an hour of peace, during which Ongnonlu explained the symbolism of the crooked seat used in initiations of the major sort.

But two lambs were still on the dung-heap, and finding nothing to eat there, bleated. The fifteen others at once rallied to the charge.

Compared to this chaos Ogotemmêli's courtyard was full of peaceful charm.

The previous conversations had brought out the pre-eminence of weaving; and the European now asked Ogotemmêli to talk of its technique. He had just seen women spinning—as he had done a score of times before since he first came to Africa

—and in so doing had witnessed a native craft in actual operation.

The apparatus of the craft consists of four vertical stakes planted in the earth and connected by horizontal bars, forming a prism, where a man and his tools can be comfortably accommodated. The warp, narrow and endless, comes from a sledge heaped with stones, passes over a horizontal support, and reaches the weaver at an angle. In the operative part between the horizontal support and the beam, round which the finished web is wound, the warp passes through the heddle and thence through the bars of the batten, the teeth of which are made of chips of reed. The heddle, worked by the foot, causes the threads of the warp to rise and fall alternately by means of a block attached to a cross-beam of the loom. The batten is balanced at the end of a small cord fastened at both ends. The shuttle, made of wood sharpened to a point at each end, is thrown by hand.

Spinning, which is woman's work, is done with a spindle consisting of a thin rod, one end of which is inserted in a thick lump of dried earth. With her right hand the woman twirls the spindle, and adjusts the thread over a skin which protects the work from dust. In her left hand she holds the mass of fibres from which the thread is drawn. She dries her fingers with white ash from a small calabash.

First, however, she will have ginned the raw cotton by rubbing the fibres on a flat stone with an iron roller a span long, thickened in the middle. The carding is done with a stick. She keeps the seeds, putting them to dry till the next sowing on the lintel of the second door of the house, where they symbolize her sex and the humidity essential for germination.

'A woman spinning,' said Ogotemmêli, 'is the seventh Nummo. The ginning-iron, like the smith's hammer, is a symbol of the celestial granary, and thus is associated with seeds. The carding stick is like the rod with which the smith sprinkled water on his fire to damp it down. The skin on which the woman spins is the sun, for the first leather so used was that of the bellows of the smithy, which had contained the solar fire.

'The twirling of the spindle is the movement of the copper spiral which propels the sun, and is often represented by the white lines decorating the middle of the spindle-whorl. The thread coming from the woman's hand, which is wound round the spindle, is the gossamer down which the world-system came to earth from heaven.

'The spindle itself is the arrow which, with the gossamer attached to it, pierced the vault of the sky. It is also the arrow buried in the celestial granary.

'The calabash containing the ashes for drying the fingers is the female Great Nummo. It recalls the calabash on the head of the celestial ram, an avatar of the male Great Nummo. The ash is the ram itself, and also its seed: the fluffy cotton from which the thread is drawn is its wool.

'The hank of thread which is drawn out to form the warp is the path of the seventh ancestor Nummo, and also the Nummo himself in his reptilian form. The large bobbin, which is wound off in spinning is the sun rolling in space.'

'Did the craft of weaving come down with the smithy in the world-system?'

'Yes, but symbolically. The north stairway of the granary represented the warp: the four beams coming out from the façade at the level of the upper storey were the four vertical stakes. The chest of the weaver was the door of the granary: the shuttle is the lock which moves this way and that as it opens or shuts. The block is the triangular bit of wood which holds together the two sections of the door.

'The craft of weaving, in which the craftsman works facing south, is the house of the seventh Nummo, and the structure of the loom is composed of all the eight ancestors. The four vertical stakes (male) mark the bedroom; the four horizontal bars (female) represent the flat roof.

'The craft is also the grave of Lébé in the primal field. The weaver's seat is the earth-platform on which the dead body was laid before burial. The warp thread stands for the opening and shutting of the door of the tomb, through which the Nummo goes in or out in the form of the woof-thread, which represents a reptile, whose tongue is the shuttle. The foot-rest of the right foot corresponds to the throwing of the shuttle by the right hand, suggesting the entry of the serpent: the left foot-rest and the action of throwing by the left hand suggest the exit. The lock of the door is the block, to which the heddle is attached.

'The heddle with its eighty threads is the symbol of the seventh Nummo's jaws. The carding-comb with its eighty slots marks the passing of the eighty heads of families, the issue of the eight ancestors and themselves represented by the eighty odd and eighty even threads of the warp.

'The web rolled round the beam, against which the weaver leans, symbolizes the serpent devouring the dead body: for the weaver is the symbol of Lébé dead and risen again.

'The typical product of the craft is the cloth which serves as a pall to cover the dead. It is made of alternate black and white squares composed of the eighty odd and eighty even threads of the warp and the eighty movements to and fro of the woof. The pall is made up of eight strips sewn together, and each strip should consist of eighty squares, but they are woven from twenty components only.

'The co-operation of man and woman, in storing the seeds, sowing and growing the cotton, has the same meaning as spinning and weaving, symbols of love.

'Spinning cotton and weaving clothing is exactly the same as a man and a woman entering the house to sleep together and produce children.

'The weaver, representing a dead man, is also the male who opens and closes the womb of the woman, represented by the heddle. The stretched threads represent the act of procreation. The cotton threads of the weavers and the numerous men in the world are all one. The making of the cloth symbolizes the multiplication of mankind.

'The craft of weaving in fact,' said Ogotemmêli in conclusion, 'is the tomb of resurrection, the marriage bed and the fruitful womb.'

It remained only to speak of the Word, on which (he said) the whole revelation of the art of weaving was based.

'The Word,' said the old man, 'is in the sound of the block and the shuttle. The name of the block means "creaking of the word". Everybody understands what is meant by "the word" in that connection. It is interwoven with the threads: it fills the interstices in the fabric. It belongs to the eight ancestors; the first seven possess it: the seventh is the master of it; it is itself the eighth.'

He repeated: 'The words of the seven ancestors fill the gaps

73

and form the eighth. The Word, being water, follows the zig-zag line of the woof.'

The weaver, he explained, sings as he throws the shuttle, and the sound of his voice enters into the warp, adding to and taking along with it the voice of the ancestors. For the weaver is Lébé, the man of the eighth family and consequently the Word itself.

Blind Ogotemmêli began to murmur in an archaic language, two lines of a funeral chant, which the Onndom weavers sing when they weave palls for the dead.

> ... *Sloth for the shapeless neck!*
> *Eighty minstrels and only one drum!*

The Nazarene returned to his house at the end of the day by way of the Dodyu-Oreil quarter, to the south of Lower Ogol, which juts out like a promontory on the shore of the pool of Bananga. In the small square, broken on all sides by the corners of houses, there were a few looms opposite the council shelter. Nearby there was an earth mound, altar of the seventh Nummo.

Denuded of weavers and of their warps, the meagre collection of stakes with their connecting bars of wood looked like rubbish thrust into a corner. The weavers, according to rule, had stopped work the moment the sun touched the horizon.

Weaving, like smithing, is daytime labour, for warp and woof symbolize a being of light and language, while the spinner's spindle turns on a skin sun, and her calabash of white ash is a fertilized sun. It is only fitting, therefore, that the sun should shine on the craft. Weaving by night would produce a web of silence and shadow. A weaver who worked after sunset, when God shuts the door of the world, would become blind.

The Word and the Cultivation of the Land

'It's a fowl that Amadigué, Gana and I bought together,' said Koguem.

Koguem had been helping Amadigué in his efforts to catch the creature, which had escaped. After a wild chase in the fields and among the rocks, the bird had found a refuge under an unapproachable rock containing sacred objects.

Amadigué accordingly sat down on the spot to wait till thirst drove his property out into the open. The others left him on watch, wishing him success.

On the swollen spur of Upper Ogol some sheep, sluggish after two thousand years of domestication, made shift nevertheless to leap from rock to rock, with tails waving rakishly, in flight from a very small shepherd-boy wearing a hat as wide as a buckler and carrying a stick and a gourd-bottle.

Leaving Upper Ogol on the left, they forebore to talk to some women on their right, who were crushing the fruit of the *Lannea acida*, because speech was thought to impair the clarity of the oil. They then came down the rocky path which led to the field of the Hogon, priest of Lébé, leaving behind them the little bare patch unturned by any hoe, which symbolizes the tomb of Lébé. To the left, climbing the sandstone slopes and entering the Guèndoumman quarter, was the slippery track by which Lébé, in the form of a great glittering serpent, passes every night to the sanctuary in the town. Further away at the edge of the field could be seen the cave in which he lives by day. They had also to pass above the heap of stones which is one of the principal altars of Lébé.

Not counting the sites of baobabs, reckoned as places with names of their own, it was necessary, in going from the camp to Ogotemmêli's house, to walk through or alongside five fields or rocks, all with names and well-defined boundaries— Tenné, Ba Diguilou, Goummo, Ogo Digou, Toummogou. In Lower Ogol it was necessary to skirt three different quarters —Amtaba, Guinna, and Tabda. The distance from start to finish, as the crow flies, was less than two hundred metres.

Each section of the ground, moreover, was divisible into places with recognized names, and in the built-up areas especially, with their houses and public squares, it was necessary to manœuvre in order to avoid places to which access was forbidden. Seen from the air, the tangle of dwelling areas, rocks, gaps, altars, and trees, all with names of their own, which made up the village of Upper Ogol, would seem to be inextricable.

Here the land was level plateau, but in the cliff area, rock walls no longer constituted boundaries; the very earth reared itself up, plots rising in tiers, some overhanging others, presenting insuperable difficulties to any attempt at land survey.

Fragmentation of land holdings was unrestricted, division of the soil proceeding apparently by virtue of occupation, as if the inhabitants had organized it rock by rock and mound by mound, impregnating it with their life, giving their names to it, and laying out each settlement, symbolically, after the pattern in which the earth had first been organized around the spot where the heavenly granary had come to rest.

On the plain, the cultivated land is like a chequer-board, the squares marked out by small ridges less than a hands-breadth wide; these look more like swellings on the earth than raised barriers. In the rocky country, where the ground is broken, the divisions are irregular, and in Sanga, Lulli's fields are cited as an example of the rules for partitioning land.

But the cutting up into squares was carried to extremes in the dry-season onion gardens, where the plots, less than a yard wide, form a series of regular pans bordered by clearly defined embankments of soil. In this way rain or irrigation water is retained at the base of the plants and does not flow away.

The basic division of land is the field.

'The land,' said Ogotemmêli, 'is cultivated in squares, eight cubits a side, surrounded by embankments of earth.'

The area of each plot, he explained, is that of the flat roof of the celestial granary; and the plot is orientated so that each side faces a cardinal point of the compass.

'The old method of cultivation,' he went on, 'is like weaving; one begins on the north side, moving from east to west and then back from west to east. On each line eight feet are planted and the square has eight lines recalling the eight ancestors and the eight seeds.'

Furthermore, inside the line the cultivator advances first on one foot and then on the other, changing his hoe from one hand to the other at each step. When the right foot is in front, the right hand on the handle is nearest the iron, and *vice versa* when he changes step.

Cultivation being thus a form of weaving, a field is like a blanket made of eight strips, the black and white squares being represented by the alternation of the mounds made at each step and the gaps between them; a mound and its shadow represent a black square.

The whole collection of fields round a village together with the village itself may also be said to recall a large coverlet, the houses with roofs shining in the sunlight being the white squares, and the courtyards lying in shadow, the black. The streets are the seams joining the strips.

If a man clears ground and makes a new square plot and builds a dwelling on the plot, his work is like weaving a cloth.

Moreover, weaving is a form of speech, which is imparted to the fabric by the to-and-fro movement of the shuttle on the warp; and in the same way the to-and-fro movement of the peasant on his plot imparts the Word of the ancestors, that is to say, moisture, to the ground on which he works, and thus rids the earth of impurity and extends the area of cultivation round inhabited places.

But, if cultivation is a form of weaving, it is equally true to say that weaving is a form of cultivation. That part of the warp which has no woof is the uncultivated land or bush. The finished web is the symbol of the cultivated field. The four stakes of the loom are the trees and bushes which are felled by the shuttle, symbol of the axe. To pull the carding-comb towards oneself is to carry wood to chop for faggots; and to draw the thread of the woof through the warp, is to bring life, water, and purity, to the desert.

77

The Word, Dress and Love

'It's Menyu's son,' said tall Allaye. 'Ever since I gave him some milk he has been coming to the camp. He has a flat head like his father.'

He passed his hand over the top of his head as he spoke, to show what he meant.

From early morning the camp was surrounded by naked children waiting for the thousand and one miracles with which the life of the Nazarenes is diversified. They were also waiting till the departure to Ogotemmêli's gave them a chance to lay hands on small articles, exclaiming in triumph to the European who could not even keep his pencil safe from their depredations. A minute being was holding it aloft like an arrow pointed skywards.

The caravan filed off by the ordinary route with a few delays caused by the porters, who stopped to blow their noses with their fingers and wipe them carefully on the soles of their feet. The party spread out in the Hogon's field, then poured into the street that divided Guinna from Amtaba, and dropped their small burdens, like a flood discharging wreckage, on the rocks and hollow stones of the courtyard. Their thin bodies then disappeared in Tabda.

'The first woven garment,' began Ogotemmêli, 'was a woman's loin-cloth. It was sewn when they took the fibres away from her.'

This garment, which has four strips in token of her femininity, is worn crosswise with the seams horizontal. It covers the body from the navel to the knees, and is wound round the wearer without any fastening.

The woman's loin-cloth is open, because her sexual parts are open. Otherwise she could not be impregnated.

The second garment to be woven was a man's trousers, the seat consisting of three strips (the token-number of masculinity), passing between the legs and covering the belly and loins, with three additional strips on each side for the thighs. The body is thus wrapped in three times three strips, a total which includes the token-numbers of both femininity and masculinity.

Trousers are closed with a cord, because the man's sex organ is closed. The knot which fastens them is a symbol of love, the right-hand end of the cord being the man and the left-hand end the woman.

The third woven garment was the so-called 'sleeved' gown, made of four long strips behind and four in front and three strips each side.

The four strips at the back recall the four male ancestors, and the four in front the female ancestors. For the man looks to have the woman he desires in front of him for coition.

The three side-strips are the male number.

The fourth thing to be woven was the covering for the dead, made of eight strips of black and white squares, which are the eight families multiplied and which reproduce the lay-out of cultivated land. The covering or pall is thus a symbol of life and resurrection. In it the dead man is folded for a short time, like a foetus in the womb, so that in it he may be immersed again in the web of the living and in the germinating fields.

The fifth article of clothing was the cap made of two strips symbolizing a pair. It was invented at the time of the organization of the world, and was originally reserved for the Hogon, that is, the chief.

Originally all clothing was white, the colour of cotton. Then men began to be afraid of turning pale like the material, and dyed their garments saffron yellow, the colour of earth, in order to look like their land. Later on, they invented the blue-black colour for the pall for the dead, for the first pall, which was wrapped round the body of Lébé.

There was much discussion about the colour to be adopted in these cases, and it was some time before agreement could be reached. But they settled on blue-black as the colour nearest to coal, which itself resembles the colour of men's skins. In the past, however, men were called *banu*, that is, red, which is what they still call light-coloured skins. But they were also thinking of the smith's skin, blackened as it was by coal-dust.

Ogotemmêli attached no particular importance to these matters of colour and number. They were simple and obvious.

'Clothing,' he said, 'man's clothing, is the seventh Nummo.'

He meant by this remark that to put on a garment (*soy*) was to clothe oneself in the words (*so*) of the Nummo, seventh (*soy*) of the name; he meant also, and especially, that a woman by wearing ornaments (*sey*) assumed the disguise of the seventh Nummo.

On this point he began with the unexpected observation that women's mouths were weaving implements.

He reminded his hearers of the teaching of the seventh Nummo when sunk in the earth; how he opened to the sunlight his anthill mouth, from which were drawn the threads of the warp.

Teeth filed to a point are the sharp teeth of the Spirit, through which the threads were drawn. The copper stud fixed to the centre of the lower lip is the bobbin of thread. The four studs (the feminine number again) on the sides of the nose are the stakes of the loom, and the pendants of beads from the septum are its pivotal axis.

When women—or men for that matter—file their teeth, they do it to recall the threading of the eighty odd and eighty even threads, which symbolize the multiplication of families. They are also indicating their respect for the Word embodied in these threads, for the moist Word coming from the mouth, and for the water we drink, the essence of the master of Speech. The zigzag line formed by each row of teeth also symbolizes the path of water and the Word.

'Thus all that adorns the Spirit of water belongs also to women.'

He meant that women's ornaments recalled the Nummo's appearance, and especially certain details of his green body. The circlet of green beads on the temple is the Nummo's glittering forehead: the necklace represents the wrinkles of his neck. The two red beads at the corners of the nostrils are his eyes.

The copper bracelets at the wrists and the bend of the arm have the shape and occupy the place of the circular bones which distend the skin of the Spirit in this part of his limbs, for his arms are flexible although they are furnished with long unjoined bones. These bracelets are four in number, the feminine number.

The row of beads or the copper ring on the right ankle recalls the circular bone at the end of the Spirit's tail; strictly speaking no ornament should be worn on the left ankle.

Copper rings are worn on the first finger, ring finger, and little finger, because these are the only fingers in a webbed hand which show circular swellings in the place of joints, and the rings imitate these swellings. But no rings are worn on the thumb or the third finger because in the Spirit they are smooth and supple so that rings would not stay on them. No rings should be worn on the toes, because the Spirit has no feet.

Ogotemmêli passed on to the ear, one of the most important apertures (said he) of the body.

The ear is bi-sexual in both man and woman. The external ear protects the auditory channel, which represents the female sex organ. The red triangular pendants are the testicles. The eight copper studs in the form of a large crescent worn on the edge of the helix are the eight ancestors.

The part played by the ear in the act of generation was to form the subject of another conversation.

The scarifications practised by women reproduce those of the Nummo. They consist usually of two lines of incisions—one vertical stretching from the level of the breasts to the navel, while the other is horizontal, lying across the belly from one side to the other. The lines are in two rows of short slanting incisions forming a series of Vs without points.

Four parallel incisions (feminine number) are made on the temples.

Each of these incisions is a representation of the organ of sex, cut with a razor symbolizing the male organ. They are always moist because they are open at the name of the Spirit of Water. It is thus that the women's fertility is multiplied.

'What of the hair? Has that a meaning?'

'Women's hair,' replied Ogotemmêli, 'is the Nummo's hair.

The comb which makes the parting is like the carding-comb which separates the threads of the warp. When the hair is dressed in the *Kou tari* style there ought really to be sixty partings in the middle and ten each side, making eighty in all, to recall the eight families; but this is not possible. Moreover, the rules about dress are not strict, and very few women wear all these ornaments.'

On the social aspects of clothing Ogotemmêli had much to say.

'The loin-cloth is tight,' he said, 'to conceal the woman's sex, but it stimulates a desire to see what is underneath. This is because of the Word, which the Nummo put into the fabric. That word is every woman's secret, and is what attracts the man. A woman must have secret parts to inspire desire. If she went about in the market with nothing on, no one would run after her even if she were very beautiful. Undressed and un-adorned she is not desirable; but dress and ornament make men desire her, even if she is not beautiful. From a very beautiful woman without adornment men turn away.'

He reflected a few moments before adding:

'To be naked is to be speechless.'

On the way back to camp Koguem commented on what had been said about dress.

'Clothes,' he said, 'give satisfaction, not only to the wearer, but also to the spectator. It is true that women attract by their dress; but they too are attracted by a well-dressed man.'

He described how the desire for clothes was causing a number of young people to leave the country. Every year, he said, the Government deplores, here in the cliffs just as elsewhere, the mass emigration of workers in the prime of life, who go to the Gold Coast to earn money and often live there for years and sometimes die there.

These young people, he said, who go off to the Gold Coast or Bamako or elsewhere, go mainly for clothes. They make money there and spend it all, the day before they come back, on gewgaws, turbans or umbrellas, and peacock about in them on market days or at funerals. Dress helps them to get married. The more clothes a man has, the more elegant he is, and the more the women go after him.

Koguem too preferred an ordinary woman decked with ornaments—mere clothing hardly counted with him—to a pretty woman without beads or bracelets.

'Ogotemmêli is right,' he said. 'Adornment excites love. It fulfils its purpose of attracting the male, as the Nummo meant it to do. And, if there is a connection between ornaments and love, that is because the first ornaments of all, those of the female Nummo, were in the centre-jar of the celestial granary, on which the smith came down; and that jar is the symbol of the world's womb.'

The Smithy

IN the rock-mass, which on the south forms the central square of Upper Ogol, in a small corner of land the smithy is hidden away. It stands on a roughly circular site with low walls of dry stones unmortared and full of openings. Resting on these and supported in the middle by a stake, is a thin layer of branches through which splashes of sunlight fall on the shadows within.

The tools and implements are scattered on the dusty ground without any apparent order. Though the smith has only just left, the smithy looks as if it has been deserted for years. The double bellows, its skins limp, points its two ducts at the dead fire. The anvil like an enormous iron thorn stands on the ground fixed in a beam, which is buried in the earth. Over against it are tongs and some shapeless pieces of iron. The hammer, symbol of the webbed hand of the Spirit of Water, is not to be seen : either it is hidden or the smith has taken it away. Against the wall there is an oven, made of puddled clay, with an opening at the bottom leading to a bowl-shaped outlet above. Close by is a hollow stone from which the water has evaporated.

In the silence and the sunlight all the poverty of the smithy is laid bare. That technique which revolutionized the world, which came down from heaven, and with its tools broke the limbs of the first smith who blew up the fire—a 'fragment of the sun'—still exists even in this decay.

The European had made a point of going to see the smithy before questioning Ogotemmêli about it. Having first studied weaving, a craft held in the highest estimation, bearer of the gift of speech, he wanted to learn from the old man the significance of this most primitive of tools.

'The smithy,' said the blind man, 'is like a dwelling-house, or again like a person, whose head is the oven and his two arms the bellows with its two ducts.'

In the primal field, in which the flying granary landed, the smithy was erected on the north side at the edge of the land which was to be cleared. That is why today smithies are always erected on the north side of the central square, which itself is always to the north of the village.

'You can see,' said Ogotemmêli, turning his head to one side, 'you can see over the wall.'

The central square of Lower Ogol was indeed there behind the ruined granary of the backyard on the left. The high central rock, the square millstone of the council house, the cube-shaped stone known as the 'Stone of the Brave' and, on the left, facing full north, a smithy sister to that of Upper Ogol, were all clearly to be seen.

But here all was according to rule, whereas in the other village the plan of the building was completely different.

'At first,' said Ogotemmêli, 'the smith did not have all the tools that he has today. He had no hafted hammer, no file and no tongs. The red-hot iron was held in the bare hand; and that is something one can still see today, when the smiths come together for funerals. As they chant the dirges for the dead, they pick up red-hot iron in their hands in memory of the practice of the first smiths.'

The chief tool, he went on to say, is the hammer. The celestial granary was a hammer; and everybody believes that it was in this hammer that the seeds came down from heaven. The hammer is the webbed hand of the Water Spirit. The arm is the cone-shaped handle, and the hand itself is the four-sided face of the tool with which it strikes.

The hammer is also the whole body of the Water Spirit, the male Great Nummo in heaven. Two of the opposite sides are his arms, and the other two his back and chest. The cone-shaped handle is the serpent's tail in which the lower part of his body ends.

The anvil is something like the implement reapers use; it is the female form of the hammer, and represents the female Great Nummo. The slab at the top is very narrow but rectangular, and it ends in a blunt point. There is often a small hole at this lower end, reminiscent of the part played by the hammer, that is, by the granary, in the organization of the world, when its interior, symbolized by this hole, was full of organs and seeds.

The beam in which the anvil is embedded is made of a medium-sized tree-trunk about a cubit in length, roughly squared. It is sunk in the earth in a line north–south, as all men's beds should lie.

The wood of the anvil is the bed of the two great Water Spirits. When the hammer strikes the iron, the two come together.

The two earthenware pots of the bellows are modelled in clay, with which wool from a white sheep is mixed. This addition gives greater cohesion to the material, which is not baked but dried slowly in the air. The sheep's wool is a symbol of the celestial Ram, avatar of the Nummo.

The two spherical pots symbolize the sun, being of the same shape, while the wool in their clay comes from the fleece of the Spirit, which is of copper, the sun's excrement. They are also associated with that luminary by the skins which cover them, and by means of which air is conveyed to the fire. The other, which the smith in flight brandished over his head, had already acquired a fiery quality from contact with its fellow-skin, and was able to sustain unscathed the discharge of the thunderbolts.

The ducts of dry earth which connect the pots with the fire-grate afford a passage for the air expelled by the skins; and this air is a breath of the sun, and so animates the fire.

From the hollow stone the smith draws water with a stick, with which to damp down the fire. The Nummo is in this puddle as in all water, and he moved in it by swimming, his movements following the rhythm of the blows on the anvil and the alternating puffs of the bellows.

The European had known for years the magical function of the sounds of a smithy. He had been present many times at rituals in the course of which at a certain point a smith would strike the rock with his hammer or with the iron part of his anvil. By producing sound from the iron, in which the mythical first smith had brought so many benefits to mankind, he was reminding his fellow-men of the supreme power of Amma and the Water Spirit. He was assisting their prayers and strengthening them by the sounds he made; he was appeasing the possible

86

wrath of the celestial Beings by this acknowledgement of their pre-eminence. When men quarrelled with one another, he would intervene between the parties, hammer in hand, and strike the rocks, thus bringing a divine note into the human disorder and calming the passions aroused.

To questions on these points Ogotemmêli made no reply, but continued to develop his exposition.

'The smith,' he said, 'in striking the anvil is asking the earth to restore to him the strength of which he had formerly emptied himself.'

For, when the smith of the celestial granary came down to the defiled earth, he put into it a great portion of his own pure strength, depriving himself in order to give the soil a life-force favourable to the great work he was about to do.

As a result he and his descendants became endowed with a special quality, which made them different from men, whether 'impure' (*puru*) or 'living' (*omo*) or 'white' (*pili*).

The 'impure' are the descendants of the first initiates of the Great Mask, the upholders of the spiritual principles of the first dead man; the 'living' are the other Dogon; the 'whites' are people like shoemakers, minstrels and men of the various peoples dwelling in the plains.

The characteristic feature of the smiths is a diminished life-force, which removes them from the category of the 'living'. But this diminishment is not like the effect of death, which separates them also from the 'impure'. Nor are they comparable to the 'whites', for these are insensitive to certain sources of impurity. Though they have, like other people, individual altars for both head and body (*kutogolo, djabyé*), they have to be constantly engaged on some other means of self-support; and this is provided for them by the exercise of their craft.

'By striking the anvil,' said Ogotemmêli, 'they get back from the earth some of the life-force they gave it. Their blows recover it.'

But blows on the iron must be dealt by day. The smith's work is day labour, no doubt because the smithy fire, being a fragment of the sun, could not shine at night. That is why it is forbidden, not only for smiths but for everybody, to strike blows on iron or stone or earth in the night-time. No blow of hammer or tap of pestle should be heard, whether loud or soft, in the silent hours. To strike blows at night would destroy the effect of the blows struck by day. It would mean the rejection of all that had been gained, so that the smith would lose whatever he had recovered during the day of the life-force of which he formerly divested himself.

The fines inflicted on those who strike blows by night are used to provide victims for the foundation altar of the village, which in former times was erected above a man buried standing, who had offered his strength and his body for the stability of the human settlement on the new earth.

Thus was restored the broken order of that relationship between the earth and the one who emptied himself to purify it and to enable men to pursue their life-giving labours.

In the primal field the smith had assigned to his own family one of the eight sectors marked out around the point of impact of the granary. But what he was concerned to do was merely to establish his right to the produce from it, for he was not at any time to cultivate it himself.

His part is to forge the implements of cultivation, but never to use them with his own hand; the hoes that he makes are for the men of the seven other families, and it is for them in return to supply him with food. So we see how, every year at harvest-time, the smith leaves his forge and goes about the country to collect the grain from the plots which the implements of his forging have worked. He knows all the fields which owe him tribute: there is nothing he does not know about their growth and their maturity.

So it is that, when the sweating peasant opens up to the sunlight the soil which lay in the shade of the growing corn, and reaps the last ear, he sees seated at the edge of the field, watching him open-mouthed and in silence, the smith.

Pottery

Pottery was born in the smithy. The smith's wife was drying in the sun a pot which she had modelled like one of the spheres of the bellows; but, finding it did not harden quickly enough, she put it near the fire. She then discovered that the clay was baking and becoming hard, and so she got into the habit of putting the pots she modelled by the fire.

She worked on a small square mat woven with eighty strings on a warp of the same number. First she made a rough model shaped like a section of an inverted cone, into which she threw with considerable force a round pebble, which made a bed for itself in the clay, and this became larger and larger until finally it took the shape of a sphere. When the inside surface of the clay was pressed it took the pattern of the mat.

Women today copy the processes of the mythical potteress; but the craft is no longer the prerogative of the wives of smiths. Any woman can be a potter, if she wishes.

'The mat,' said Ogotemmêli, 'on which the woman works, is a symbol of that of the first human couple. The craft of pottery is like a person on a mat. In moulding the clay the woman is imitating the work of God, when he modelled the earth and the first couple. She is creating a being, and the round pot is like a head resting on the mat, a head or a womb. A pot without ornament symbolizes a man, a pot with two small breasts a woman.'

Ogotemmêli had before him one of the pots used for brewing millet-beer. He passed his hand over its belly as he spoke to feel the pattern imprinted on it.

'The mat on which the potter works has eighty threads one way and eighty threads the other. It is woven like one square of the pall that covers the dead, but with fibres of baobab instead of cotton.'

Baobab fibres are much used among the Dogon for cords and plaited objects of all kinds. One sees rings a couple of cubits deep round the trunks of trees from which the bark has been torn.

'This fibre-plaiting is men's work and resembles weaving. The best work is done in Banani. Patterns made on pots in this way make one think one has one's mat with one for repose wherever one goes.'

'And what,' said the European, 'of the pebble with which the clay is struck?'

'The stone,' was the reply, 'which the woman rolls in the clay is the symbol of the food which will be cooked in the pot.'

'How was meat cooked before there were clay pots?'

'Before pottery was invented,' said Ogotemmêli, 'men ate their meat raw.' In an earlier conversation he had compared the moon to a pot heated a quarter at a time. This symbol has another application.

'Before the clay has been baked,' he went on to explain, 'the open end of the pot recalls the circumference of the moon. After the baking it represents the circumference of the sun. That is intelligible enough,' he added, 'for one must suppose the moon is less completely cooked than the sun.'

So a humble pot is an epitome of the universe, with its own mat on its surface.

The Large Family House

OGOTEMMÊLI'S house was not a typical specimen. Its external appearance was poverty-stricken, with dusty niches filled by altars commemorating dead children. No odours of stored grain emanated from its wretched cellars. There were only holes where swallows nested, opening towards the west in expectation of future flights.

Amadigué's house, on the other hand, was chequered with flat surfaces and recesses, a combination of doors, holes, and the traditional cone-shaped decorations.

The front elevation was twelve cubits wide and eight cubits high; it was pierced by ten vertical rows of eight square niches, their sides measuring a handsbreadth; these niches extended from ground level to a horizontal line of swallows' holes which lay under the shelter of a roof of small wooden billets no larger than a cubit in size. The whole façade was finished off by a series of slender columns like sugar loaves, each one topped by a flat stone intended to catch the rain; but the water had worn them away so that some of them had come to look like hourglasses.

In the centre, two doors, one above the other with two niches between them, divided the chequer-board into two parts; the door on the ground floor, a little wider than a man's chest and less than a man's height, was made of two bare planks; the one in the upper storey, which was the same width but considerably lower, was decorated with several rows of sculptured figures in relief and was fastened by a conspicuous lock surmounted by two geometrical figures.

The plan of the building was a square with sides measuring eight cubits (the same dimensions as the agricultural plots) flanked by four rectangles of equal length. It might also be compared to a Greek cross with very thick, short transverse arms. But in Amadigué's house the front was wider, and in each of the angles formed by its extremities was a recess.

The square constituted the principal room, used by the married couple for sleeping and by the woman for work. Four posts in a square on the diagonals supported the ceiling. To the left a platform of earth was placed in the corner against the wall. In the room, above the door, cotton-seeds in their white fibres were heaped on the lintel.

The rectangle at the front of the house formed the vestibule, the entrance to it facing the door of the room. The rectangle at the back served as a kitchen, and the two side rectangles were store-rooms.

These four rooms, consisting in fact of narrow passages, opened on to the central room by doors in the middle of the walls, which in the case of the store-rooms were mere bays. The sole entrance in the centre of the front wall was in a line with the openings into the principal room and kitchen.

The hearth was composed of two large stones placed two handsbreadths from the back wall and two handsbreadths from one another. A round pot rested on them and against the wall.

The plan of the upper storey was the same, except for the kitchen, the ceiling of which was higher than the roof of the building, which it overlooked by means of an opening that also served as an outlet for the smoke. Like most of the houses in Upper Ogol, Amadigué's house faced west so as to avoid the rains brought by the prevailing winds. It formed one side of a narrow lane, the other side of which was a series of granaries with carefully closed doors. But in front of the central door there was an opening leading to the dung-heap of a rich man. At the top of the façade, attached to beams projecting beyond the mud wall, hung bronze-red bunches of the millet known as 'eyes staring out of their head' because of its big round seeds.

It seemed to the European that he was coming into an ordered accumulation of riches, overflowing roofs, floors, niches and cellars alike.

Indeed, all kinds of produce, in measured quantities, were drying on the roofs—red pepper, purple-fruited sorrel, yellow millet, which makes a clear sound in falling and is called 'tinkling gold'.

'The front wall with its eight rows of ten niches,' said

Ogotemmêli, 'represents the eight ancestors and their descendants, numerous as the fingers on their hands.'

In the vertical direction the two series of five columns, he explained, are the ten fingers, and when one looks at the front elevation of a house one sees two hands spread out.

The niches are the homes of the ancestors, who occupy them in order of birth beginning with the highest row. The niches should never be closed, for the ancestors need to breathe the outdoor air. On the carved door of the upper storey there are, or should be, eight rows of eighty figures, picturing the men and women of the whole world descended from the original ancestors.

The lock is the altar of the ancestors, and the two figures above it are the custodian and his wife. The pair of taller figures that are sometimes carved above the panel, represent the original human couple.

The circular holes in the pediment, ten in number like the fingers of the hand, are occupied by swallows' nests, the poultry yard of the ancestors. They are called 'swallows' holes'—and so euphemistically are all the niches in the front wall—out of respect for the old people, of whom one must not speak lightly.

The eight small columns on the top of the wall are the altars of the ancestors, beginning with the first ancestors on the left. In a narrow house with only two or three vertical rows of niches the columns are fewer. In a wider house there may be ten or more, but the traditional number is eight, one for each ancestor.

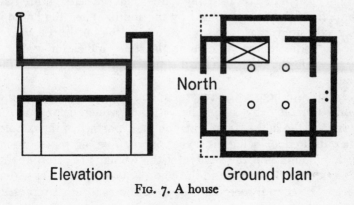

Elevation   Ground plan

FIG. 7. A house

The whole façade, with its eight rows of ten dark holes separated by lighter plane surfaces, is a symbol of the pall used to cover the dead, made in eight strips of black and white squares, which itself is a representation of cleared and marked out land.

This façade gives its name to the tallest mask, the top of which is ten cubits above the wearer's head. The pole of this mask is divided into ten sections each consisting of a perforated rectangular grating with four or five bars; between each of these is a flat plane. The pole itself is a symbol of the warp in weaving, and is lowered towards the east and the west in imitation of the daily course of the sun.

The European recalled the hortatory chants intoned in the 'storeyed house' ceremony:

> '*They say the houses of Molu in Tomboké are fine,*
> *That the houses of Molu are fine.*
> *In Molu the houses have storeys.*
> *But it is the men who are fine,*
> *Not the storeyed houses!*'

'The soil of the ground-floor,' said Ogotemmêli, 'is the symbol of the earth and of Lébé, restored to life in the earth.'

The flat roof, square like that of the flying granary, represents heaven, and the ceiling which separates the upper storey from the ground-floor represents the space lying between heaven and earth. The four small rectangular roofs around it indicate the four cardinal points, as does the hearth itself.

The hearth derives its living flame from the celestial fire that came from the fire purloined by the smith. When the house is correctly sited, that is to say, is open to the north, the pot on the fire indicates the same point, the stones indicating east and west, while the wall, the third support for the pot, marks the south.

Inside the house, the several rooms represent caves of this world inhabited by men. The vestibule, which belongs to the master of the house, represents the male partner of the couple, the outside door being his sexual organ. The big central room is the domain and the symbol of the woman; the store-rooms each side are her arms, and the communicating door her sexual parts. The central room and the store-rooms together represent

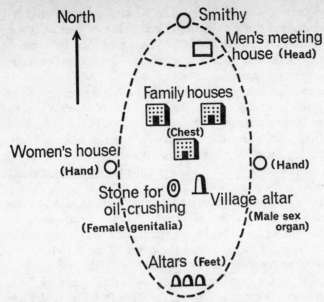

North

Smithy

Men's meeting
house (Head)

Family houses

(Chest)

Women's house
(Hand)

(Hand)

Stone for
oil-crushing
(Female genitalia)

Village altar
(Male sex
organ)

Altars (Feet)

FIG. 8. Diagram of village

the woman lying on her back with outstretched arms, the door
open and the woman ready for intercourse.

The room at the back which contains the hearth and looks
out on to the flat roof, shows the breathing of the woman, who
lies in the central room under the ceiling which is the symbol
of a man, its beams representing his skeleton; their breath finds
its outlet through the opening above. The four upright poles
(feminine number) are the couple's arms, those of the woman
supporting the man who rests his own on the ground. When a
child is to be born, the woman in labour is seated on a stool in
the middle of the room, her back to the north, and is supported
by women. The infant is delivered on the ground and takes
possession of its soul in the place where it was conceived.

The earthen platform that serves as a bed, lies north and
south and the couple sleep on it with their heads to the north,
like the house itself, the front wall of which is its face. The man
lies on his right side facing west, and the woman on her left side
facing east, which are the positions they will occupy in the grave.

The man lies on his right side and touches the woman with his

95

left hand, never with his right. The woman sleeps on her left arm, and touches the man with her right. They never lie in any other position. A woman is buried lying on her left arm, a man lying on his right, just as they sleep. The funeral covering is spread over the pair.

Under the bed are put all the seeds for sowing except cotton seeds, which are placed on the lintel of the second door, symbol of the female sex.

In sexual intercourse the man is sowing; he is like a Water Spirit causing fertilizing rain to fall on the earth and on the woman, on the sown seeds. Thus agricultural and conjugal acts are linked.

When the pair lie with a covering over them, as in death, the bed is also a grave; it is the grave of Lébé, into which the seventh Nummo enters, and from which he emerges, by means of the two openings set between the doors of the façade.

Just as Lébé returned to life within the earth by the efforts of the Spirit, so the seeds are made to germinate, and children are procreated, by the action of the couple lying under the funeral pall, symbol of numerous lineages and cultivated lands.

But a house of this sort is only one feature of the village, which consists of a tangle of dwellings surrounded by granaries and outbuildings. Streets run through it in every direction, splitting it into blocks. Each village is divided into quarters, and in each quarter there is an extended family possessing a large house of its own. Each quarter has its council shelter built on a small open square; but the village has a more important shelter, belonging to one of the quarters but built on a larger square where important ceremonies take place.

'The village,' said Ogotemmêli, 'should extend from north to south like the body of a man lying on his back. Lower Ogol is almost correct. The head is the council house, built on the chief square, which is the symbol of the primal field.'

It appeared also, from the blind man's earlier explanations, that the village should be in the form of a square with one side facing north and the streets running from north to south and east to west. But this is not possible except in the plain; on the contorted plateau and in the scree of the cliffs the village has to be adapted to the irregular terrain.

On the north side of the square is the smithy, as was that of the bringer of civilization. To the east and west are houses for menstruating women; they are round like wombs and represent the hands of the village. The large family houses are its chest and belly; the communal altars at the south of the village are its feet.

The stones on which the fruit of the *Lannea acida* is crushed, placed in the centre of the village, represent its female sexual parts. Beside them should be set the foundation altar, which is its male sex organ; but out of respect for the women this altar is erected outside the walls.

Within the village each quarter is a complete whole, and should be laid out in the same way as the village, like a separate entity. Seen from the air, the village is like the ancestor's house with its eighty niches, or like the great pall for the dead with its black and white squares. The buildings are the filled in areas of the façade of the house, while the courtyards and approaches are holes. The flat roofs shining in the sunlight and the shadows thrown on the ground reproduce the black and white colours of the pall. The streets running from north to south are the seams joining the strips together.

The men's shelter, which is to be found in each public square and particularly in the central square of the village, is a very different building from the dwelling-houses. In Sanga it consists of a square stack composed of several layers of trussed millet-stalks, the whole resting on a rough framework of tree-trunks balanced on three parallel rows of dry-stone or wooden pillars. The men meet in the shelter during the heat of the day to rest and chat. The elders in particular confer there and take decisions on matters of public interest. In the past, when a village was founded, the shelter and the women's houses were the first buildings to be erected.

It was under some such shelter as this that the eight ancestors used to take counsel in the days when they had human form before their transformation into Water Spirits.

Today shelters may be circular, with a millstone shaped like a section of an inverted cone on top; but otherwise they are, or should be, orientated according to the cardinal points. They have, or should have, three rows of pillars lying north to south, the two side-rows having three supports and the middle-row two supports, arranged in the form of a quincunx. These stumpy pillars, made of firmly balanced stones, sometimes covered with a coating of whitish grey mud, stand like the trunks of the eight ancestors when seated in council with their heads in the rafters of the roof.

To an observer sitting inside the building and facing north these columns appear in numerical order, the first in the north-west corner, the second in the west, the third in the south-west, the fourth in the south-east, and so on round the points of the compass. The seventh is in the middle to the north, and the eighth behind it.

Thus the ground plan of the series of eight pillars resembles a serpent coiled along a broken line and surrounding the symbols of the seventh ancestor, the master of Speech, and the eighth ancestor, who is the Word itself.

The Sanctuary

IN earlier conversations Ogotemmêli had let it be understood that the dwelling-house had not been the first building to be constructed. The very first was a Binu sanctuary erected in the Dâlé region by the priest of the ancestor Dewa-out-of-the-Stick. To be exact, it was near the Guibêlé marsh in Kunnu that this took place; and the shape of this sanctuary was later taken as a model for dwelling-houses.

'But,' Ogotemmêli had added, 'a sanctuary is a tomb, whereas a house is a place to live in.'

A Binu sanctuary is erected in honour of an ancestor, Binu, whose name is a contraction of two terms, one of which means 'gone' and the other 'come back'. This ancestor was apparently dead, that is to say, gone to another world, then returned to the world of men, to his own people to protect them and to help and succour them.

The conversations with Ogotemmêli presupposed a knowledge of this important institution, which may in some degree be called totemic in default of a better term. A subsequent conversation was to confirm the European's reservations on the subject of Dogon 'totemism', but he felt that the term was useful and less open to objection if properly defined.

He felt also that the ideas and images revolving in the mind of his remarkable informant were all that mattered, and that neither his own ideas nor the speculations of Western students were of any interest.

The symbolism of a Binu sanctuary was to be the programme for the fifteenth day, and it was with keen interest that the European made his way to the dung-heap which was the scene of the old man's revelations.

He recalled the hundreds of sanctuaries which he had studied in the course of his travels over the plateau and cliffs. In particular he remembered the two great towers in the form of shells, which framed the façade of the temple of the Nummo of Nandouli, situated under the baobabs at the head of a dry valley in harsh surroundings suggesting the creation of the world. He had had to discard every stitch of clothing and enter naked a third tower, the shape of the white crown of the Pharaohs, where, among other extraordinary objects, he found smith's tools decorated with cattle-bells, iron sandals and an iron crown resembling that of the Lombards. There, before the altar-throne of the Water god he was at the heart of the problem.

In the south of the plateau, at Dyombolo, he had seen the square house with rounded corners of the Binu Arsana, and was dazzled by the red, black and white colours of its paintings that represented masks, a sun, and a base of alternating triangles forming a zigzag pattern. A huge serpent, in relief, with a speckled body, entered the building by a hole in the wall and came out somewhere else.

At Banani and Yugo Pilu, villages of the scree, at the foot of the towering rock-walls, he had seen temples that were no more than façades laid over a hollow in the rock or an open shed. They were approached by means of ledges from which the

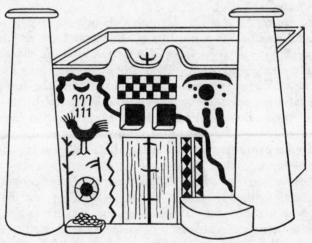

Fig. 9. Totemic shrine and its paintings

scree could be seen descending to the plain, with thinly scattered trees as in an orchard.

In Yugo Dogoru all the altars were grouped together in a narrow gorge which became even narrower as it entered the heart of the mountain-mass. They seemed to be thrust like stoppers into chinks in the horizontal galleries open throughout on to empty space. The rock ledges were so narrow that the altars were reduced to the thickness of stage sets, bearing on their façades a few drawings of chevrons.

At Bababi the priest offered sacrifice in the sight of all the people; but at Yugo Dogoru he disappeared into the bowels of the rock.

But, whether it is an actual building exposed to the sunlight or a recess at the end of a gorge, the sanctuary always contains a simple chamber either square (often rounded at the corners) or circular. The sanctuary of the Sodamma quarter of Upper Ogol, a village which is full of altars, measures four cubits by five. Its front is pierced by a door surmounted by two holes and crowned with four excrescences like rounded sugar-loaves. This building stands in a small courtyard, and like all those similarly placed, is very small.

The temple of Binu Sangabilu in the Do quarter, on the other hand, is built on a fairly large open space away from the dwelling-houses. It is a cube measuring some six cubits a side, its front wall flanked by towers at the corners, slightly conical in shape and topped with two mounds, between which there is an iron hook. The door, measuring one by two cubits, is surmounted by two square niches placed on the same level. To the right of the door is a platform of earth which serves as a seat for the priest during ceremonies. To the left are placed some hollow stones, in former times used for grinding, and now containing stone axes or round pebbles.

The roof is a flat one, from which the rain is led off by a wooden gutter, while the two corner towers are topped by flat projecting stones which protect the roof-ridges from rain. Inside the sanctuary are the cult objects—a hollow stone full of water or thunder stones, earthenware vessels of various kinds, iron or wooden implements and altars made of earth.

'A sanctuary,' said Ogotemmêli, 'should face north. But, as with the big house, it is the rain which decides the orientation.'

The two flanking towers and the central cones are the large and small altars of this world. Those in the centre receive libations of millet-gruel and the blood of sacrificial victims. At the time of sacrifice the white gruel and the red blood trickle down the front of the building and drip in long lines to the ground.

'Where you see the iron hook between the mounds,' said Ogotemmêli, 'is the place where the ancestor smith began to work at his smithy in the primal field.'

'But the hook? What is that?'

'The hook is the anvil. It is buried in a cross-beam.'

'A cross-beam of the roof?'

'No! There is a short piece of wood on the pediment, not to be confused with the roof timbers. It is the symbol of the beam in which the anvil is fixed.'

The roof of the sanctuary, it appeared, is the symbol of the primal field, and the interior of the building beneath is the tomb of Lébé.

The platform outside is the place where the dead body rested before it was buried. The door is the hole by which the men entered when they wanted to exhume the bones in order to take them into new countries. The two niches above the door are where the seventh ancestor came and went when he cast his human skin and took the form of a serpent: he entered by the aperture on the right when he came to swallow the dead man and regenerate him, and he came out by the one on the left.

Within the sanctuary, the hollow stone full of water, pebbles, and cowries contains the seventh ancestor's vomit, the waters of torrents and marshes, the dead man's bones changed into covenant-stones, and his nails changed into cowries. The sanctuary is the chamber of the swallowing, where the seventh ancestor consumed the human nature of Lébé and cast out the outline of the organization of the world.

But the sanctuary is also a smithy. The hook on the pediment is the anvil, and the hollow stone outside the building recalls the one from which the smith pours water to cool his red-hot iron. The two hemispherical altars in the sanctuary, the priest's personal altars, dedicated the one to his head and the other to his body, are the pots of the bellows. They are placed close by a red ochre mark which represents the fire which the bellows quicken. The hammer is represented by a conical altar.

But the most important of all these objects is the iron hook fixed in the pediment which is the anvil of the smithy. The hook is most often a double one, each of its branches ending in a tight curl. This is the horned forehead of the celestial ram, whose curved horns hold the rain-clouds. The two curled ends are also thought of as two hands which will retain moisture and secure abundance.

Instead of a hook, however, there is sometimes a square or cylindrical iron shaft, as thick as a thumb and a handsbreadth in height, narrowing from its middle point into a cone, ending in a blunt point. Halfway up the shaft two small flat pieces of iron extend like arms on either side; these are slightly curved upwards and widen out at their ends into a sort of flattened hand, edged like the teeth of a saw to represent fingers.

This object, which is also called a 'hook', has a slight resemblance, because of its vertical shaft, both to the anvil and to the hammer of the smith, while because of its branches, which are arms, it is a symbol of the Water Spirit, already represented by that same hammer and anvil. These two arms raised slightly have the same function as the curled hands of the hook: their curved shape retains the rain and with it the crops necessary to men.

Because of the beneficent properties of these iron hooks and in memory of the eight ancestors, eight ears of corn gathered at the harvesting of the field belonging to the sanctuary are hung up at the top of the façade. For the same reason, when sowing is to begin, the ears which are to provide the seed are spread out on the roof. There they absorb the moisture and the forces of renewal are inherent in the curled horns and the outstretched arms.

It is from this roof, that is to say, from the primal field, whose depths once witnessed a death and a resurrection, that the ears, heavy with life, are flung to the people mingled with the seed corn.

Paintings on the Façade
of the Sanctuary

THIS iron Christ fixed in an anvil beam on the pediment of a tomb had robbed the Nazarene of his sleep. To tell the truth, the slumbers of the whole community were apt to be short. The revelations of the Bambara transplanted to Sanga, linguistic study, and exacting researches into the main cycles of Dogon activity, left little time for repose or peace of mind.

On his return from the last conversation the European had sprung the news on his companions.

'Now I understand the spear of Orosongo,' he said. 'You know that very long iron spear we photographed nearly ten years ago. Well, it must be a variant of the hooks, it is of the same spirit.'

He was alluding to an object which had for years excited his curiosity and which he had seen in a temple on the Wazuba plateau. Fixed on the point of the weapon was a human figure, half the size of a hand, in forged iron, with its arms outstretched as on a cross.

He was still curious about the curving arms of this anvil-Christ.

'No doubt,' he said, 'Ogotemmêli sees in this a system of hooking together. The arms are to hold water and seeds and abundance. The anvil in fact, if I may say so, has its arms full.'

But he thought of the seventh ancestor's last revelation, of the string-game between his webbed hands for the demonstration, which was a kind of weaving, of the armpit drum. This iron planted on a tomb was, as it were, a reminder of the third Word, a musical word.

But Ogotemmêli would never utter a word about this.

In the course of the sixteenth conversation the Nazarene asked why the different objects in the sanctuary (which was also a tomb and a smithy) were so scattered that it was impossible to understand their meaning.

'The objects are scattered,' replied Ogotemmêli, 'in order to conceal their symbolism from those who would like to understand them.'

In short for the uninitiated, the interior and the whole structure of the building and its accessories constituted a riddle without an answer.

But there was another riddle for the onlookers; at the time of sowing, the façade of a sanctuary is transformed into a picture of white, and sometimes also red and black, figures. With millet-gruel, ochre and coal the titled sacrificing priests decorate the walls for the new agricultural cycle.

Owing to the ignorance or inadequate instruction of these people, and for other reasons as well, fancy appears to reign unchecked in the choice of the subjects, objects and figures represented. But the rule governing the arrangement was known to Ogotemmêli.

Viewed from the front, the façade of the temple is divided into three parts—the right, reserved for female beings and cult objects, the left, reserved for males, and the space above the door.

The principal figure on the right is a ram, shown in profile, urinating, looking to the left and, above him, a series of spots representing stars.

'But the right is reserved for females!'

Ogotemmêli raised his head.

'Between his two horns,' he said, 'the ram wears a calabash, which is a symbol of woman and of the sun, who is female. That is how the ram comes to be on the right.'

He had already made frequent mention of this animal, well known to the peoples of the French Sudan as an avatar of the Water Spirit. Everyone mistrusts the rams which prowl around the marshes, especially if they are wearing a glistening calabash, to which the oil of *Lannea acida* lends red reflections. The calabash, it is true, acts as protection against the rays of the sun; but the ram uses it mainly as a bait to attract men.

Someone sees a calabash between the horns of a ram; what an

astonishing sight! But it is beautiful, he thinks, shining like the sun. He wonders why such a pretty thing, so red and shiny, should appear on the head of a ram; perhaps the ram should be caught before he breaks it. (A Dogon's attention is always attracted by material objects.) So, quick as thought, he rushes at it, but the calabash has vanished like a dream from the ram's horns and is floating on the water, drawing its rash pursuer into the power of the spirits who drink his blood from his nostrils.

But these are earthly manifestations. There are a hundred well-established local legends of enterprising rams who prowl around ponds and pools in the wet season, seeking to attract girls and luring their unhappy victims into the water, among the water-lilies.

'Who is this ram?' said the stranger.

'It is the Great Nummo of heaven, the Nummo Pair.'

'A pair?'

'The ram is the male and the calabash the female. It is a ram of gold. Before every storm in the rainy season he may be seen moving in the vault of heaven.'

The European grumbled at this new complication. A ram of gold? That was the first mention so far of gold.

'Gold,' said Ogotemmêli, 'is a younger brother of copper.'

Was gold then a by-product, a metal of secondary rank?

'The fleece,' continued the old man, 'is really copper; and copper is the cluster of rays coming from the rain-clouds when the sun is hidden. Copper is excreted by the Water Spirits in the damp atmosphere of heaven.'

He dilated on the notable part played by the sun in sucking up the clouds, and on the transformation into copper of the luminous rays excreted by the Nummo.

'The Ram Nummo,' he said, 'rolls in his own excrement.'

'When he appears in heaven,' he added, 'he wears a calabash between his horns. It is like a soldier's cap, and glistens with *Lannea acida* oil.'

The ram is also a symbol of the world-system; the calabash is the sun, his body is the earth, his forehead is the moon, his eyes are the stars in the sky. The copper fleece is also a fleece of water, for copper consists of wet rays. It is also a fleece of leaves, for water and vegetation are of the same essence.

His nose and mouth represent the breathing of all living creatures in the world, for his hindfeet are those of the large animals, his forefeet the small ones, and his tail the reptiles.

But the calabash is also the female Nummo, the essential Woman, whose breasts on the body of the beast are the two excrescences of the throat.

The ram puts the calabash (woman) on his head to hold her between his horns, which are testicles, and to have intercourse with her by means of the organ on his forehead. The Nummo, having taken the form of the ram, urinates from his lower member showers and mists, and with his frontal member he fertilizes the feminine element of the sun, and the woman and the sown seeds.

In all this Ogotemmêli saw the fundamental truth of the universal life process.

'The sun's rays,' he went on, 'are fire and the Nummo's excrement. It is the rays which give the sun its strength. It is the Nummo who gives life to this star, for the sun is in some sort a star.'

It was difficult to get him to explain what he meant by this obscure statement. The Nazarene made more than one fruitless effort to understand this part of the cosmogony; he could not discover any chink or crack through which to apprehend its meaning.

He was moreover confronted with identifications which no European, that is, no average rational European, could admit. He felt himself humiliated, though not disagreeably so, at finding that his informant regarded fire and water as complementary, and not as opposites.

The rays of light and heat draw the water up, and also cause it to descend again in the form of rain. That is all to the good. The movement created by this coming and going is a good thing. By means of the rays the Nummo draws out, and gives back the life-force. This movement indeed makes life.

The old man realized that he was now at a critical point. If the Nazarene did not understand this business of coming and going, he would not understand anything else. He wanted to say that what made life was not so much force as the movement of forces. He reverted to the idea of a universal shuttle service.

'The rays drink up the little waters of the earth, the shallow pools, making them rise, and then descend again in rain.'

Then, leaving aside the question of water, he summed up his argument:

'To draw up and then return what one had drawn—that is the life of the world.'

But one could not remain for ever on these metaphysical heights. Moreover this ram had the power of movement: once he had risen to the heavens, he moved about there. He went about his business: he did not merely stay still and urinate. He moved among the high clouds leaving a track of four colours from the earth shaken off his hooves. His left forefoot made a black track, his right a red track, the two others one green and one yellow. That fourfold track was called 'the Nummo's track'. It is the rainbow.

But the rainbow has an end. The Golden Ram came down by it from heaven, and plunged into the great pools of the earth.

'You can see him, when there is a violent storm, plunging into the Bananga marsh south of Lower Ogol. Have you never seen him?'

The old man pointed with his wizened hand to the south, as he added:

'He plunges among the water-lilies, crying: "The water is mine! Water is mine!"'

Paintings on the Façade
of the Sanctuary (continued)

THE chief figure on the right-hand section of the façade should therefore represent the Water Spirit, the Nummo, in his marvellous form of a golden or copper ram in a bed of stars.

One point, which Ogotemmêli had forgotten, is of interest to mammalogists.

'The horns of the beast are straight or curved: they can be either, but the curved sort are the oldest.'

The millet-gruel spread on the mud wall with chicken's feathers or brushes made of asses' hair was intended to give the impression that the fleece was made of leaves and, to draw attention to the processes of germination, the tail ending in a serpent's head was shown above an ear of millet standing erect.

To the right of the ram, two footprints, often shown in relief, represent the sandals of the priestly master of the sanctuary as well as the footprints of the first man. They are also the sandals of the Nummo Pair. As their bodies end in a reptile's tail, one sandal does for each, the left for the male and the right for the female.

On each sandal are eight spots recalling the cowries put in the place where the feet of the ancestor Lébé rested in the tomb of the resurrection. They also represent the eight ancestors, the eight seeds and the eight covenant stones. Lastly they are the eight cowries adorning the ritual sandals worn by candidates for the priesthood on the day of their inauguration.

Above the ram and the stars, three horizontal lines, coloured red, white, and blue-green, curving downwards at either end, represent the rainbow. Thus the painting on the right-hand side of the door is a complete picture of the sky with its light and its rain.

The objects or creatures shown on the left are of the earth. A prominent feature is a serpent who, in Sanga, is the seventh ancestor. He is often depicted as a wavy line, indicating the movement of water, which is also very commonly seen in the form of vertical zigzag lines representing the course of terrestrial streams as well as the way in which the Nummo falls on to the earth from heaven in the form of rain. And this movement may sometimes be suggested by the picture of an ostrich, whose body, shown by concentric circles, is marked with chevrons, and whose zigzag course, when pursued, is unlike that of any other winged creature of the plain.

Zigzag lines also appear in the form of vertical registers containing saw-teeth in single or double series with the points opposite each other, giving the whole design the appearance of a stack of hour-glasses.

In the upper part of the façade, as a pendant to the calabash on the right which represents the sun, is a drawing of the moon, either full or as a crescent. This is a reminder, on the left-hand side, of the celestial regions.

In the remaining space on the wall there are various ritual objects and animals in no particular order: the priest's forked staff, which is a symbol of both masculinity and femininity; the shaft itself, which is breast-high, is male, the female part is the fork in which the priest rests his forefinger, itself a symbol of the male; the priest's seat, often shown as a solid circle surrounded by a rim; the short, straight staff of the ancestor who first bestowed masks; the hooks which are actually seen elsewhere on the flat roof; throwing-sticks in the form of crooks, which symbolize the sons that every family wants; these are the doubles of the real crooks hung on the pediment; a ritual 'robber's crook', the handle of which is decorated with a line of chevrons, while its short, curved arm is open like a mouth with red lips, recalling that they held the fragment of sun that the smith stole; hoes; bunches of large millet and ears of small millet; the prohibited animal associated with the cult of the ancestor to whom the sanctuary is dedicated; a sheep or a fowl, the usual sacrificial victim offered on altars; a water-bird which recalls the priest's quest before his installation, when he

PLATE I

(a) Dogon granaries

(b) The layout of Dogon land

PLATE II

(a) Woman spinning

(b) Dogon woman wearing
Nummo ornaments

had to explore the marshes and torrents to find the covenant-stone that had been hidden at the death of his predecessor; a tortoise, portraying the one that every family, large or small, possesses; when the family-head is absent, the tortoise takes his place and eats the first mouthful of food and the first sip of water every day. This drawing of the tortoise is a reminder of the family-head and also signifies that the shell represents the dwelling-place of the Nummo, that is the vault of heaven. The diamond-shaped drawings of tortoiseshell symbolize the façade of the Nummo's dwelling, the squares of the covering for the dead, and the zigzag lines of falling rain.

Masks such as the 'storeyed house', the 'equine antelope' or the 'unfolder of bush-wings' are often depicted on the left-hand panel. These are the wooden masks, male objects possessed of more power than the braided cowls, which indeed contain a certain amount of effective moisture since they are made of fibre; but the wooden masks contain even more, which they derive both from the wood in which they are carved and from the fibres in which those who wear them are clothed. Being wetter, they are closer to the Nummo.

Above the door of the temple is depicted a chequer-board of white squares alternating with squares the colour of the mud wall. There should strictly be eight rows, one for each ancestor. This chequer-board is pre-eminently the symbol of the 'things of this world' and especially of the structure and basic objects of human organization.

It symbolizes:

the pall which covers the dead, with its eight strips of black and white squares representing the multiplication of the eight families;

the façade of the large house with its eighty niches, home of the ancestors;

the cultivated fields, patterned like the pall;

the villages with streets like seams, and more generally all regions inhabited, cleared or exploited by men.

The chequer-board and the covering both portray the eight ancestors.

Inside the sanctuary, besides the red patch representing the fire of the smithy, on the right of the door as you go out, is a painted serpent representing the eighth ancestor, and on the left a crocodile symbolizing the oldest known man of the family. This last device is proper to Sanga; each region makes pictures of the being to which it is attached.

Thus the world-system, with its creatures and appurtenances, celestial and terrestrial, is painted on the temple in millet-gruel and rice.

'And what, you ask, is the use of the paintings?' said Ogotemmêli. 'It is this: they help the plants to grow, they promote germination. The day before the sacrificer wets his brushes, the ears for the sowing are spread out on the roof, the symbol of the primal field.'

In this way, at the start of the cycle of vegetable growth, the still unfertilized seeds are taken and incorporated in the universal cycle, in the general movement of clouds and men.

But the stranger was burning to ask a question.

'I have never seen a picture of a ram on the front of a temple,' he said, 'I have never seen a temple decorated according to these rules.'

'I do not know,' replied the blind old man, 'where I could find anyone able to draw the ram. If only I could see myself! . . . Temples are no longer painted according to the rules.'

In the first place, he explained, ignorance accounts for it. The priest and his sacrificer may be quite young, and may have had very little instruction in the rites of their own religion. There are many who are completely ignorant concerning the symbolism of the paintings, and particularly the picture of the celestial ram. But there are some priests, he added, who, even if they knew the rules, would not follow them. Indeed, since the pictures have power, and the more complete they are, the more powerfully they affect the grain crops, the priest has an interest in not showing too much of them, lest they should be copied by neighbouring priests on the watch for anything that could influence or charm the celestial powers. Accordingly he makes his temple façade a sort of riddle for the benefit of the uninitiated, who recognize certain details. As for his fellow priests, they only perceive the usual designs; the more important ones are not noticed.

Ogotemmêli was not very explicit on these matters, and information had to be sought elsewhere.

Since the intention and, above all, the words of the ritual play an essential part, it may be supposed that the celebrant, in painting the current pictures, puts into them in thought and word much more than his hand delineates.

But more than ignorance or mistrust, a strictly religious factor militates against, since it suppresses, expression, and is in fact the most serious obstacle to the spread of knowledge; and that is the marked reluctance, arising from respect and fear, to mention the names or picture the forms of supernatural powers.

It is a well-known fact that one cannot mention the name of one who is absent without bringing about considerable effects in the unseen world. The usual explanation of this phenomenon is that the mention of a name invokes the being whose name it is, and compels it to appear, though its presence may be unwelcome. But nothing is said about the reason why the being should hasten to answer the summons of its name. The reason is that to utter a name is to bring into existence a form and a habitation—the best form and the most suitable habitation to receive the life-force of the being invoked.

In uttering the word the speaker no doubt projects a force of his own, which is carried on the breath issuing from his mouth and is in fact one with it. But this force merely represents the force of the one invoked, it offers it a form and a voice. This form, which will be that best suited to the one who is called, traps, as it were, his life-force, compelling him to appear, to arise in answer to the call.

The same considerations apply to the paintings, especially if the material used in making them is efficacious and if the words which accompany the actions of the painter's hand are explicit and compelling.

Where names are concerned, these ideas lead to silence or the use of euphemisms; in the case of pictures they result in the avoidance of direct representation. Just as the name of the Water Spirit is never uttered, so his likeness is never drawn. To do so would be offensive to him, because to portray him would be to compel him to appear, just as if he were called by name. This would disturb him in the carrying out of his purposes and interfere in his activities as director of the universe.

There is good ground, therefore, for any priest to depict on the façade of his temple only those figures that are connected with his own Binu or are in general use and known to all.

Thus round an invisible ram, master of germination, with a fleece of leaves and copper, the artist paints a series of accessory objects, celestial or terrestrial, without order of any kind, in which only the initiated can perceive a whole world order.

The Cult of Lébé

It was market day, and the usual commotion proclaimed the fact. At night and again at dawn, the braying of asses had aroused the west. The market-place came to life in the sunlight, as on every morning, but now attended by preliminary excitements.

At Ogotemmêli's home a kind of board meeting was taking place between the master and an intelligent man squatting under the niches of the ancestors. Koguem and the European were sitting in their usual places listening to the two men.

'Ogotemmêli,' Koguem explained, 'says he wants to eat an ox-head. He has called in Dyougodyêh to get him to buy the head. Dyougodyêh is explaining that he once bought a head for seventy-five francs which he cooked and ate his fill of, and then resold for ninety-one francs.'

'The profit,' said Ogotemmêli, 'is not enough. You should buy my head from another man, and get it cheaper.'

Another solution, it was suggested, would be to abuse the butcher who charged too much.

'To show you he deserves it,' said Ogotemmêli, 'I once bought a head from him and four feet with it. He wrapped them in a skin and, when I got home, I found only three feet. The butcher had stolen one. One should be on one's guard against that sort of man.'

'I know,' he went on, 'one of my brothers has bought a live ox, and is going to resell it today. You should ask him for the head. It will be all right with him. But one can still curse the dishonest butcher!'

Dyougodyêh agreed, except about the cursing.

'It is not worth while,' he said, 'in order to save less than fifty francs, to have the sun blazing on one's skull all day, and cook an ox-head for six hours.'

As for the dishonest butcher, he would not curse him—only abuse him.

'I also once bought an ox-head,' he said, moving away and talking as though to himself, 'for 110 francs. It was from the same butcher. Well! After my meal I resold what there was of it for eighty-five francs. Had I eaten twenty-five francs worth? Not a bit of it! Barely ten francs! I was done that time.'

He was still grumbling as he made his way across the courtyard.

'Curse him!' called Ogotemmêli after him. 'Curse his father!'

It was the most irrevocable of curses. The man turned round, and said:

'Abuse will be enough.'

He spat on the wall and went out.

Ogotemmêli lowered his voice to answer the Nazarene, who was questioning him about Lébé, his present-day cult, and his priest, the Hogon.

The Hogon lived next door behind the granaries, and it would have been a disgrace to be overheard above the mud wall. This was his private house: his official residence was in Upper Ogol.

The European was well aware of the main lines of the cult of this, the oldest, ancestor, eaten by the seventh Nummo, but himself the eighth Nummo, confused with the seventh but nevertheless distinct.

His covenant-stone, coming from his own skull, was the badge of his pre-eminence over the eight other principal stones, and *a fortiori* over all other smaller stones serving as the mark of subsequent ancestors.

Without going into the overlapping of territories, the interminable quarrels, the questions of the precedence of persons, families or tribes, and the unending reckoning of ancestries, rights, and claims, it might be said that there was in each region a Lébé with a priest (who was always the oldest man in the region) and an altar, which in the case of Sanga was set up in the principal public square of Lower Ogol, in a place which was never trodden by any uninitiated person, and which was approached by officiants only on solemn occasions.

This altar, in the form of an umbilicus, was not made of

ordinary earth, or rather its earth had received, when it was founded, power from afar, both in time and in space.

The mythical Lébé had been buried in the primal field and, when men, feeling cramped in their settlements, decided to migrate, they determined to take his remains with them to the new countries they intended to explore.

When they opened the grave, the eldest of them found there the covenant-stones and also a large live serpent. This elder was called Dyon, which means 'digger'. Dyon concluded that this earth must be good, since in it a dead body had been brought back to life. He thought that by borrowing some of it he could transport to their future home this leaven of resurrection and impregnate it with the ancestral essence.

Loaded with soil, Dyon, with others following his example, moved away by mysterious routes passing underground. He was followed by the serpent, the living form of the seventh ancestor and of Lébé, who bore on his skull in a long crack an ear of millet.

The subterranean journey ended south-west of the cliffs, where Dyon emerged from the hole of a bamboo, as is shown by the motto he gave to his descendants : 'Diggers! Grown from the hole of a bamboo!'

Others came out at Amani below the scree. Others at the foot of Bamba peak. Some had followed ordinary routes in the same direction, and joined up with the first party.

At Kani-Bonzon, south of the cliffs, Dyon-the-Digger founded the first altar of Lébé. The earth he had brought with him was placed below a squared stone, which they covered with mortar. Later, each of the leaders of the migration took a little earth from the altar, and founded another altar at a distance; and these other altars served as starting-points for any number of others. In this way the virtue of the primal field was spread throughout the new clearings, cleansing the impurity of the land and helping the men to establish themselves on it. And the Lébé serpent, omnipresent, one yet many like a God, followed each founder.

This is why there may be seen, on the rock-table of Upper Ogol to the north-west, a cave called 'Cave of the Steady Women', out of which he (the serpent) comes in the evening, and to the east another called 'Cave of God's Baobab', to which he returns at dawn. Some, whose eyes are not as those of ordinary men, have sometimes been able to see him in full daylight, coiled, bright beige in colour, in the piece of land called 'Place of Rest' which is left fallow in the field of his priest.

He has an enormous task to perform; as the mainspring of germination, the protector of placentas, the purveyor of vital force, he labours day by day with bursts of energy at critical times.

'Every night,' said Ogotemmêli, 'he visits his priest, the Hogon, travelling by the western street, which separates Sodamma from Do. In the early morning he returns by the eastern street between Guêndoumman and Do. That is why the Hogon must be in his house at night, and does not go outside the village.'

'What does he do at the Hogon's?'

Ogotemmêli was silent for a long time. Then in a still lower voice he said, what all the village knew, that Lébé licked the Hogon's body.

'This,' he whispered, 'gives him the strength to live for one day.'

This strength is for the benefit of all. The Hogon is, as it were, the representative of the serpent towards man; but he is also the representative of man towards the serpent. He is entrusted with all the life necessary for men and for the land.

For Lébé's saliva has in it the power of moisture, the voiced breath which issues from every mouth. For the whole of one day the old man is endowed with speech.

The blind man's voice became no more than a breath; he paused in order to hear the noises of the streets, to detect the presence of others, to penetrate the silence of those who were watching on tiptoe, open-mouthed, in the corners of the neighbouring buildings. Now he continued:

'That is why no sweat must flow on the Hogon's body. It would rob him of his strength. Moreover, if sweat were to flow from his body, it would mean that he had deceived Lébé, and broken his tabus. The saliva is the life-force. It would vanish, if the tabu were broken, and the Hogon would die.'

Some weeks earlier, one of the European women had gone in great haste, at a moment's notice, to the installation of the

Hogon of Ninu, and had been able to observe the precautions taken to keep the candidate from suffering fatigue or sweating. The ceremony took place in the caves of Kunnu-Sese, and the old man had been carried to his temple on a man's back through a mass of rocks and over slippery inclines, which a pedestrian might think twice before venturing to climb.

Ogotemmêli, questioned as to these proceedings, declared that, in addition to the danger of sweating, there was the risk of contact with the soil. If the Hogon had touched the ground, all the millet would have become red and dry. He would have 'scorched the earth'.

For the Hogon originated, in a sense, from the nature of Lébé, thus of the Nummo, and of the heavenly powers and their fire (for the Great Nummo are the smiths of heaven) and so from the sun; therefore he must not move about on foot outside the reserved territory. That territory is the village and the area outside the walls as far as the fowls wander, some score or so of cubits in extent.

'But the Hogon might equally well "scorch" the village,' said the European.

'Yes!' was the reply, 'but he wears sandals. Sandals are reserved for priests and especially for the Hogon. No one may go into the Hogon's presence with sandals on his feet. In the same way, no one may go into the smithy except barefoot, because the fire of the smithy was stolen from Heaven. It is sun, like the Hogon.'

'To put on sandals,' said the European, 'is to pose as the sun. Very well! But why should sandals prevent him from setting the earth on fire?'

'The first sandals,' said Ogotemmêli, 'were made of iron—not of copper, for copper is water and also rays of light. The sandals were iron, because iron is the colour of shade.'

Shade, he went on to explain, is cool and fresh. It is the absence of sun and helps to fight against him. Iron, the colour of shade, is a good protection for soil trodden by feet of fire. At Nanduli on the plateau, the priest, at the supreme moment of consecration, when he is wholly identified with the Nummo, puts on the two iron sandals which lie on the altar.

But there we see the first fumbling attempts at walking. What was wanted was sandals comfortable to wear and supple like the foot. The first were cut out of the used skin of the bellows of the smithy.

'It was the Great Nummo who suggested leather, because the skin had held the fire stolen from Heaven at the time of the smith's descent.'

Skin was thus proof against fire. It was itself fire, or rather, it was inoculated against fire. It was the ideal screen between the foot and the soil to be protected.

Thus leather sandals enabled those who possessed celestial attributes to walk on the earth without injury to germination. Sandals were reserved to such people and no other person might usurp the right to wear them.

Another accessory peculiar to the Hogon and indicative of the origin of his power is his red cap.

'The red cap is like a sun on the Hogon's head. No one else may wear a red cap in Sanga.'

Koguem smiles. 'When I was a rifleman,' he confided to the stranger, 'I always took my military cap off when I reached the boundary.'

'Another reason,' said Ogotemmêli, 'why the Hogon does not go outside the village is because of the copper.'

When a Hogon dies, a copper ring is put round each of his ankles and his arms. These rings come from the original primal field, the grave of Lébé. They were made of metal excreted by the seventh Nummo after the swallowing.

Once again Ogotemmêli explained the nature of copper.

The rays falling from the clouds are changed into copper on touching the ground. Not on the surface of the ground, however, but deep in the earth, too deep for men to be able to lay hold of it, the transformation takes place. Lébé's copper was found, because it was in the grave they had dug for him.

The rings made of the metal are the property of Lébé; they are put on the Hogon when he is buried, but afterwards they are taken from him and given, not to his successor, but to the oldest man after the latter, who will be appointed in his turn, when the office falls vacant again.

Consequently every Hogon had had the rings in his possession while his predecessor held office. He is impregnated with copper. He is like copper, and therefore may not cross any water, for that is one of the Nummo's chief prohibitions. The

Nummo being, in a sense, copper in virtue of his celestial and luminous essence, takes back to himself all copper that passes over watery places which are his preserves.

The European, for himself, had no difficulty in accepting all these symbolical representations, these different methods by which man sought to manipulate the invisible and was himself manipulated. But he was thinking of those who, in other countries, might one day be curious enough to study Dogon metaphysics, and whenever he had an opportunity he checked Ogotemmêli's explanation of the universe by offering some objection.

'Copper,' he said, 'belongs to the Nummo: he *is* copper: he excretes copper. Very good! But then he could take back the metal at any time and in any place, and not merely when anyone carrying it passes by water.'

'Did I not tell you,' was the answer, 'that copper is also water? To pass with the metal near certain waters is to risk seeing it return to the water, and to be carried away with it oneself.'

In fact, if copper is closely connected with the Nummo and he is water, the liquid and the metal are of the same essence.

Ogotemmêli then resumed his concrete explanations of the foundations of Dogon thought.

'The sun,' said he, 'is a burnt-up land surrounded by a spiral of copper raised to a state of incandescence which gives it its diurnal motion, which in turn gives light and life to the universe. The sun is, so to say, molten copper, in proof of which the metal in the fire throws off rays like those of the sun. But these rays, as I have told you, draw up moisture and make clouds. They are the channels by which the water passes: they *are* water. Proof of this is the fact that they are visible only in times of warm mists and storms. That is why solar rays are called *mênn di* (copper water).'

'Mêndi,' said the European, 'is also the name of a mountain.' Ogotemmêli looked up. Decidedly, he must be thinking, these Europeans are sometimes not as stupid as we Africans usually suppose.

'Yes!' he said. 'Ignorant people say *Mênti*; but the proper pronunciation is *Mêndi*.'

Mêndi stood up like a dome above the northern plateau not far from Tintam, two days' march from Sanga. The European had seen it some time before in a dry mist, swollen like a volcano about to erupt.

'It is called "Copper water", because it contains copper and is an abundant source of water; and that is why the souls of the dead go there before starting on their journey to the south. They provide themselves with copper there, which they drink on their long journey. That is what they do for water.'

The European recalled what he had been told, when he saw the mountain. The souls of the dead, his informant had told him, come there in large numbers. They come on foot, on horseback, on pack-oxen, and nowadays in packed lorries, to fetch water. They all crowd to Mêndi.

'One useful thing about the Nummo,' said Ogotemmêli, 'is his having given copper to men.'

The Cult of the Binu

It might be supposed that the institution of Lébé was the centre of the Binu worship, that 'pseudo-totemism', as the Europeans were for a long time in the habit of calling it.

Investigations carried out during this most recent expedition had only tended to confirm what had been published up till then by the research team. Binu worship venerates the souls of the eight ancestors and of certain men of note, who followed in the wake of the eight in later times, and secures their favour on behalf of the living.

After a long time, after the revelation of the third Word and the present-day organization of the world, Death made its appearance on the scene. Up to that time men were immortal, or at least, after a long life, underwent a transformation like that of the eight Great Ones—that is to say, they went down into the anthill and were seen no more, the only traces they left being the bowls lying by the opening. But, instead of becoming Nummo and going up to heaven, they remained on earth.

When Death appeared, only a few very old men were able to transform themselves in this way. The others submitted to the destruction of their bodies, and new rites were introduced for regulating the spiritual forces liberated by their deaths.

From this time onwards men were subject to hitherto unknown dangers, and their ancestors, who had not experienced death, came to their aid and returned to their people—whence their name of Binu.

In order to reveal himself, a Binu would appear to one of his descendants in human or animal form, and give him one of the covenant-stones (dogué) found in the tomb of Lébé. These stones had been carried away by the old people in their migrations, or had been left in the earth and, by mysterious routes, had found their way to the present country of the Dogon.

Armed with this stone and with various objects which had belonged to his ancestor, the man selected for the revelation would build a sanctuary and found a cult, of which he would be the priest.

Before his death he would hide the stone in the gorges or marshes, and his successor, inspired by the Nummo and the spirit of the Binu, would go in search of it, wandering among the rocks and searching in the waters till he found it, and proved thereby the authenticity of the call from heaven.

Even today, in the villages, one may come upon such men, with their shining eyes, who leave their work to get up in the middle of the night to pursue this unwearying search, which often goes on for years and years. The European had seen in the Dodyou Oreil quarter one of the most intelligent and well-educated youths in Sanga, who was a candidate for the succession to the office of priest of the Binu Ogoiné. This young man was seeking to revive a cult, the previous priest of which had been dead more than a century, and since that time the necessary ritual objects had never been found.

Each family belonging to one of the eight big ancestral groups has a Binu belonging to that group. This ancestor may be common to a number of scattered families, which together form a large aggregate. It may also happen that the ritual objects of one sanctuary are shared among several families.

Regular sacrifices are offered to the Binu at sowing time and at harvest, in order that the people may derive benefit from the powers of the ancestor, powers instinct with life since he never experienced death.

From the very beginning of their investigations, which went back nearly fifteen years, the research team had been led to study this institution. The appearances were convincing; at the turning-points of the myths, animals appeared, spewing out the covenant-stones given them by the ancestor and becoming for that reason forbidden or 'tabu' as the Europeans say in their anthropological jargon. Some of them seemed to figure simply as auxiliaries, as the bearers of messages or as saviours. Others, on the contrary, were identified with the ancestor himself. The myth of the Binu Tiré, ancestor of Ogotemmêli's family, which originated in the Sodamma quarter of Upper Ogol, was a good example of this.

The ancestor, when he became an old man, was in the habit of looking after the children in his eldest son's house, while the adults were away at work. One day he changed himself into a serpent, which frightened the children. As, however, he resumed his ordinary appearance when the men came back from work, the whole thing was put down to childish fantasies. But it happened again, and one day the eldest son, returning unexpectedly from the fields, surprised the old man in his metamorphosis. The latter, ashamed at being discovered thus, at once changed into an antelope of the kind called equine, in order to run away faster. Pursued by his son, he made for the cave of Kommo Dama, south-west of the Ogols, and disappeared into it.

The son, not daring to follow, remained at the entrance of the cave, listening to the sound of the galloping hooves of the animal growing fainter as it disappeared into the bowels of the earth. He was about to go away, hearing nothing more, when he became aware of a murmur, which gradually grew louder. From a murmur it became a rumbling, and then a storm, till finally a huge wave broke out from the depths of the cave, died away at his feet, and immediately withdrew.

Looking at the ground when it had gone, the man found a stone which the flood had deposited there. It was the covenant-stone left by the old man before his disappearance into another world. The man picked it up, and later entrusted it to a member of the family, who was found to be possessed by the spirit of the ancestor and by the Nummo, and became the first priest of the Binu Tiré of Sodamma.

It was natural to suppose that Dogon totemism, though it might have particular features of its own, would nevertheless conform to the criteria prescribed by the anthropologists. Moreover the natives themselves lent weight to this supposition by a misuse of words: they gave the name 'Binu' indiscriminately to the ancestor and to the prohibited animal. But some doubt persisted. It was the human ancestor alone who played the chief part in the cult. The animal seemed always to be an accessory; the links between the man and the animal were not at all clear. The team of Europeans had come to the point of avoiding the word 'totem' and experimenting with the invention of new terms. How would 'binuism' do? Till the question of the relations between man and animal was settled, no decision in the matter was possible.

Ogotemmêli was to offer a solution—a provisional solution no doubt, but so original as to reopen the whole question of totemism.

He began the discussion, however, with certain aphorisms which were not of such a kind as to throw light on the problem.

'Animals,' he said, 'are superior to men, because they belong to the bush and do not have to work. Many animals feed themselves on what man grows by painful toil.'

He even went so far as to say that animals were more perfectly made than men, seeing that they lacked speech. It was an excellence in them to be without the power of speech.

Did he mean by this that speech, the instrument of progress, the foundation of the world-order, was in the last analysis a disaster? Did he mean to say that speech was, in a sense, the fruit of disorder, inasmuch as it was necessary for the restoration of the normal movement of things? Did he mean that, if the world had developed without hindrances from its original basis, there would have been no need for speech, no need for technical processes, for the two things were bound inextricably together? Did he mean that animals were immune from human misfortunes?

To all these questions Ogotemmêli never made any answer.

It appeared from his earliest statements that the part played by animals was connected with the original system of twin births, and that it was a form of reparation, of reorganization, of compensation.

'Man,' said the European to himself, in an effort to sort out his ideas, 'loses the system of twin births. The Nummo intervenes, and gives each child two souls of different sexes. Objection: the creature is both male and female, whereas it should be either one or the other. Solution: circumcision and excision. The parts in which the second soul resides, prepuce and clitoris, are eliminated. Objection: one soul remains disembodied. Solution: the prepuce becomes the lizard called "Sun", and the clitoris becomes the scorpion. Objection: these animal carriers are crude, too close to the primitive creatures

PLATE III

(a) A large house

(b) The Dogon cap

PLATE IV

(a) Priest wearing Covering of the Dead

(b) Patriarchal tortoise

of the dawn of the world. The second soul, which continues to be in contact with the person concerned, is not adequately provided for. What is the solution?'

Ogotemmêli pondered. They were at the root of one of the oldest human institutions.

'When the eight ancestors,' he said at last, 'were born to the first pair, eight different animals were born in heaven.'

'Born to whom?'

'To pairs of animals created in the beginning by the God Amma. Up to this time they had had no connection with the earth. When the eight men appeared, each of them shared a soul with an animal; but the man remained on earth, while his animal associate remained in Heaven. It was not till after their metamorphosis in the anthill and their transformation into Nummo that the ancestors went up to heaven and rejoined their animal associates there, though without becoming one with them.'

As for the men who came after them, they were transformed in the same way, but did not go up to heaven, so that they were separated indefinitely from the associates who had been born at the same time as themselves in the species of animals linked with their respective families.

When Death came into the world, the new world-system had already come down in the form of the celestial granary, on which all the animals figured. Consequently the metamorphosed ancestors were in some sense represented by their animal associates, who from that moment lived in the uncultivated areas round the villages and no longer in heaven.

'The animal,' said Ogotemmêli finally, 'is, as it were, man's twin.'

And an ancestor could use the animal which was, so to speak, his twin, to make himself known to the living men whom he wished to help. True, the animal was distinct from him, born elsewhere and to all appearance different in form, but it was of the same essence and was recalled to heaven in the same batch.

The ancestor, by revealing himself, gave valuable help to men, one of its most efficacious elements being the revelation of the unknown twin, to whom each man was linked without being aware of it, and who was to be venerated by becoming one of the prohibitions observed by the family. Thus, from revelation to revelation, the whole Dogon people settled into a new system, in which each man possessed two supporters for his second soul: one from his birth, consisted of the animal and the other, after circumcision, was the 'sun' lizard.

Ogotemmêli had much to say of the function of the animal regarded as man's twin, and of the distribution of spiritual powers, and of a man's duties towards his related animal, the object of prohibition, the pledge of life outside himself. But suddenly, in the course of the old man's discourse, the amazing complications of the system became apparent.

'I said,' he observed, summarizing, as his custom was, the account he had given, 'that the first children and the animals in heaven had no successors.' (This was a mistake on Ogotemmêli's part. What he had said, and what he meant, was that there were no relations between them.) 'Relations began with circumcision and excision. At every human birth, therefore, a prohibited animal is born. But the animal itself has a twin, a prohibited animal; and this animal likewise, and so on. Every human family is thus at the head of a whole class of animals.'

Ogotemmêli emphasized this important point. Every human family was part of a long series of creatures, and the whole aggregate of human families was connected with the whole animal kingdom. And behind that was a dim suggestion of vegetable series.

'When man is born,' said the old man, 'since he is the head (that is, the chief) of all the prohibited animals, all the prohibited animals' prohibited animals are born at the same time.'

In each of the eight families, therefore, man was the originator of beings whose life had repercussions extending to the last term of a series affecting the eighth part of creation.

This whole order of things rested on the assumption that the obligation imposed by the prohibitions, so far as man was concerned, extended to the whole species. In fact it applied only to one or two animals and one vegetable: otherwise men would have found themselves involved in a network of impossible contingencies.

'When I was born,' said Ogotemmêli, in illustration of his argument, 'an equine antelope was born too. The antelope's prohibited animal is the panther. A panther also was born. But the panther's forbidden animal is the antelope. The circle was thus closed and complete.'

'But,' he added, 'although a man is not concerned with all the creatures of the series, it is nevertheless true that every childbirth sets in motion the birth of all the animals and vegetables associated with the family of the child.'

That meant that when a child was born in any one of the eight families, the whole of creation went into action.

The European took his leave. The first sounds of the braying of the asses returning from the pastures could be heard in the direction of Lulli.

Behind every man he met in the narrow streets he seemed to see the shadows of an eighth part of all the living creatures of the world.

Sacrifice

ON his way through the streets of Lower Ogol, from Dodyou Oreil to Tabda, by way of Guinna and Amtaba, the European was thinking of that unplumbed mystery, the blood sacrifice.

In Binu temples, on Lébé altars, on the earth mounds set shamelessly on a thousand sites in the middle of courtyards or against the side of walls, animals were dying at the prescribed seasons throughout the year. They all shed their blood for the sake of those relationships with Heaven which man persisted in maintaining. Fowls poured it out with their heads hanging down and their wings outstretched, their feet held in the strong fist of the man who cut their throats. Quivering sheep were handed down at arm's length from the rooftops to be held above the pediments studded with iron hooks and anvils with extended arms. Their blood sputtered from the bubbling wound, and flowed over the façades in dark red trails which turned brown as glowing iron becomes dark.

When the victim was too heavy to be moved from the ground on which it lay in its death-throes, its blood was collected in calabashes as it spouted from the throat as from a fountain, and the sacrificer like a gardener sprinkled it on all the consecrated objects of iron and wood as if he were watering plants.

It might be said that every domesticated animal in Sanga perished on the altars except a few cattle kept for a year or two for the market.

The Nazarene, on his way through the labyrinth of streets, where women in the gentlest of voices were exchanging morning greetings, thought of all the ink that had flowed on the subject of this blood and all the hypotheses put forward to explain man's ruthless determination to sacrifice.

He felt strongly that the only people who could understand

it, the only men who could explain themselves, were precisely those who did not know how to write.

Some years before he had grasped the theory of ritual killing: a fifteen-year-old Dogon had put a member of the team on the track, and suddenly all had become clear. In all its different forms, whether of consecration, expiation, divination, purification, upholding the invisible or securing salvation for one's self, sacrifice for the Dogon had one unchanging effect—the redistribution of life-force.

But it was not simply a matter of taking a victim's life-force to put it somewhere else, or to increase the life-force of some other being, visible or invisible. The object was rather to create a movement of forces within a circuit composed of the sacrificer, the victim, the altar and the power invoked. In the case of the ordinary service of a power like the Nummo, Son of God, or of the God Amma himself, the mechanism could be clearly seen.

At the critical moment, that is to say, when the blood flows, the man utters a prayer, by which he invokes the power, for example the Nummo, and explains what he is doing. The prayer is spoken aloud. It is therefore itself an expulsion of force, which follows the lines of the breath issuing from the speaker's mouth. This force serves, in the first place, to arouse the Nummo and, in the second place, to direct the force that flows from the wounded throat of the victim and pours out on to the altar.

On the altar the virtue of new, fresh, blood combines with what has been left there by a long series of ritual murders: for the altar is a store-house of forces, on which man draws at the appropriate time, and which he keeps constantly fed. It is also the point of contact between man and the Invisible.

So long as the altar is fed, and its power is renewed by fresh offerings, the Nummo, when he hears the Word comes to drink, to draw strength and maintain his life. The Dogon word for sacrifice does in fact come from a root which means to 'renew life'.

But in investing the altar with his presence the Nummo brings with him an influx of fresh forces. The result is an emulsion, a boiling mixture, from which two currents proceed. One of these is caught by the Nummo, and is his share in the benefit of the sacrifice. The other, which is the most important from the human standpoint, goes back along the flow of the victim's blood, enters its wounded throat, follows the channels of the blood, and lodges in the liver, which is a privileged organ, the hidden crucible of the personality.

The victim is then cut up, prepared, and eaten. But the liver, now full of virtue, goes to the sacrificer, whose own liver is filled with a reinvigorating influx. By consuming the liver of the victim he assimilates a part of the Nummo's force, thus closing the circuit opened by the Word, which itself came from his own liver.

The Nazarene remembered all these details, which he had already learnt from accounts given to him by the actors in this age-old institution. He noted that what came from the liver returned to the liver: the man expectorated only to ingurgitate again, and in the cycle of this spiritual sustenance, which wore the likeness of the system of physical nourishment, the victim and the altar of the God both had their place.

But was the cycle really completed in this way?

Ogotemmêli had never said much about the sacrificial procedure. He assumed that the European had solved the problem, partly because he knew the latter was well-informed on the subject, and partly because the whole thing seemed to him self-evident. He had further revelations to offer concerning the institution, but he had waited till the European was acquainted with the various practices and ritual actions. He was sure, moreover, that his explanations would have been unintelligible without a knowledge of the Dogon conceptions of the Word and its effects.

The European, who was about to enter Tabda and take the turning which led to the blind man's home, stopped suddenly and signed to Koguem to look. In the dark angle of the street a black chicken with a tail like a trapeze upside down was in frantic pursuit of some invisible object. It jumped in every direction, almost turning a somersault in the air, then stopped abruptly only to go forward cautiously, scraping its beak on the ground. When the stranger halted, however, the chicken flung itself against a bright spot, which appeared for a few moments on the wall; it was the reflection of the yellow screen attached to the lens of the camera which the European always carried about with him.

In the courtyard Ogotemmêli, in his brown rags, was advancing with careful steps. His feet knew all the pitfalls in the rocks and the dust. In his right hand he held his long staff, which reached up to his shoulder. His left hand held close to his side the black leather bag, well known in all the surrounding neighbourhood, which contained secret remedies.

After a lengthy greeting, he sat down in his usual place in the embrasure of the storeyed house. His voice that day was scarcely audible, for he was still speaking of Lébé and of his priest, the Hogon. He wanted to teach the European the meaning of the annual sacrifice, the first phase of which took place on the outdoor altar in the middle of the big square of Upper Ogol known as 'Lébé's Terrace'.

This altar was a mound of grey earth, and all the inhabitants of the village skirted it with care, because it contained a piece of the earth taken in the old days from the altar of Kani-Bonzon, the first place where the Dogon stopped in their migrations; this altar itself was made with earth from the grave brought from the primal field. This mound therefore represented in a sense the grave of Lébé.

On the appointed day, after the ceremonies that opened the sowing season, a goat had its throat cut on the altar.

'A smith is there,' said Ogotemmêli, 'with his anvil. He stands before the man who is going to eat the liver.'

'Who is going to eat the liver?'

'The oldest of the "Impure".'

The 'Impure' are released from most of the prohibitions, and in particular those connected with death. Each family includes a number of such persons, who are designated by divination. They alone are able to handle with impunity the forces emanating from the dead.

'Why an "Impure"?'

'Because the sacrifice takes place on earth from a grave. Also because an "Impure" is, as Lébé was, neither dead nor living.'

An 'Impure' is therefore the person best fitted to receive temporarily the force that will pass from the victim into him when he swallows the liver.

'As soon as the throat is cut,' went on Ogotemmêli, 'the smith beats the ground with his anvil, and does not cease doing so till all is consumed. His beating helps the forces to pass.'

The life-force of Lébé, contained in the earth of the grave mingled with the earth of the altar, passes to the rhythm of the beats into the liver of the goat, and thence into the liver of the 'Impure' who eats it after it has been cooked.

'The blows of the anvil start the movement.'

Ogotemmêli meant by this that the blows of the anvil performed the function of the warning prayer and gave the movement its direction. Also they recalled the blows dealt by the smith who fell from heaven at the time of the subterranean swallowing and resurrection.

'When the "Impure" eats the animal's liver,' continued Ogotemmêli, 'it is as if he were eating the skull of Lébé, the skull of his old father: for it is the force of Lébé's skull that passes into the sacrificial animal.'

This observation recalled the placing of the stones cast up in the tomb by the seventh Nummo after he had eaten Lébé. Whereas the stones that indicated the joints were destined for the Binu cult, the stone that marked the place of the head was the sign of the cult of Lébé himself, as the honoured representative of the eighth ancestor, and identified with him.

'The "Impure" eats the liver cooked,' said the old man, 'because fire rids it of everything ill-omened. The bad part of the bile contained in the gall-bladder disappears in the flames, and the good principle remains.'

Then, lowering his voice still more and having satisfied himself that neither the Hogon's wife nor his own could hear him, Ogotemmêli added: 'The "Impure", by eating the liver, gives his own life.'

It was a turning-point of the enquiry. Ogotemmêli spat and took more tobacco. For some minutes he spoke only of some obscure matter concerning a field to the north of the Sammtigou hollow on the right of the rock known as the 'Tâ Cave'. Ogotemmêli was vehement about the case, which to him was as clear as day, and he insisted that the people of the Go rock were impostors. He would not even name them: he called them 'the Go people'.

'You were saying,' the European reminded him, 'the "Impure". . . '

'The "Impure", by eating the liver, becomes Lébé himself, who died, who was eaten, and who rose again for the restoration of the world. He is the same as Lébé; he has in his liver the life-force of Lébé. He is emptied of his own life in order that he may be filled with that of the ancestor; and, since it is in the liver that the Word is born, everything that is said by the "Impure" at the sacrifice, and for a considerable time after, is as though said by Lébé. When he speaks the "Impure" imparts the good Word to everyone.'

So much for this part of the sacrifice. They had now heard all about the cycle of the movement of forces, starting from the sacrificer, passing through the invisible Power, the altar, and the victim back to the sacrificer. That might seem a sufficient account of the operation; but Dogon philosophy did not stop there. The qualities set in motion continued their course. By the words of the man who was identifying himself with the dead author of the third revelation, the vital forces spread out to all humanity within range of his voice.

In this action the oldest 'Impure' was not alone. He was seconded by other men of the same kind as himself, who consumed the rest of the victim. They too received the power of words, but not to the same extent. Their voices were effective, however, and also operated for the good of the community.

Meanwhile Ogotemmêli continued his disquisition, which was concerned not so much with sacrifice in general as with the sacrifice offered to Lébé at the time of sowing. The immolation of the goat on the outdoor altar was followed next day by a second sacrifice. This took place in the Hogon's house on an altar which, apparently, was not dedicated specially to Lébé, but also, and perhaps chiefly, to the seventh Nummo, who had swallowed Lébé.

This altar had probably not been built with earth from the grave, for the Hogon, who was very distinctly 'living', himself consumed the liver of the victim after pronouncing the following prayer, in which the aspirations and expectations of the whole of the Dogon country were summed up:

> Oh God! Receive the morning greeting!
> Ancestors! Receive the morning greeting!
> We are here on the chosen day,
> We are going out to sow the seed,
> We are going out to cultivate.

Oh God! Cause the millet to germinate,
Make the eight seeds sprout,
And the ninth calabash!
Give a wife to him who has none!
And to him who has a wife without children
Give a child!
Protect the men against thorns,
Against snake-bites,
Against ill winds!
Pour out the rain,
As we pour water from a pot!
Millet! Come!

Ogotemmêli did not say whether the Hogon identified himself with the seventh Nummo. But the point was immaterial, for the union of the seventh Nummo, who had eaten Lébé and raised him from the dead, with Lébé, who had been eaten and raised from the dead, was effected in the course of the day: the 'Impures' who, the day before, had communicated in the flesh of Lébé, and the oldest of whom had undergone a real transubstantiation, appeared at the Hogon's house at the moment of the sacrifice to demand that the union of the seventh Nummo and Lébé, representing the family of the eighth ancestor, should be maintained unbroken, that the Word and the master of Speech should continue to be closely linked together.

The rite of sacrifice thus ensured that the order established at the time of the resurrection in the primal field, should continue and that the seeds sown in the earth should bear fruit.

But Ogotemmêli did not wish it to be thought that the sacrifice to Lébé at the sowing was the only one that allowed the dissemination of good words.

'The effect of every sacrifice,' he said, 'is the same as that of the sacrifice to Lébé. First one feeds and strengthens oneself, and then, by means of the Word, gives strength and life to all men.'

Even in sacrifices offered for one's own welfare, which everyone offers on his personal altars, representing his head or his body, the meal of the sacrificer benefits all.

It is the same with every sort of sacrifice or libation which men offer at foundation altars in villages, at altars of the several quarters of villages, in family shrines, on earthen vessels commemorating twins or ancestors, at the Great Mask or on fire altars.

All sacrifices, therefore, have the same effects as the corporate ritual celebrated at the communal sowing. After he has communicated, man speaks, and his Word, impregnated with the virtue of the ancestors, goes out to others.

'The altar gives something to a man, and a part of what he has received he passes on to others,' said Ogotemmêli. 'A small part of the sacrifice is for oneself, but the rest is for others. The forces released enter into the man, pass through him and out again, and so it is for all . . . ' As each man gives to all the rest, so he also receives from all. A perpetual exchange goes on between men, an unceasing movement of invisible currents. And this must be so if the universal order is to endure. 'The Word,' said Ogotemmêli, 'is for everyone in this world; it must come and go and be interchanged, for it is good to give and to receive the forces of life.'

The Fertilizing Word

THE conversation of the previous day had made plain the power of the human word. The voice of man can arouse God and extend divine action.

This, no doubt, was only to be expected, since God himself, acting through his son the Nummo, had three times reorganized the world by means of three successive Words, each more explicit and more widespread in its range than the one before it. There had been also the regeneration of the eight men and their rebirth as Water Spirits through the voice of the Nummo who, by speaking to himself, fertilized himself.

Where did it come from, this Word, which diffused itself along the spiral curves of the breath as it issued from the face, and what paths did it take within the human being?

It was not in the nature of Ogotemmêli to give direct answers to such questions.

'The Nummo,' he said, 'who is water and heat, enters the body in the water one drinks, and communicates his heat to the bile and the liver. The life-force, which is the bearer of the Word, which *is* the Word, leaves the mouth in the form of breath, or water vapour, which is water and is Word.'

He repeated what he had said the day before, that the Word came from the deepest and most secret part of the being, namely, the liver. But he preferred to follow the original line of his thought, and not to answer questions.

He reminded them that the first Word had been pronounced in front of the genitalia of a woman; the first skirt had been plaited, that is, 'spoken', by the Nummo in front of his mother.

The Word finally came from the anthill, that is, from the mouth of the seventh Nummo, which is to say from a woman's genitalia.

The second Word, contained in the craft of weaving, emerged

from a mouth, which was also the primordial sex organ, in which the first childbirths took place.

'Issuing from a woman's sexual part,' said Ogotemmêli, 'the Word enters another sexual part, namely the ear.'

In the symbolism of the body already discussed by the old man, the ear was bi-sexual: the external ear was male, and the auditory aperture female. But in fact the Word, according to its nature, can enter by two apertures in a woman—the ear or the sexual organ.

Bad words enter by the ear and pass into the throat, the liver, and finally the womb. The unpleasant smell of the female sexual parts comes from the bad words heard by the ear. The smell, apparently, completing a cycle of words.

On the other hand good words, though taken in by the ear, go directly to the sexual parts where they encircle the womb as the copper spiral encircles the sun. This Word of water provides and maintains the moisture necessary for procreation, and the Nummo, by this means, introduces a germ of water into the womb. He changes the water of the Word into a germ, and gives it the appearance of a human being but the essence of a Nummo. Or rather, the Nummo, present in the moist sexual organ, as in all water, by means of efficacious words which mingle with the woman's seed, moulds a tiny watery creature in his own image.

Thus at the very beginning of human life is to be found a divine germ which lies waiting in the womb of every fertile woman. It is shaped by the Nummo: but the living matter of which it is composed is produced by human action. All good words, whether spoken by the mouths of men or women, enter the bodies of all women, and prepare them for future mating and childbirth.

This is because the germ thus formed of water cannot grow or develop; it is in a state of expectation. It can however be destroyed by evil influences. It is motionless, and the flow of good words, even if it were unceasing, would do no more than preserve it in this condition. It awaits the dawn of its being.

Ogotemmêli did not explain why this celestial germ could not develop in accordance with its essence. If asked, he would no doubt have answered that the 'why' in the destinies of the universe was no part of his philosophy and that, if women brought perfect and celestial geniuses into the world, those destinies would not be what they are.

The germ must therefore be given a fresh start. It must also be given another substance, for its celestial nature was not fitted for life on earth. It is at this point that the man intervenes.

But it seems that this intervention, though necessary, bears the mark of certain primordial events. The amorous struggle of the human couple, in which the woman resists while her partner plays the aggressive part, reproduces the primal struggle between the jackal, God's eldest son, and his mother the earth. The male of today is the jackal digging into the anthill in search of the ant, an avatar of the earth. The woman is the incestuous mother, who finally confesses herself overcome by her son's superior strength, and mates with him.

The mating of the human couple in the darkness of the inner room with its four posts is consummated on the earth-platform, placed so that the man faces west, lying on his right side, while the woman faces east. The bed, symbolizing the primal field with the seeds in it ready for germination, is full of expectant life.

At the moment of union the Nummo guides the male seed, which encircles the womb with a spiral motion, as the Word did. This seed, coming as it does from an organ made of earth, is itself a symbol of the earth. It is also earth, because it comes from the man's joints, which were indicated in the original tomb by the covenant-stones cast up there.

'The stones,' said the old man, 'were put at the points where the joints lie, because the joints are the chief thing in the body of a man.'

The Nummo moulded this earth with the water of the germ, which is itself the produce of the words taught by Heaven.

'The water of the woman,' said Ogotemmêli, 'which the Nummo formed in his own image, is mingled by him with the seed of the man, who is earth.'

As usual he went on to enlarge on a difficult point by re-touching his first statement.

'Just as God shaped man out of earth and water, so the Nummo shapes the seed of the man with the water of the woman.'

'The Nummo,' he added finally, 'with the words and the

woman's seed forms a being of water after his own image. The man's seed enters into this germ as a man.'

He meant that the human nature in its totality, 'as a man,' entered the being of celestial essence that was awaiting life in the womb.

The man's seed, originating in the joints, transmitted them, providing the being, whose limbs were supple like those of the Nummo, with a man's elbows and knees. Thus the male seed, extracted from the eight joints, directs itself within the embryo to places corresponding to those it occupies in the limbs of the man, in this way giving the first indication of the human frame.

It is also, by its earthly quality, both reminder and evidence of the debt which each of us owes to the earth, because it was of earth that the first pair were made; and this debt has to be paid by the shedding of blood, in circumcision and excision and in menstruation.

But Ogotemmêli postponed discussion of this debt till later and reverted to the effects of the Word in generation.

'Words spoken by day enter the bodies of women. Any man speaking to any woman is assisting procreation. By speaking to a woman one fertilizes her, or at least by introducing into her a celestial germ, one makes it possible for her to be impregnated in the normal way.'

He compared a pregnant woman to an ear of millet beginning to swell within its leafy spiral. Such an ear is said to have 'found its voice', perhaps by analogy with a fertilized woman, who also has found a voice, that is, the voice of a man.

But he insisted that the word, if it was to be good, must be spoken in the daytime. 'Words of the day are the only good words; a word spoken by night is ill-omened.' And that was why it was forbidden to talk loudly or shout or whistle in the villages by night.

'Words fly away,' he said. 'No-one knows where they go; they are lost and that means a loss of force, for all the women are asleep at night; no ear, no sexual part will catch them.'

Where could they vanish away, these words without echo and with no one to hear them? Was it right to utter, over enclosing walls, in the cracks of doors, in empty streets, words addressed to nobody?

But there was something even worse than lack of hearers. In

fact in any village there are always some women who are not asleep. Words spoken by night may enter their ears. They say: 'Who was that?' They never know. What is said at night is the word of an unknown speaker, falling into their wombs at random. If any women were impregnated in this way, the embryo would be the fruit of chance, like that of promiscuous and irregular unions.

But words spoken by night do not fertilize women, and just as blows on the ground at night undo the work done by the smith on his anvil by day, so the word of the night, entering a woman's ear and passing through her throat and liver, coils itself round the womb in an inauspicious way, unwinding the efficacious spirals formed by the word of the day.

Bad words therefore make women temporarily unfit for procreation by destroying, or rather disturbing, the 'germ of water' which is waiting to receive the contribution of the male.

But its effects were more far-reaching. Ogotemmêli had already said that the bad word did not merely occupy the womb; it passed out thence in emanations, which also played a decisive part in the act of procreation.

'Bad words smell,' he said. 'They affect a man's potency. They pass from the nose to the throat and liver, and from the liver to the sexual organ.'

They caused a man to feel aversion. Ogotemmêli then turned to the question of feminine hygiene, which could (he said) to a considerable extent, combat the effects of bad words. He referred to the celestial granary, in the middle of which was a round jar, symbolizing the womb and the sun, which contained the covenant-stones intended to mark the joints in which the human seed originated.

On this round jar was a smaller pot serving as a lid, full of *Lannea acida* oil intended for toilet purposes and symbolizing the foetus. This vessel had on top of it an even smaller pot containing sweet-scented roots.

Starting from these objects, Ogotemmêli developed rules of hygiene, which included details of the various measures taken by woman in order to attract men. Scent (he said) acted like a good word in combating the bad smell resulting from a bad word. From this theme he reverted to the uses of dress and ornaments, which he had already discussed at length.

In conclusion he dwelt on the continuous part played by words in the pitfalls and struggles associated with procreation. The same word which predisposed the womb for mating, also exerted an attraction for men in the folds of the loin-cloth, the warp and woof of which enclosed in their threads the words of the eight ancestors.

The Blood of Women

THE European asked a question point blank, which seemed to have nothing to do with the subject of the conversation.

'Why,' he asked, 'do the eight families observe different prohibitions? Why all these animals?'

Ogotemmêli, who was never disconcerted, gave an answer which made his interlocutor smile with satisfaction.

'The prohibited animals,' he said, 'are different, because wombs may be of four different forms and the male sexual organ of three; the children produced by different combinations of these forms are therefore different. The animals, which are in a sense the twins of the different sorts of men, must therefore be different from one another.'

At the beginning, he reminded them, the first created couple had eight children, of whom the four eldest were males and the four others females. The latter ranked fifth to eighth in the family; the wombs were assigned to them having the qualities associated with Nos. 5 to 8.

Form No. 5 is called *pobu* in allusion to the fruit of the tree of that name.

Ogotemmêli and Koguem both chuckled slyly at the word, which is one of the worst insults one can hurl at a woman.

The *pobu* form is egg-shaped, round below and somewhat pointed above. In the arrangement of the celestial granary it corresponds to compartment 5, that is, to the seed of the bean, and is of the same oblong shape. It is ill-omened, and its offspring are malformed, because it is not deep enough and does not allow of normal development.

Its number is that of abortion and of sickly children.

Form 6 is called 'antelope's foot'. It is three-cornered, so that it has the shape of the male number 3, and should in theory give birth to male twins (2×3, twice the number of the male). It is propitious, as are the two following forms. It corresponds to the native sorrel.

Form 7, called 'split', is longer and thinner than form 5. It is split along its length like rice seed, to which it corresponds. It gives birth to twins of different sexes (4 + 3).

Form 8, called 'chest', is a trapezium upside down like a man's chest. It has four sides (the female number), and produces female twins (2 × 4). It corresponds to the *Digitaria*.

No one knows how the different forms of the male organ were attributed to the first four ancestors, but the three forms are known as 'thick', lizard's head' and 'long'. The first of these, which is propitious, is especially suited to the female forms 5 and 8. The second, which is spear-shaped, 'pricks'. It is unpropitious for all forms. The third suits forms 6 and 7, but is unpropitious for the others.

These four female and three male forms are of course found in all the eight families. But at the dawn of humanity they were the origin of classifications.

Does this Dogon idea throw any light on what the linguists call nominal classes? The system is based on a classification of living creatures, objects, actions, and modes of being, into categories. In those African languages which have been preserved, a distinct class of nouns, with special characteristics, appertains to each of these categories. The Dogon language, at first sight, does not seem to display this distinction; but, on the other hand, it provides striking examples of categories of beings, objects, or abstractions, apparently disparate, but having names derived from the same root and, moreover, closely linked in the myths and in rituals as well as in the minds of those who participate in them. Thus the conversations with Ogotemmêli had brought to light the close connection, not merely verbal but also expressed in the objects and actions themselves, that linked cloth — clothing — speech — ornament — seven — sun — cow — mother—lizard (avatar of the prepuce)—four—granary—steal.

It would also be possible, though perhaps rather rash, to suggest a linguistic connection linking *Digitaria exilis*—menstruation, and voice—spiral—copper—rain, which are fundamental to the Dogon religious system.

But these ideas merely passed like a flash through the mind of the European, as he listened to the confidences uttered by Ogotemmêli in a low voice or a whisper according to the volume of noise from the street.

'After God made woman,' he was saying, 'he gave her bad blood, which has to flow every month.'

This tiresome affliction might be explained as a perpetual punishment for the primordial incest of the jackal's mating with his mother the earth. The jackal had laid hands on his mother's skirt, which the Nummo had plaited. Until then the fibres of this garment had been light-coloured: afterwards they were purple.

'The red colour of the fibres,' said the old man, 'is that of the menstrual blood which was thus introduced on the earth. But, as it is disrespectful to speak of the earth menstruating, it was said that there had been a shower and that the fibres had got damp, and were now being put to dry in the sun.' The consequences of this exposure of blood will be referred to later.

The flow of menstrual blood is the result of the mating of son and mother, a thing forbidden.

In another connection Ogotemmêli compared this blood with that shed in circumcision which is regarded as the payment of a debt to the earth: woman, having been made of earth, owes the earth this debt. God imposed on her a debt of blood, and she has to pay it in the 'water of God's bosom'. Such was the name he gave to menstrual blood out of respect for women.

The earth remits payment of this obligation only during pregnancy and suckling, for the child itself counts as payment.

During these bad periods a woman has to be separated from the community. Contact with her would defile the men, and her presence in places where people live would weaken the altars. She therefore lives on the edge of the village in a round house, symbol of the womb, and only leaves it at night to wash herself. She has to go by a prescribed path to the waters she is allowed to use, for if she goes anywhere else the area would be polluted, the pools would be troubled, and the headwaters of streams would boil.

'Woman is the Nummo's principal prohibition. He desires

clean blood, and not this foul flow. He flies at the approach of a woman.'

And this is why the footsteps of a menstruating woman will drain all life away from places where she is forbidden to tread. She herself is, to a certain extent, the seat of disturbances comparable to those she would cause if she broke the rules. The flow from which she suffers is the excess blood ejected from within her by a superabundance of bile; and the bile is produced by the bad words which have entered into her.

'Not only do they unwind the fertilizing spiral of good words,' said Ogotemmêli, 'but they also accumulate in the gall-bladder and exert pressure on the blood.'

It is as if the Nummo, present in the liver and unable to leave it without causing death, expelled from the body the unwanted blood, itself a symbol of the evil word.

'Pregnancy, on the other hand,' continued the old man, 'is the sign that good words have entered and have not been uncoiled from the womb. It is a sign that all is well.'

The Blood of Women and the Threshing of *Digitaria*

DOGON institutions are full of unsolved enigmas, guarded on all sides by mysteries, correspondences and symbolisms without end.

Much work had been done before the contact with Ogotemmêli had been made. Considerable sections of this civilization had been discovered and studied in detail. The operation of the masks was known; the cult of the dead, certain sacrificial procedures, the Binu and Lébé cults had been analysed. Researches carried out by teams of specialists had indicated certain avenues of approach in the vast field of facts that seemed to converge on a central point, where lay the clue to men's secret motives, the connecting links in the network, the whys and hows in the delicate intricacy of Dogon thought. But this central point appeared at times like an inaccessible rock, at times like an insubstantial mist.

Ogotemmêli had performed the miracle of unveiling this famous central point to which everything was linked; more than that, he had indicated the transverse lines connecting institutions with one another, rite by rite and law by law. In his account, Dogon civilization appeared in the likeness of a huge organism, every part of which had its own function and its own place, as well as contributing to the general development of the whole. In this organism, every institution was integrated; none was outside it; and each in turn, however divergent it might seem and however incompletely understood, was found to fit into a system whose structure revealed itself day by day with increasing clarity and precision.

For years the Nazarene had been faced with the problem of the *Digitaria exilis*, known in the Western lingua franca as *fonio*, a graminaceous plant, the cultivation of which differed from that of any other. Fifteen years before he had heard for the first time the trumpets sounding at sunset for the nocturnal threshing.

First came the lowing of a cow-horn in the Ba Diguilou field facing the walls of Dodyou. Its muffled sounds brought the young men out from the streets, each armed with a short stick. Then, in the last light of the setting sun, the troop disappeared in the direction of Gôna, only to return later in the night, heralded from a long way off by the sound of antelope horns with their two piercing notes, which seemed to rise from the depths of the past.

The *Digitaria* with its tiny round grain is harvested in great haste the moment it is ripe. Its stalk, which reaches up to a man's calf, bends with the slightest breath of wind as soon as it is dry, and the grain falls off. It is necessary therefore to stack it and thresh it quickly, if possible on the same day. In practice this is done in the early hours of the night and, as it has to be done in such a hurry, the young people collect by quarters, and for several weeks thresh the crop of each family-head in succession. The young girls join in this work : they sweep the grain on to the rocks as it falls, and carry the harvest in goatskins on their heads. Some of the stronger ones take turns with the young men in wielding the flail.

In certain respects this work seemed to have peculiar features of its own. During the reaping, which was done by the adult men, assisted by the women who carried away the cut stalks, songs of unusual immodesty were exchanged between the sexes. From time to time the reapers would make a concerted dash towards the edge of the field, or to meet other workers coming to join them, and this lent a special note to the work. But the most extraordinary thing was the way the grain was used; it was forbidden to a great number of men and only the 'impure' could eat it with impunity, ordinary 'living' men could be exempted only in certain circumstances. Priests, on the other hand, could be severely defiled by merely touching it, the one reason why the Hogon might never be touched was because a person might have *fonio* dust concealed under his nails and so might contaminate him.

It was no easy thing to induce respectable women to pound

it, and it had to be winnowed outside the walls in places set aside for the purpose. The grain was hard and very small, yielding very little nourishment in return for a great deal of labour. It was said that women would seek divorce to avoid the labour of preparing it. Lastly, it was one of the strictest prohibitions of the Water Spirit.

So the European experienced the liveliest curiosity when Ogotemmêli quietly remarked that *Digitaria* and menstruation were one and the same thing.

On the previous day, when he had been talking about the blood-debt owed by women, he had said nothing to suggest such a turn in the conversation.

'*Fonio* and *menses*,' he said: 'all one!'

The two words in Dogon are from the same root.

But this time, said the European to himself, the connection between the two things will be difficult to make out. For he profoundly mistrusted linguists who simply study words without considering what they represent.

Ogotemmêli was seated, as usual, on his threshold, looking at the ground, his hands crossed behind his head. He never displayed animation in the course of the conversations except to curse the noise of the cocks or to reach an agreement with the men who cried their wares to him. Apparently he felt no emotion of any kind when speaking about these things which lay beyond the bounds of time and thought. In his hands a round pot became a sun with eight spirals of copper, and an old basket a universe. All these things were so familiar to him.

When he spoke of the *Digitaria* his voice was very low, as was only fitting in reference to a forbidden grain connected with the intimate matters of women's life. The connection, he explained, went a long way back, in time and space alike. It dated from the time spent by the eight ancestors in heaven after their transformation into Water Spirits. In heaven the eight new Nummo had to live apart from one another. But the first ancestor, who later became the smith, used to visit the third, the ancestor of aristocratic people. They thus transgressed the prohibition and, becoming impure in consequence, had to separate themselves from the others. To enable them to live, however, God gave them the eight seeds, including the *Digitaria*.

It was then that the first ancestor solemnly declared before all the others that he would never eat this small plant; instead he gave it to his friend the third ancestor. One day, however, having eaten all the other seven, he was forced to beg for the food he had despised. In spite of the expostulations of the third ancestor, who reminded him of his solemn pledge, he persisted in eating the grain about which he had spoken evil.

He asked his friend to say nothing of all this, and the two of them swore to keep faith and to support one another about the *fonio*, and they prayed God to kill the one who broke his oath. But the others suspected what had happened; and, considering that a Nummo, even if impure, ought not to break his word, they were ashamed of him for eating the grain, and put their prohibition on it.

'But why was it put in the granary which came down to earth?'

'It was there for the evil word. It *was* the evil word.'

The baneful element had to have a place in the new world-system. Ogotemmêli meant that, since the evil word had been uttered more than once, it could not cease to exist or be left out of the world-order; and nothing could better represent it than the *Digitaria*, concerning which the first ancestor had given the pledge by which he bound himself, and had sworn his false oath.

It was the symbol of the evil word that charms a woman and prevents her conceiving; which unwinds the coils of the good word round her womb and coils itself there in their place. It was the symbol of menstrual blood, sign of the temporary barrenness which these bad coils induce.

This is why the *Digitaria* was put in the eighth compartment of the granary, which has the rank of the Word and corresponds to the gall-bladder in the body.

But it should be understood that the seed also preserved its beneficent power, the good word which God put into it when he created it. In the same way the gall-bladder is good because it plays a part in the normal functioning of the body, but its contents are baneful when they are excessive.

Another point to be noted was that the rank of the compartment in which the *Digitaria* was put was that of the womb of the 'chest' type, which engenders perfect twins. The best and

151

the worst were therefore in the same place, and of the same rank. It was right that they should be found together, and that they could be dissociated by the same action—the nocturnal threshing—which attracts the good and wards off evil.

The climax to which this subtlety of thought was tending and the logical development it was to follow, were yet to be seen.

The grain being there in the universe, it had to be used. Furthermore, it had to be used in the very function assigned to it in the matter of procreation. Thus the cultivation and especially the threshing of *Digitaria* were organized.

At the sound of the trumpets calling them together, all the young men and girls of the quarter are aroused. No one may be absent under penalty of a heavy fine payable to the head of the elders' age-set. The hour of sunset is chosen, partly because all the villagers will then have returned from work outside, and none of those liable for the threshing will be able to shirk it.

The boys start first and go to the scene of activity, where they begin to thresh the stacked crop with their sticks. Standing in a circle, their arms rise and fall in a rhythm of three beats, one-third of the group threshing at each beat, so that the sound is like the hoof beats of a galloping horse. As they work they chant verses, some of which recall the obscene songs chanted during the day by men and women reaping together. From time to time a couple of the boys step out to let one of the girls who have arrived on the scene enter the circle.

The songs and the beating of the stalks have the same object. 'Threshing the grain,' said Ogotemmêli, 'is savagely beating the force, that is, the words, which it contains; the good words, which they have from their creation, come out and mingle with the chanting. The songs thus form a network of sound, in which the beneficent force, the good words extracted by the blows, is caught. The songs are strengthened by it, and will thereby become more apt to coil their fertilizing spirals round the womb, particularly as the meaning of the words is clear and the references to sex are frequent.'

This network of sound receives the beneficent force emanating from the grain, and the girls and boys carry it to the village, thrilling to the sound of the trumpets which, from afar, announce their coming to the men and women who have stayed at home. The good force of the grain comes out and follows the words and songs of the threshers.

The heavy blows of the flails, the songs and the trumpet-calls all work together for the same end, the production of children. Though they are sounds of the night, they have the same good effect on the womb as words spoken by day.

But the European had found what looked to him like a gap in the ordered unfolding of these visible and invisible proceedings. The qualification 'though they are sounds of the night' had not escaped him, and he took the first opportunity to ask slyly, 'Was it not forbidden at ordinary times, except for certain games or rituals, to beat the ground, shout, sing or make noises of any kind by night?'

'Usually,' said Ogotemmêli, 'beating the ground is forbidden; anyone who does so is fined, and the fine is used to buy a victim which is sacrificed on the foundation altar of the village. For this altar sanctifies the ground on which it stands, and the blood of the sacrifice restores to the soil the force which it has lost because of the blows. But the blows which the young men give are not ordinary blows.'

He was silent for a moment. He thought he had heard footsteps stopping in the street. When he spoke again, it was in a very low voice.

'Threshing *fonio*,' he said, 'is like a man cutting the throat of a victim on an altar.'

The European listened holding his breath.

'It is a sacrificial act.'

But how did the blood come into it? By what twisting of symbolism was it possible to arrive at this comparison?

'The eighth seed,' said Ogotemmêli, 'is the symbol of bile and of menstrual blood.'

He repeated the explanation he had given at the beginning of the conversation. The seed in the eighth compartment (gall-bladder) of the celestial granary contained both good and evil words. All that was good in it was extracted and mingled with the songs; what was evil stayed in it and fell to the ground with the grain under the blows of the flails like blood dripping from a victim. Just as in a sacrifice there was a separation of the spiritual principles of the victim, so the songs caught the good quality, while the scattered grains retained the evil principle, the menstrual blood representing the debt due to the earth.

'The threshing of the grain,' he said, 'is like a woman giving her blood to the earth to drink.'

So that the symbolic sacrifice of the *Digitaria* beaten to death had two aspects: in the first place it was paying the fine due for the blows of the flails by night; secondly, it was paying to the earth the original blood-debt of women.

This secondary effect was moreover complementary to the fertilizing action of the good words extracted from the grain. Since the songs, pregnant with these good words, were putting the women in a position to conceive, that is to say, to cease from menstruating, it was necessary to complete the symbolic action by paying the blood debt to the earth beforehand.

Thus the women, during the threshing of the grain, were bathed in an atmosphere appropriate to generation, and all the young men and girls, the hope of the community, had to take their part in this work and those songs, from which they themselves drew strength for future love-making. The fine which they would have had to pay for shirking was intended to punish, not so much the loss of their labour as their failure to profit by the communal revivification of the forces of generation.

The Dual Soul and Circumcision

THE harvest had long been over. The men had beaten down one by one the head-high stalks, had reaped the ears or bunches of grain and allowed the stalks, freed from their burden, to spring up straight again. There was nothing in the fields now but tall yellowing canes. In huge trusses carried on men's heads and in stacks piled on the backs of diminutive donkeys, which they completely swallowed up, the harvested crops had found their way along the streets of the village brushing against the mud walls as they went, to be deposited in heaps in the courtyards and swell the dung-heaps.

There had been a short period, now at the end, when the long dry canes were stripped by naked children, who then ran round the villages brandishing great spears, with leaves fluttering in the wind like pennons. They formed groups of five or six and rounded up the dogs, driving them into blind alleys where they proceeded to beat them, with the result that for a good week afterwards any dog made off, scraping the walls as he went, at the first sight of the smallest child.

These games had now ceased for lack of spears. Trodden underfoot by men and sheep, the broken bits had joined the courtyard dung-heaps. The children meanwhile had taken to a new game of watching for the premature fall of the baobab fruits.

'The uncircumcised,' said Koguem, 'think of nothing but disorder and nuisance.'

The thing was quite simple for him, but for Ogotemmêli the state of childhood was more complex. One realized, as one listened to him, the untiring solicitude of adults for the young, and the feelings of both men and women in presence of what certain sociologists have been pleased to call 'the barbarian invasion', which, by means of new-born children, submerges society every year.

Children are in a sense outside the group. They have their own life, their own paths, their own possessions, their collections of beetles and of grasshoppers with their wings broken by way of precaution. They know the value of a straw, a pebble, a water-lily stalk, a reed. They are naked and unashamed. They are indifferent to danger, but terrified by trifles. They also display a mysterious inclination for death.

'Nothing in them is rigid,' said Ogotemmêli, and he explained at great length that this, like everything else, dated back to the original Creation. 'In order that everything should be well,' he said, 'twin-births should be the rule.'

The source of all disorder was the loneliness of the jackal, God's first-born. Unquestionably the jackal was bad, because his loneliness drove him to his mother. Because of this, in order to avoid loneliness, the Nummo at each child-birth prays to God for the birth of twins. But the Nummo's prayers are not always answered, and that is why he has given two souls to every child at birth.

It had always seemed surprising to the European that the word for 'soul'—to use the traditional European term—was a repetition of a single word, *kinndou-kinndou*, which should really be translated 'soul-soul'.

The Nummo then creates two twin souls for a single being. He is present at its birth in the inner chamber of the big house between the four supporting posts. The woman sits on a low seat or on an upturned mortar; two older women help her. The child is delivered on the ground, which he must touch with his four limbs.

The Nummo has previously drawn on the ground the outlines of two souls shown in human form. The first outline is female, and the second male. As the new-born child touches the outlines, the two souls take possession of him. His body is one: but the spiritual part of him is two.

As to the origin of these souls, and the limitless source on which the Nummo must draw for these endless gifts, Ogotemmêli had no explanation to offer.

The infant then arrives in the world endowed with two principles of different sexes, and in theory belongs as much to one as to the other; his personal sex is undifferentiated. In practice society recognizes in him by anticipation the sex which he has in appearance. Symbolically, however, his spiritual androgyny is still present.

The mother, after delivery, remains secluded for four (five-day) weeks. She then goes out in the village with the new-born child on her back, and for three weeks she carries in her hand an arrow, if it is a boy, or a knife, if it is a girl, apparently for protection against visible or invisible dangers. Note that these two periods of four and three weeks are the female and the male numbers respectively.

During the first four weeks the woman who has given birth to a girl spins cotton. This is a representation of the chief work which the future woman she has borne will be doing.

The woman who has given birth to a boy also spins, but not so much. The idea is simply to show the fellowship of the male weaver and the female spinner.

The feminine spindle at work indoors and the masculine arrow displayed in the streets by the mother of a son are both intended to demonstrate the celestial origin of humanity.

'When a girl is born,' said Ogotemmêli, 'the mother takes her spindle in her hand as a reminder that the granary which came down from heaven was attached to a spindle planted in the sky. The thread she winds is that which was unrolled in the descent.

'As for the mother of a boy, the arrow she carries in her hand is the arrow which the smith held to defend himself on his journey through space. But the two things have the same meaning, for the smith's arrows were pointed spindles, and the one he shot into the granary became the axis, of which the granary itself was the huge-spindle-whorl.'

Thus the actions and objects which surround a birth recall the reorganization of the world; they signify the integration of the new-born child into the system revealed by the smith and by the seventh Nummo. They are a manifestation of human nature, which is made for work.

'But what about twin-births?' said the European.

This far-reaching question demanded a lengthy reply, which Ogotemmêli reserved for another occasion. Later he would deal with the fundamental cult of twins.

The European gathered, however, that when twins were born, each was given two souls, and the same customs were observed as in the case of single births; but there was one important difference: though the period of seclusion was the same, the period of the mother's going out 'armed' was extended to four weeks, making eight weeks in all before she resumed normal life.

Equipped with its two souls, the child follows its destiny, but during its early years its personality shows signs of instability. In so far as the child retains the prepuce or the clitoris—characteristics of the sex opposite to its own apparent sex—its masculinity and femininity are equally potent. It is not right, therefore, to compare an uncircumcised boy to a woman: he is, like an unexcised girl, both male and female. If this uncertainty as to his sex were to continue, he would never have any inclination for procreation.

The clitoris of the girl is in fact a symbolic twin, a male makeshift with which she cannot reproduce herself, and which, on the contrary, will prevent her from mating with a man. Just as God saw the earth's organ rise against him, so a man who tried to mate with an unexcised woman would be frustrated by opposition from an organ claiming to be his equal.

Nor can the individual act normally under the double influence of the two principles: it is essential that one of the two should decisively take first place. The child cannot behave like a responsible being, nor can he be treated as such until he has been circumcised.

He cannot, for example, be given his full title, or establish a cult, or take the remedies which the healers give against disease, or use amulets. All these things indeed presuppose the traffic of forces too violent for a being whose soul is not yet stabilized. But the duality of the individual is not the only cause of his instability; God having made him of dust, man has contracted a debt to the earth, which he must pay in blood. He has to offer himself as a sacrifice on the earth from which he was made: the shedding of blood in circumcision, said the blind man, is like the offering of a victim on the altar, and it is the earth that drinks the blood.

Till this account is settled, the soul is not stable, the individual does not truly possess it. From birth the child is, as it were, attached to the earth by a link called 'The thread of God', which grows from the prepuce or clitoris and enters the soil.

This link is established at the moment when the new-born child touches the ground; it is a link of blood. It moves with the child and enters the soil at his feet; at circumcision it is severed.

'Who then is the earth?'

Ogotemmêli did not give a direct answer.

'Blood is shed,' he said, 'in order to return to the earth what has been lent. But it is not the earth only that receives its due. The Nummo comes to drink the blood and he calls Lébé, who follows him and also comes to drink. But the sacrifice is not offered to them; it is made for the earth and for everything that is of the earth, including therefore the first pair made by God.'

'But the Nummo? And Lébé?'

'The place where the old man was (that is to say, the grave of Lébé), the soil from which God formed Man, Lébé rising from the dead in the earth—all these three things are one.'

The principle which Ogotemmêli was proclaiming was the unity of the universe. The tomb of resurrection was earth: man is earth: the old man raised from the dead was of earth, and it was into the earth that he was thrust alive. Lastly, the one who raised him from the dead, himself dead and buried beneath the smithy, came to life again in the earth.

'But why wound man in his sexual organ?'

'Because in the prepuce or the clitoris resides the soul which must depart; also, because it is by means of the sexual organ that the foetus originates.'

In the womb, he explained, the nucleus of life is a sex-organ, to which a head becomes attached, the body developing afterwards. The sexual organ is the high altar of man's foundation. Thus God does for every being what he did at the first creation; he erects the 'altar' of man just as the founder of a village erects a foundation altar for the village.

But it is not only the body that is of earth. Some say that God formed souls like bodies, and it is on the ground that the outline of the soul is drawn at birth. It seems also that the idea of a debt to be paid is associated with the notion of an inauspicious force taken up by the individual together with his earthly condition. This element has to be got rid of at the end of childhood, and sent back to the place whence it came.

There are, therefore, a number of different reasons for the practices of circumcision and excision: the need to rid the child of an evil force; the need for him to pay a blood-debt, and to pay it once and for all in terms of sex; to these may be added the feeling that, for the sake of fellowship, a man, like a woman, should suffer in his sex.

Preparations for the operation begin from the time of the child's birth and, as it is a question of stabilizing the soul, the family altars are used to keep it as near as possible to the child.

In the eighth week after the birth, the arrow which the mother of a boy carried is put on the altar of the nuclear family. The father cuts the throat of a victim with the words: 'Oh God! Receive this blood and bring forth from it the fortune of my son!'

From this time on the souls of the ancestors, who have come to the altar to drink, help the child to be spiritually assimilated into the family, and impart to him a portion of their strength by infusing it into the victim's liver, which the child is given to taste.

On the day before the circumcision, prayer is again offered before the altar for the stabilization of the soul; and at the moment when the prepuce is cut, the male soul transfers itself to the altar, and remains there during the whole period of seclusion. When the child again approaches the altar after the wound has healed, another victim is sacrificed for him, and he eats the liver; at this moment his soul returns to him.

The first effect, therefore, of circumcision is an outrush of spiritual force; on the one hand the severed prepuce, seat of the female soul, is transformed invisibly into the lizard called 'Sun'. The child is thus freed from the element of femininity. On the other hand his male soul, like that of a victim, leaves his body and takes up its abode in the family altar. Throughout the period of seclusion, which the circumcised boy has to undergo, he is without any element of spirituality, and that which he is to receive again waits meanwhile with the dead. The circumcised boy is himself as one who is dead.

'When the circumcised boy recovers his soul from the family altar, is he completely rid of the female soul, which has departed with the lizard?'

'No!' said Ogotemmêli. 'He still has its shadow, which is like a diminished female soul and which he shares with the lizard. The shadow is stupid, whereas the soul is intelligent.'

Once more the Dogon speculative philosophy revealed itself as a series of actions and compensating reactions side by side.

'The "Sun" lizard,' continued Ogotemmêli, 'is the symbol of the female prepuce surrounding the male penis. Its short tail resembles the penis. It is red in colour, which is why it hides from the light, so as not to be compared with it.' This lizard, in fact, lives in the earth, and is seldom to be seen.

'The lizard,' he said, 'is female; but the back of its body is like a penis. It is a prepuce, but is also like a penis with the prepuce drawn back. Surrounded by this female called "Sun" and round and red like that luminary, which is itself female, the penis ends by acquiring femininity.'

'What is the meaning of the sistrum made of pieces of calabash, which the circumcised person wears during the period of seclusion?'

The sistrum is made of a stick or wand, on which are threaded circular slices of calabash, symbol of femininity, with jagged edges. Children shake them to scare away evil spirits and women.

'The stick of the sistrum,' said Ogotemmêli, 'is the sex organ without the prepuce. The rounds of calabash, in number equal to the number of circumcised boys, represent the prepuces of the group. The boy shakes the sistrum with one hand; in the other hand he holds a walking-stick decorated with a helix of eight coils cut in the bark. The stick is the Water Spirit, who guides his footsteps: the helix is a reminder of the spiral coiled and uncoiled round the sun.'

So the child holds in his hands femininity, water, and light.

Personal Altars

THE camp was infested by animals. At night unknown marauders stirred forgotten dishes, overthrew gates, and fled at the appearance of shadows larger than their own. It might well be that these disturbances were not due to any ordinary animals; but nothing could be done about it. In addition there were internal troubles, the remedy for which was known but never applied.

'If you have been given a cock as a present,' grumbled the European, 'eat it the same day! Or cover it up with a mat with a weight on top! Otherwise it will wake you at four o'clock in the morning.'

Every night for a week past, a cock with a particularly piercing crow had triumphantly defied all obstacles and, long before dawn, would flap its wings outside the walls and fences, with which it was surrounded every evening.

'It is worse,' said the European, 'than Doneyrou's ram.'

The ram, a present from Doneyrou, the Canton Chief, was a tempestuous character. When loosed in the courtyard, he had made straight for the wall of the enclosure, regardless of the rest of the world; then he backed a few paces in a straight line and, with one bound, launched himself in a relentless charge. Taking advantage of a projection in the mud wall, he had cleared it, not as a horse jumps, but like a panther. He had then disappeared, followed by two men shouting and waving their arms and a mob of children who asked for nothing better.

There could be no question of following up this whirlwind. It was not till the evening, the time when all nature subsides into peace, that the fleece and horns appeared again at the end of a rope.

'First he ate the millet at Bâ Biguilou, which is cultivated by the Hogon's future successor. Then he tried Ogo Digou, which belongs to the Hogon himself. He ate the millet. Then he went into Dodyou Oreil, and went straight to Ongnonlou's place, and worried and killed a lamb. He has terrorized Dodyou Oreil all day. Here he is!'

It might have been supposed that the animal would be cut in pieces then and there, but nothing of the sort happened. Human inertia continued to let him out again each morning with the same clamour of shouts and yells.

There had also been minor incidents caused by frogs. There was one who hid in a shoe and another in a soap-dish, who showed themselves in response to a beckoning finger.

There were certain recesses where it was necessary to walk carefully and without a sound so that a couple of field-mice, as small as a thumb, could make their nest in the pocket of a coat. While they were away, the bits of grass and thread could be removed to a sock hanging up on the same spot; but soon afterwards they were back again in the coat-pocket.

'Field-mice,' said Ogotemmêli on being informed of these incidents, 'like clothing. They also make nests in saddle-bags and hanging pots.'

He knew all about their habits and their avoidances, as he did about all birds and animals wild or tame. He brought to light an unknown world, which he was very ready to talk about, having been a hunter for many years.

The Nazarene would have liked to follow him into this world of the bush, where each animal and plant has its part to play, its fears and its passions. But time pressed; it was necessary to follow the main lines of the Ogotemmêlian philosophy, and leave for subsequent enquiries the development of institutions.

In the weather-worn niches in the façade of the house there were placed, among a few wretched objects, clods of earth heaped on flat stones. In some of these a small cup-shaped hollow had been made; others had iron hooks or small pieces of forked or notched wood stuck in them. They were the furniture of the personal altars of Ogotemmêli's family. Their number showed that he had had many children, and that, contrary to the usual custom, he had not destroyed their things when they were dead.

Ogotemmêli had often mentioned these personal altars, and the European was well acquainted with them; each individual has two; the altar of the skull and the altar of the body. The former is made by the father a few days before the boy leaves for the circumcision enclosure. The moulded clod is placed against the boy's head and is consecrated by a libation of millet-gruel while the following prayer is said:

The child is going into the bush,
Altar, receive your water and wood!
Let not the good power depart with the blood!
Let the evil power depart!

The altar is then sprinkled with the blood of a cock or hen, whose throat is cut for the occasion. The liver and heart are taken from the birds and grilled; a portion is put aside and thrown on the clod of earth, while the rest is eaten by the boy.

In the case of a girl, the altar of the head is set up by the father in his own house, when the girl leaves it to go and live with her husband.

The altar of the body is made of a clod of earth with which are mixed parings of nails, eye-lashes, hair, and a few drops of blood taken from the initiate. The father generally consecrates it before the other altar, when the body of the boy needs strengthening as a result of his experiences, or when the girl at puberty is marriageable.

At first sight these two altars constitute a sort of external reserve of personality, on which the individual can draw, and which can be increased by sacrifices and libations. For the ordinary Dogon, sacrifice on his altar of the head is tantamount to sacrificing on his own head, the seat of thought and volition and the most important part of his body.

'When the head is well,' the saying goes, 'the rest is all right.'

Accordingly the Dogon frequently sacrifice on these altars at regular intervals corresponding in part to the religious cycle of the community, but also when the occasion requires it. Illness, defilement caused by transgressing a prohibition, loss of strength, for example by procreation, are all counteracted by the life-giving flow released at the altars by the sprinkling of blood which, incidentally, benefits the sacrificer who, in a sense, communicates with himself by eating the victim he sacrifices.

But this arrangement, which is accepted by the ordinary Dogon, was incomprehensible to the European. How could one offer a sacrifice to oneself? If one detached a part of oneself and made an altar of it, the sacrifice did not attract force of any kind. There was, of course, the force of the victim; but a meal of roast fowl would have the same effect, and would as surely increase the strength of the sacrificer.

Accordingly he decided to ask Ogotemmêli the question which usually arose in this kind of enquiry:

'Who comes to drink the blood of a sacrifice offered on altars of the head or the body?'

This question, which seemed harmless enough, had been the most difficult question to frame in the whole of his ethnological career. For it is necessary to consider carefully the form of a question if it is to yield the information desired. It was in fact such a simple question that no one had ever thought of asking it.

The first time he had asked this question, it had simply put his informant to flight; he was a timid man, terrified of evoking the invisible. Later it had been more successful, and the investigator was able to fling it like a firebrand into the jumble of reticences, falsehoods, and concealments presented to him by his informants. This question produced only two responses: flight or the truth.

For Ogotemmêli, the willing instructor of a European, the question was a perfectly natural one.

'When a victim's throat is cut on a personal altar,' he said, 'there are two who come to drink the blood—the first man created by God and Lébé.'

He went on to say that in a sense the first man and the dead and risen Lébé were one and the same person. But the European intended to plumb the meaning of this subtlety later. 'Why,' he asked, 'is one the head and the other the body?'

'When a victim is sacrificed on an altar of the head,' was the answer, 'it is the force of the first man's skull and of Lébé's skull which passes back up the blood and enters the liver. If the sacrifice is offered on an altar of the body, it is the force of the first man's body and of Lébé's body which fills the liver eaten by the sacrificer.'

Then the two altars were set up in the name of the first man and of Lébé, and not only in the name of the beneficiary.

'What,' said the European, 'is the formula uttered at the consecration?'

'In making the altar of the head,' said Ogotemmêli, 'and in touching the child's forehead with it, the father asks for the old man's help.'

'What old man?'

'The first man created, and also Lébé.'

Ogotemmêli repeated his assertion as to the identity of the two, and quoted the words of the consecration formula: 'Ho! Skull of the old man, come and help!'

For the altar of the body the rite was similar, but the appeal was no longer addressed to the skull:

'Ho! Old man's body, come and help!'

The European's question had been completely answered. But he was only one step nearer to enlightenment. Why the separation of skull and body? Why these personal altars, when the great public altars regularly received at the prescribed dates the libations and blood sacrifices of the community?

'When these altars are modelled,' said Ogotemmêli, 'the story of Lébé is recalled.'

He meant the resurrection of Lébé and his being ejected by the seventh Nummo in the form of the outline of stones.

The altar of the head is made separately from the altar of the body, because in the grave of the old man one stone was found in the place of the skull, and the eight stones and the other smaller ones in the place of the skeleton.

The stone in the place of the head was separate from the others and ranked as No. 9, which is the number of chieftainship; and so the altar of the head is made separately. Copper is added to it also to recall the Nummo's excretion after swallowing the old man.

But there was another complication. Stone No. 9, which the Nummo had cast up in the place of the skull, had had a special destiny of its own. It had become the emblem of the function of the Hogon, priest of the cult of Lébé. Symbolically, therefore, the altar of the head could represent Lébé. But the stones of the joints, which had outlined the body of the risen Lébé, also had their own destiny. They had become emblems of the functions of the priests of the Binu.

'The altar of the head is Lébé,' said Ogotemmêli, 'and the altar of the body represents the Binu.'

So in this cult of self-help, every man had within his reach and for his private use a religious system of Lébé and the Binu, representing in miniature the world-system thrown up in the tomb of the primal field. He had, in short, a representation of the tomb itself in the form of the two clods of earth heaped on flat stones. Without upsetting the social system, or disturbing the serenity of the great altars erected in the sanctuaries, he could take action to protect his own modest interests, manipulate beneficent forces in private, and promote the working of

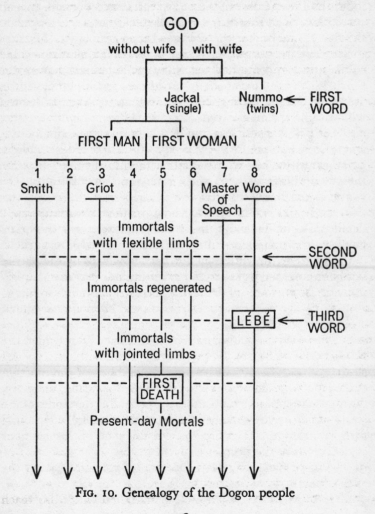

FIG. 10. Genealogy of the Dogon people

the cosmos, all with his feet in the dung-heap of his own court-yard.

But there was even more to it than this. In the light of certain allusions made in earlier conversations, the Nazarene could understand why the person concerned introduced nails and hairs into the composition of his altars, and why he touched one of them with his forehead. If the altar of the head represented the skull of the first man, of Lébé, and of the man of today, and if the altar of the body represented the bodies of all three, that must mean that one identical nature belonged to the first created man, the first dead man restored to life, and the man of the present day. That was why an altar dedicated to the first two contained the nails, eye-lashes and hair of the third. When the sacrificer consumed the victim immolated on a part of himself, he was communicating, in religious reality, with the first human work of God. He was communicating also with the ancestor restored to life as a celestial power, whose body had provided the design of the new order of things. In other words, he was assimilating the life-force of both, and thereby, in his private life and on his own behalf, ensuring the course of this world's destiny.

Thus, it was possible to see how, in the authoritative and detailed Dogon economy, the whole is present in every part; how the great national cults can be fragmented into particles fine as dust the individual pieties, each of which, by the play of symbols, embraced the whole immensity of the ordered world of men.

Appearance of Death

DEATH had not yet figured in the conversations with Ogotem-mêli. All the mythical events relating to the revelation of the three reorganizing Words had taken place while men were still immortal. The death of Lébé, the death of the seventh Nummo had been no more than artifices of Divine Providence; they wore the appearance of death only, and the double resurrection had restored the normal course of things.

For many years past the team of Europeans had known the myths which tell of the entry of Death into the world and the operation of institutions which had had to meet that tragic development. But there was still much that was obscure in the information they had gathered.

The European knew that all events were linked together in the unfolding of universal history, and that the physical end of man existed in germ from the beginning; it was implicit in the fibres out of which the Water Spirit had made a skirt for his mother, the earth.

One notable myth concerned the adventures of the fibres throughout the world. Reddened by the menstrual blood which flowed after the incestuous union of the earth with her son the jackal, they were put to dry on the anthill. The red colour was so bright that a passer-by seeing them exclaimed:
'Is it the sun? Is it fire? What an astonishing thing!'
A voice from the anthill replied:
'It is not the sun, it is not fire, it is something new.'
Time passed, and the fibres were stolen and put to human use. A woman got hold of them, put them on, spread terror all around her, and reigned as a queen, thanks to this striking adornment which no one had ever seen before. In the end the men took them from her, dressed themselves in the royal garment and prohibited its use by women, with a few

exceptions. All the young men danced wearing red fibres, and the women had to content themselves with admiring them.

But the possession of these stolen goods, acquired by force, carried with it its own penalty; those who had robbed the woman had concealed their exploit from the oldest man, thus breaking the tradition of respect and submission due to their natural Chief. The old man, having reached the term of his human life, had, like the ancients, been changed into a Nummo Spirit; but, in accordance with the rule, he had not gone up to heaven and had continued his earthly life in the form of a great serpent. One day when the young men had dressed themselves in their fibres, which they kept hidden in caves, and were on their way to the village, the serpent met them and barred the way. Angry at having been flouted, he violently reproached them, speaking in the Dogon language so that they could understand; and this was the cause of his death. For, since he no longer possessed human form, the language of which was the third revealed Word, he ought to have used the language proper to spirits, into whose world he had come, that is to say, the first Word. By speaking to the men in language that was familiar to them, he was transgressing a prohibition, and cutting himself off from the superhuman world, in which he was now an impure element, and so could no longer live there. It was equally impossible for him to return to the world of men. Accordingly he died there and then.

His death was therefore the result of infringing a prohibition, itself caused by the breaking of a rule. This was something universally recognized; all religions ascribe the loss of immortality to a sin involving a breach of order. But, for the Dogon, how exactly had the disaster come about? What happened to the forces embodied in the serpent-ancestor? What had taken their place?

'The fibres worn by the young men were dry,' said Ogotemmêli. The old man's explanations often began with an enigmatic remark, which was the starting point for a logical development from known principles.

'They were the symbol of the fibres reddened by the blood that followed the earth's incest, which had been put on the anthill to dry in the sun. But they were also the symbol of the fibres moistened at the beginning by the Nummo, which refresh the wombs of women. It was wrong therefore to expose them to heat and light, for they should always be moist to protect the genitalia and encourage procreation.'

He emphasized the need for moisture.

'Damp fibres are refreshing; they ought not to dry. Dry fibres make a woman dry—that is to say, barren.'

The European wondered where the old man's argument was leading, and how he would arrive at the problem of Death.

'Nowadays,' the old man went on, 'whenever a man puts on a fibre skirt to dance in a public place, he moistens it with a little water before tying it round him, saying as he does so: "The long words of men!" This was intended to show that an ancient saying of the ancestors was being followed and a very old custom observed.

'Putting water on the dance-skirt is good for women: it is like moistening their genitalia to help them bear children.'

Where men were concerned the practice had further significance; they were not merely demonstrating an essential condition of procreation.

'When men wear the fibre skirts, it is as if they were dressing up as women, for this dress represents the female sexual parts; furthermore, when dressed like this they represent, not women in general, but pregnant women; it is as if they were moist with the moisture of the female sexual organ.'

Ogotemmêli seemed to attach some importance to convincing the European of the need for moisture.

'When put in the sun, the fibres became hot and dry. They were thought to be the sun or fire. They no longer contained water, for the sun had drunk it all up. But they still had a certain amount of force, thirsty and ready to attract and absorb moisture.'

They represented, so to say, absence of life and desire for life. But they were impure because of their colour which was due to menstrual blood, and no doubt they could not fail to absorb impurity, the force released by the infringement of prohibitions.

'When the old man-serpent abused the young men, the fibres drank in his words; they drank in the breath which came to them and because of them, for they were the occasion of the reprimand.'

What little force remained in the fibres was a small quantity of water, that is to say, of the Nummo.

'As there was a little water left, the Nummo drank the force of the old man. He drank the old man's blood. This force, this blood, came with the old man's words which passed from his mouth into the fibres.'

This was how the serpent died, dried by the fibres and drunk by the Nummo.

Just as the earth's moisture is drunk by the sun, so that of the old man was absorbed by the dance-skirts. It was as if the moisture of the words had been breathed in by the sun from the fibres.

The serpent lay across the path dead. The young men were frightened and fled to the village, from which they returned with the elders. It was decided to take the carcase to a cave, and to wrap it in the fibres which had been the cause of its death. But this was only an apparent solution, though valid for appearances; it did not regulate the invisible. The soul of the old man left the dead body, taking with it what remained of its strength. As putrefaction proceeded, the spiritual principles liberated sought an abode. They found it in the person of a pregnant woman who, for some obscure reason, was wearing a red skirt like those in which the body of the serpent was wrapped. The woman gave birth to a child, who was red like the fibres and spotted like the reptile, and did not become normal until he had been dedicated to the ancestor who had vanished as a result of human disobedience.

The dedication took place in the course of a long period of seclusion which the adolescent child underwent. For the ceremony a great log of wood was cut to the shape of a reptile and painted the colours of the dead serpent, and to this the spiritual principles, for which the child could no longer provide a home, were attracted by a suitable sacrifice. The child himself was attached to the cult which the community instituted in honour of the ancestor.

These events and actions produced great consequences. The European pondered long over them, while Ogotemmêli was absorbed in the serious business of taking tobacco.

With the death of the ancestor, prelude to the death of men, came the obligation laid on the living to provide a habitation for the souls and liberated forces of all who came to die. They also had to find among themselves a child to be responsible for the cult that was established in every case. The world of the dead was now to be organized in all its complexity. It was to lay a heavy burden on the living; it gave the first impulse to art, through the carving of wooden images representing the dead person, and later of animal masks, for animals also perished, killed by the hands of men; it gave rise to personal anxieties by reason of the increasingly intricate network of rules and prohibitions in which everyone was involved. It might be said that the series of errors and offences which had resulted in death had introduced a new order of things, in which the individual, and no longer simply the group, had a part to play. While the general responsibilities common to human nature remained, those offences, in which might be recognized the first notions of sin, imposed on mankind the isolation of the individual, caused endless divisions in society, and reduced to the measure of each man's capacity the burden of expiation or of maintaining the new order.

It was no part of the European's intentions to discuss again in detail the numerous rituals, attitudes, and representations arising from man's loss of immortality. The institutions relating to the dead were well known; but in every case the question of origin arose, and only a man like Ogotemmêli could throw light on that.

One of these institutions demanded attention on account of its widespread occurrence and imposing ceremonial. This was a festival celebrated every sixty years by the entire population, and which, from year to year over a long period, affected in turn every part of the Dogon country. This itinerant ritual, which was called Sigui, started from the Yugo region.

The whole area of cliffs and plateau, from north-east to south-west, participated. It was the occasion of long days of dancing and ritual performances. The collection of the food-stuffs consumed demanded months of effort. Every family in the territory whose turn it was to demonstrate, lived for a long period beforehand in a state of feverish anxiety.

Two essential features of the festival are the shaping of a long wooden serpent out of a single tree-trunk—one of those brought back by the European for the Musées de France measured ten metres—and the drinking of millet beer, the drinkers sitting on a special kind of seat called 'mask-seats', which are not used on any other occasion.

The meaning of the shaped log was clear. It was intended to provide a new resting-place for the spiritual principles of the first dead man, which were still present in the world of men. The wood of the first 'Great Mask' cut by the ancients was of course worn out, and the man appointed to care for it was dead. These two developments threatened the peace of the human race. The spirit of the ancestor needed another home, and his cult required a new initiate. A child had therefore been chosen from among the descendants of the one who had been born with the mark of the dead ancestor. The new child was initiated, together with a number of companions, in the cave where the Great Mask had been put. He was dedicated, by a blood-sacrifice, to the new log, which, to the accompaniment of suitable rites and prayers, had replaced the old one.

The same procedure had been followed every sixty years; and in old villages might be seen, ranged at the back of caves, the tall poles of the past sixty-year periods, the more recent ones still bearing traces of colour, while the older ones were falling into decay and crumbled into dust at a touch.

But, if the periodic carving of the mask and consecration of new initiates could be explained, it was not so with the beer-drinking, in which all the males of the district participated, ranked according to age and sitting on seats of an unusual shape. The actual drinking no doubt had a mystical meaning; it was a general communion, shared by the new Great Mask, dripping with libations, and the whole male population, from the wizened elder to the infant born that very day. The whole community was consecrated to the mask and thereby assumed responsibility both for the expiation of the offence against the ancestor and for the cult of the new home for his spirit.

On the other hand, there had never been any explanation of the meaning of the 'mask-seat', a sort of short crutch in the form of a Y, with the two branches wide apart, often nearly horizontal, thinned down and notched at the edges. The communion was not valid unless the communicant was sitting on this seat, which had been previously consecrated by a special libation.

'The mask-seat,' said Ogotemmêli, 'represents the Water Spirit.'

Once again it was necessary to go back into the remote mythical past.

Before his transformation into a Nummo the ancestor who was the first to undergo death, had had a long-standing dispute with a man of his own age-class about precedence. Each wished to take precedence of the other, and each claimed to be the stronger.

Both belonged to the fifth family, which is now settled at Yugo. When the time came for their transformation they had still not been reconciled and, after being transformed into serpents, they renewed the quarrel, each crying in the language of the Spirits 'It is I who am the stronger!' Eventually, after a struggle, the first serpent killed the other and ate him.

It was at that time that the incident with the young men took place, and the serpent died in a state of defilement. The enemy he had swallowed, and who was only apparently dead, now came out of the body of the victor. As, however, he had been in contact with the carcase and had risen from a dead boy, he too perished from the contagion. But his death could not be compared to that of the other. His conqueror had died impure; he himself died without being defiled, but merely from contagion, as was subsequently to be the case with the majority of men. His skeleton was picked up, rough-cast and made into an altar. A copy of it can be seen, said Ogotemmêli, beyond the Samtigou field near the new village of Go.

The European knew this high red landmark, on which years before he had seen an animal spread-eagled, sacrificed, opened and stripped by birds of prey. For months he had tried to find some way of breaking through the wall of silence erected by the Sangabinou family, the guardians of the mystery. Disconnected scraps of irrelevant information had been the sole reward of his persistence. The Sangabinou elders, bristling and showing their teeth, or turning their backs and shutting their eyes, had closed their ranks in defence of their celebrated altar with its coating of coagulated blood.

The Sangabinou in this part of the country were a minority group of the Aru tribe. They claimed to be the oldest members of it, which was in fact the truth. For centuries they had owned the village of Go, which however they had abandoned for some decades in order to build a new village on the site. They showed with pride a heap of stones, not far from their council shelter, which they said was the oldest altar in the country and had been erected by the Tellem, the former inhabitants who had been peacefully edged out by the Dogon.

'This altar,' said Ogotemmêli, 'comes to them from Yugo, where there is the original altar built in the olden time.'

It was like a tomb. Highly important as it was for the whole Dogon people, it was nevertheless entrusted to a single family. But there was another object symbolizing the ancestor, an effigy of which belonged to participants in the Sigui festival. This was an iron stake, to the top of which a small tongue, like a slice of melon with blunt points, was attached at its centre point.

'The stake,' said Ogotemmêli, 'is the lower part of the Nummo's body in his reptilian form. The flat iron cross-piece represents his arms slightly raised. The head is missing.'

'But did not the ancestor die in the form of a serpent?'

'Yes! Both the enemy ancestors died in the form of serpents. But that was their visible form. Their real form was the invisible form of Nummo Spirits.'

'If they both had the same invisible form, why shape a log of wood for the first and a mask-seat for the second?'

'The first died defiled through having infringed the linguistic taboo. So he was represented in the earthly form of a serpent. The other only died by contagion. Moreover it was he who took precedence over the other, because he was the older. Consequently he is nearer than the first to the celestial form of Nummo; and so in the iron stake he has been given the form of a Nummo without a head.'

'But what about his head?'

'It was not forged because the stake is a seat, and one does not sit on the head of an old man. All wooden seats are made after the pattern of the iron one.'

'Why this form of seat?'

'When a man drinks the Sigui beer sitting on the seat, he is the old man himself. It is as if the ancestor was there. The seat is the body, and the man sitting on it is the head of the dead Nummo. Each is a resurrection of the old man.'

Ogotemmêli seemed tired; he had caught cold the previous night having slept on the rock without a covering. From time to time his voice was indistinct. But he continued:

'The wife of the ancestor of the seat was the same woman who discovered the red fibres. That is another reason why this ancestor was more important than the other. At the end of her earthly life this woman too transformed herself into a Nummo Spirit like all the notable old men. Her symbol is the calabash which every man takes with him during the Sigui Festival, and from which he drinks his beer.'

So, at the celebration of this recurrent ritual, the drinkers, who danced the serpentine movement of the Spirits, were honouring in the new great log the ancestor who had been victorious in the quarrel. They brandished in their hands the wooden seat and the calabash—the calabash-woman, in which they were to drink the life-giving liquor, and the ancestor of the seat, whose head they represented. In their representation of the two dead ancestors they were miming their resurrection.

Returning by the path between the two Ogols, the Nazarene passed in front of the baobab, in whose branches the Great Mask had been set up during the Sigui Festival. He walked across the open spaces where the dancing and the communion drinking had brought the whole male population together. He was lost in thought as he went.

He had long since recognized the significance of this great peripatetic ritual, celebrated by each region in turn. But he had only now discovered the symbolism of the mask-seat that suddenly illuminated the whole of a religious system, poised between life and death and built upon the constant interaction between one and the other.

On the side of life there had been an alliance, an intimate union between two beings, one heavenly and one human, in which one fed on the other. Both had risen from an apparent death and, one by means of the other, distinct in essence but merged one with the other, had shown forth a new world-order. Today both inspired a cult of life and appeared in material form on the sanctuaries; the one, eaten in the form of a man and regurgitated as a figure outlined in stones, could be seen as the sinuous serpent modelled in the sun-dried mud of façades, living and drinking the blood and gruel of sacrifices. He was Lébé, the shining one, gliding through the lanes by night, intent on his task of spiritual support.

The other, as an anvil, its two arms forming a cross and its head pointing to heaven, crowned the pediments; he also lived and caught in his curved embrace the fertilizing rains. He was nearer to heaven than the one who had been eaten as a human body.

On the side of death there had been the combat between two spirits of the same family, in which one had eaten the other. One, victorious in the struggle, had died in a state of impurity and had been represented in his serpent form by a great wooden pole, shaped afresh every sixty years. The other, being of more heavenly form, had emerged alive from the maw of his conqueror, only to die at once. He was represented in the same form as the iron crook on the pediments of the sanctuaries of life, with a body and two arms but no head. This head was represented every sixty years by man himself drinking the beer of the cult of the dead.

In the world of the dead lay an answer to the world of the living.

The Cult of the Dead
Fermented Liquors
The Living Dead

EVERY market-day drunken men reeled along the streets and grunted meaningless phrases over the walls. Most of them were elderly men, and no one took exception to their behaviour or to their remarks. On the contrary they seemed to be regarded with a certain respect not unmixed with apprehension.

When asked, the Dogon replied that it was unseemly for young people to drink too much millet beer, but that there was no objection to grown-up people, and especially the old, coming home drunk from the market or from family drinking-parties. In any case no one ever abused a man who was under the influence of drink, even when he used rude words, which was frequently the case.

Observing signs of amusement on the faces of the bystanders, the European was moved to ask what the drunkards were saying.

'What do people say when they have drunk too much beer?' was the answer, 'why, they say: "The dead are dying of thirst".'

That seemed like a joke. On the other hand, it was not easy to see why the remark should have been regarded as a great insult if it had been made by someone who was sober.

But in fact the matter concerned nothing less than the cult of the ancestors and the attitude to it of the drinkers of alcoholic drinks.

There was, besides, much to be said about the drink itself. In rituals it was reserved for things connected with the dead, 'things', as they were called, 'of the bush'. Ancestors on the other hand, being regarded as living beings, were given blood and millet-gruel. Altars were never deliberately sprinkled with beer.

'If the altars were given beer,' said Ogotemmêli, 'the ancestors would get drunk, for they are living persons. It can only be given to altars dedicated to "Impures", who are living dead.'

This regulation implied far-reaching explanations and Ogotemmêli supplied them all. The European, accustomed as he was to the old man's logic, the rigid ordering of his argument and his scrupulous distinctions, could not help being astonished at the closely-knit system of thought displayed before him every day.

But he wanted to know the underlying meaning of the drunkards' insulting words: 'The dead are dying of thirst'.

He knew that a man's soul often leaves him long before his death, and returns only at the critical moment to stay in the dead man's house during the period of mourning, which is ended by a funeral rite that causes the soul to depart, thereby releasing the family and the community from the prohibitions imposed on them. Great quantities of food and drink are provided, and masks are made. Generally speaking, the scale of the ritual depends on the age and standing of the deceased. The relatives are expected to offer the mourners provisions in proportion to the number of mourning ceremonies of the same kind that the dead man had celebrated.

The most important part of the ceremony is a masked dance on the flat roof of the dead man's house. On the small rectangle of earth, which symbolizes the heavenly places, the whole series of masks, representing the world of animals and men, social functions, crafts, and neighbouring peoples, draws the soul of the dead man into the pattern of its action and leads it away beyond the domain of earth.

Some days later other rites sever the last bonds of the deceased who, from being one of the dead, now passes into the category of ancestors as soon as the child whom he has designated as the inheritor of his life-force has set up the altar-pot, from which he will henceforth come to drink.

All these meticulously regulated ceremonies are designed to put an end to the unstable situation of the dead man who, as *defunctus* in the literal sense of the word, has ceased to function, has done with life, and is now wandering uncertainly in the unknown. It is to the advantage of the community to carry out these rituals within the prescribed periods in order to ensure peace and religious order, but it does not always do so; in fact families have to incur heavy expenses in organizing the end of mourning.

'Families always wait,' said Ogotemmêli, 'till there are several dead, before they celebrate the end of mourning and set up the altar-pots.'

In this way the expense is shared, but as a result there may be an increasing number of unsatisfied dead, whose condition is unstable, and who linger in the world of the living uncertain and mistrustful.

'When left like this in suspense,' said Ogotemmêli, 'the dead lose patience and cause disorder in the villages.'

By 'disorder' he meant a state of moral insecurity in the families concerned which hindered the normal course of life.

'The Dogon,' he went on, 'is much concerned about this matter of the erection of altars.'

He is torn between his desire to satisfy the dead, and the need to extricate himself as best he can from the difficulties caused by the funeral expenses.

But the annoyance caused by this dilemma was not enough to explain either the individual or the general uneasiness. Among the Dogon, personal feelings in matters of religion are almost always the result of external factors. The first point to establish was the reason for this latent discontent on the part of the unstable dead.

'The dead,' said Ogotemmêli, 'are impure from the fact of their death.'

There was, so to speak, an explosion of the individual's spiritual forces at death. The soul was separated from the life-force, whose will and consciousness it was; the vital force itself was split up. It was in fact a composite entity, made up of portions of the forces of its genitors, a 'god-father' ancestor, and various ancestors of the group and the clan. During its life-time it had been sustained by sacrifices offered on the altars dedicated to these different personages. While forming a coherent whole, and thus permitting action on the part of the body that housed it, the life-force, in virtue of its multiple origin, continued to be bound to all those from whom it was derived.

One effect of death was to disperse the vital force and return its component part to the altars from which they had come. In a sense it was this dislocation of force, this stripping of the soul, that constituted the impurity of death. But it must be admitted that the word 'impurity' was unsuitable, inaccurate, and misleading in that connection; there was, however, no other.

Accordingly the soul, being in this condition of anxiety and confusion, sought to recover its balance and collect its scattered forces, so as to regain that 'purity' which characterizes life as opposed to death, to recover life, in fact.

'Being impure,' said Ogotemmêli, 'the dead create disorder everywhere.'

But this disorder is simply a warning addressed to the living, for these disturbed souls are not seeking vengeance but appealing to men to regularize the position of the departed. Being impure and temporarily possessed by death, the departed raise the alarm by means of something which, in all rituals, is reserved for the dead—millet beer.

During the period of mourning, before its cult has been established, the homeless wandering soul seeks to slake its thirst in the fermenting beer that the relatives are preparing for secular or religious purposes. Wherever smoke and steam rise up from the great vats filled with water and millet, there the souls gather.

They alight on the edge of the brewing vat and impregnate the fermenting liquor with what little force they still possess. This force, mingling with the millet and water, gives the liquor its intoxicating property, and is assimilated with the beer by the drinker; it is strong enough to disturb him, though not to the extent of making him impure. There is, as it were, a struggle between it and the drinker's own force.

The ferment of disorder introduced into the beer by the dead, excites the drinker, but his own force resists it and finally rejects what is impure. He casts out the disturbing element by means of words, disordered but effective.

'The drinker,' said Ogotemmêli, 'returns the impurity to those who put it in the beer, but also, and especially, to those who are guilty of keeping the departed waiting too long without altars.'

The words find their way over walls and through doors till they reach the people responsible for the delay. The men staggering in the streets may stutter meaninglessly, sing, or shout insults; but their words are heard by all, and some will certainly have an end of mourning ritual to perform or a funeral account to pay. Even if the words of the drunkards are uttered indistinctly, they are clearly understood by all those careless people whose granaries are not full enough to start the rites and by all those poor people whose efforts are in vain.

The dead are dying of thirst!

When the family conscience is heavily burdened in this matter of delay, every illness and every unfortunate incident is interpreted as a second warning, and an urgent one, from those who are kept waiting. People who fall ill, people whose cattle die, go to consult diviners; and the diviners tell them to end their mourning, and to set up the jars from which the dead will come to drink.

The very fact of establishing their cult means that the dead will receive regular succour from their own people, and from the moment of the first offering they will gather together their forces and draw to themselves all the parts dispersed by death. From impure dead they will become living ancestors.

'Then drunkenness has its uses?'

'The words the drunkards speak move people to set up altars, and that gives satisfaction to the dead.'

'Then it is a good thing to drink too much beer?'

'For the old, drunkenness is a duty; it seems like disorder, but it helps to restore order.'

The Living Dead

But this institution of fermented liquor and religious intoxication was not held to be sufficient to ensure that the duties owed to the dead were kept in mind by the living. Another institution, that of the 'impure', the living dead, provided for the constant observance of the rule.

After the body of the first dead man had been carried into the cave, a copy had been made of it by shaping a big serpent in wood—the 'Great Mask'—and the child designated by the departed had been consecrated as its guardian, together with a number of his companions.

Since a cult had thus been established and a new dwelling-place provided for him, the dead man, though in a state of impurity when he transgressed the prohibition, had now become a living ancestor. Even though he presided over the cult of the dead, his fate had been a normal one. But this impure condition had a decisive effect on the young initiates, who had themselves acquired the same quality. The fact that, in course of time, the condition of the Great Mask had changed, did not alter in any way the position of the children; they were to remain for the rest of their lives 'impure', or, in a sense, dead persons.

'These initiates,' said Ogotemmêli, 'are by nature the same as the ancestor of the Great Mask, but whereas he became alive as soon as an altar was set up for him, they remained "impure" because they were consecrated in the presence of the dead man while he was still "impure".'

When they died they became the 'godfathers' of other children, and so today every family has a large number of 'impure' members, who are exempt from most of the prohibitions imposed on other men, who are called 'living'. They play an essential part in all cults, but they have one permanent function, which devolves on them in virtue of their nature itself. They are also substitutes for the first dead man as he was when he had not yet been given an altar. These 'impure' persons and the 'impure' dead man who became the Great Mask are all one. They are also substitutes for the dead who have no altars. So much so that any good done to them benefits the departed, and, in particular, their participation at sacrifices feeds all those dead persons who are wandering about in search of food. When the 'impure' eat the flesh and drink the beer of sacrifices, it is as if the dead who have no altars were eating and drinking. The 'impure' are therefore like dead persons who are permanently fed in order that they may leave the villages in peace.

'But that is an illusion,' said Ogotemmêli.

He meant that it was not enough to feed and slake the thirst of the 'impure'. It was essential ultimately to provide actual altars for those who were no more and who were suffering from their unstable condition. They must be given cults and promoted to the rank of ancestors.

'What happens to the "impure" when they die?'

'They are like everyone else. When the family sets up an altar, they become ancestors.'

So these men, going about their several occupations, complaining of the price of meat in the market, toiling in the fields, just like anyone else, were really dead and, when they drank, were drinking for the dead.

They only became alive when they became ancestors and when their bodies were mouldering in the grave.

Dancing

MORE than once in the course of the conversations Ogotemmêli had spoken of dancing. In various rituals, dancing, with or without masks, was often the central liturgical action. In the funerary cult particularly, both at the burial and at the ending of the period of mourning, it was the supremely significant gesture.

The origin of the ritual dance went back to the first days of the world, when the incest of the earth, changed into an ant, had given the jackal possession of the fibre skirt and made him the enemy of God.

'Clothed in the skirt,' said Ogotemmêli, 'the jackal went on to the roof of his father's house, believing him to be dead.'

The father of the jackal was God; and, God being temporarily asleep, his son, who was also his rival, thought he was dead. Prefiguring one of the essential actions of the funerary rites which men were later to institute, the animal went up on to his father's terrace to mourn for him.

Dressed as he was in the fibres taken from his mother, the jackal danced and as he danced, he spoke, for the fibres were full of moisture and words. They had in them the first Word revealed by the Nummo to the earth, and it was this water and this Word which made the animal speak.

God's son spoke his dance. His steps left traces in the dust of the terrace which indicated the meaning of his Word.

'In his dance,' said Ogotemmêli, 'he left three tracks lengthwise and three crosswise, representing God's Roof, the inside of his house, and the recess where the altar of the dead is placed. He planted little pieces of wood, placed stones and traced signs.

'The son of God in celebrating the memory of his father, whom he believed to be dead, acted, spoke, and traced out the world and its future. He spoke the first Word, and he laid bare the future of the world. In his anger he revealed the secrets of God.

'For he honoured his father and flouted him. He had taken his mother's fibres, which were full of the Word that contained the designs of the celestial powers.'

The terrace where the jackal danced was the first divining table. Later men copied it in the sand round about the villages.

The reference was to the rectangles of smoothed sand, on which diviners write their questions, and the jackals lured by bait come by night and write the answers.

So the first attested dance had been a dance of divination; it had told in the dust the secrets of the Word contained in the fibres worn by the dancer. It was also a dance of death, for it was to honour and flout his father, whom he believed to be dead, that the jackal had invented it.

Ages passed. Men had appeared on the scene, and the revelation of the third Word had moved heaven and earth. Ogotemmêli had already told how, to the rhythm of the anvil and bellows of the smithy, the seventh Nummo had risen from the dead, how he stood erect on his serpent's tail and how, stretching out and folding back his arms, he had passed through the underworld like a swimmer.

This resurrection dance had led the master of Speech to the tomb of the ancestor who represented the Word. The end was a swallowing followed by a rhythmic vomiting, which ejected into the tomb the outline of the new world-order.

All these marvels had taken place in the primal field, where the celestial granary had descended, and in which the smithy had been set up to the north of it. This scene, these sounds, this movement and action were to be reproduced in the life of men, and to be enriched by new meanings and new movements.

The smith, inventor of the first rhythm of resurrection, found other rhythms corresponding to new dance-figures. Anvil and bellows were combined in this work, but they were soon symbolically represented in the basic concord of instruments: when they had been revealed by the seventh Nummo, drums replaced the bellows, iron hand-bells the anvil, and drumsticks the hammer. At first only smiths beat the drums; but gradually others took their place.

'Beating the drum,' said Ogotemmêli, 'is the same as blowing the bellows, which is a symbol of the sun.'

The sun-drum, like the sun itself, throws out heat and loud-sounding steamy vapour on the dancers. The dancers are warmed in their armpits, which breathe like the nose. The heat enters the bile and spreads from there over the whole body. It is to encourage its action that the spectators cry: 'Hotter! Hotter! Hotter!' The heat is also the speech of the ancestors revealed by the drum. The sweat which flows from the armpits and the body is the ancestors' words overflowing.

Thus inflamed, the masked dancers with their girdles of red fibres become fragments of the sun. Certain movements imitate those of the sun. The *sommo* dance is the nearest copy, and the *gôna* dance is the next closest. When the tall mask called the 'Storeyed House', which symbolizes the family house, the covering of the dead and the warp of the loom, turns on a horizontal line, it is the round sun itself which is seen.

The wearer of this mask also performs another mime in which he kneels, facing towards the east, lowers his pole in front of him, then raises it and lowers it behind him towards the west, as if the head were broken. The lowering and raising of the pole represent the sun's daily course from east to west: the man is the copper spiral which causes its motion. But this was an elaboration of the original figures, which were simpler.

'It was the seventh Nummo,' said Ogotemmêli, 'who taught men to dance.'

He had begun by repeating his first rhythmic movement in the underworld. He danced with the top half of his body, standing upright on his serpent's tail. At first men danced on one spot, rotating on themselves or imitating swimming motions, but these movements were exhausting. Gradually they began to move their legs, imitating the slow walk of the chameleon, who has all the Nummo's colours, that is to say, the colours of the rainbow. Then the movements became more rapid. The *gôna* figure recalls the Nummo's vomiting in the tomb; dancing is a relief, like vomiting. Later men took to leaping, raising one leg and then the other. The leg stretched out, while the body was lifted in the air, represented the tail of the serpent on which the Nummo stood erect.

To get to the dance-floor, the dancers run in Indian file forming a serpentine line with broken segments.

'The zigzag line,' Ogotemmêli explained, 'represents the line of the Nummo, that is to say, the line of a river flowing full.'

Dances first took place, he said, on the primal field in front of the smithy, which provided the music for them. The primal field was the first main square. Nowadays the dance-floor is the main square of the village, situated on the north with the smithy at the edge of it.

So the team of dancers, the orchestra, and the setting all reproduce the scene and the actors of the original dance. To recall the mingled ringing sound of the iron and the muffled breathing of the bellows, small bells are attached to the drums; and when the drumstick, a symbol of the hammer, smites and skins, the roll and reverberation of the drums recalls the noise and clamour of the mythical smithy. The beating of drums is the bellows and anvil quickening and striking the 'fragments of sun' that dance.

And the team of dancers, the society of masks, are a picture of the whole world, for all men, all activities, all crafts, all ages, all foreigners, all animals, can be represented in masks or woven into hoods. The masked dancers are the world; and, when they dance in a public place, they are dancing the progress of the world and the world-order.

Thus the whole complex of dancers, orchestra, and the place where they dance constitutes a picture of the smithy beating out the rhythm of the movement of the universe.

'But the spectacle on the main square,' said Ogotemmêli, 'is transitory.'

He was anxious nevertheless to find points in its favour.

'It shows,' he said, 'the world-order in colour and in movement.'

Had the European seen that, he asked, in the ceremonies for the end of mourning?

'Yes!' replied the European. 'I saw the ceremonies for Monsé, the hunter who died on October 20th fifteen years ago; and I have seen many such ceremonies since then.'

He remembered unforgettable scenes in the squares and on the terraces of funerary huts. He recalled the procession of 150 masked dancers of the two Ogols which had materialized out of the quivering mirage of the sandstone flats and been swallowed up in the dust of the tracks across the fields, most of them girdled with scarlet fibres which parted to reveal shining black or straw-coloured fibres underneath. The men had false black breasts on their chests or strings of cowries conspicuously white. Their faces were hidden under plaited hoods, some of which had a short fawn-coloured plume or a red tuft in the Roman fashion at the top. They represented the young people, smiths, Fulani, Samo, leather-workers, drummers, Moors, ritual thieves, hunters. Others wore masks of carved wood painted in the three basic colours, red, white and black, representing the equine antelope, the deer tribe, foraging birds, 'bush wing-waggers' with high Lorraine crosses, and lastly the long poles known as the 'Storeyed House'.

All held green branches in their hands as tokens of their own freshness. For months these men had laboured in thickets and the cracks of the rocks. They had started out armed only with their knives and hatchets. They had cut, crushed, steeped and woven fibres, bark and stems. They had pounded pigments and applied them with brushes of asses' hair. They had jested about the red colour of their skirts, with which their hands were stained, likening it to the menstrual blood of women. Their peasants' clothing, in which they had started, had been torn by thorns and frayed by use; and now they were returning, a brilliant spectacle in the dun-coloured bush, helmed and visored with the head-dresses and faces of the world of the dead, and girt with the scarlet skirt, symbol of the sun.

On the main square of Lower Ogol they converged in small files, all similarly adorned, with fly-whisks or coloured basket-work in their hands, dancing their special dance-figures or joining in the general dance to the rhythm of the drums and the iron bells, in clouds of dust, encouraged by songs in the common tongue and orations in the sacred language, such as:

Shed tears for my dead father!
The water is falling, falling from my eyes!

On the terrace of the dead man's house, to which they mounted by notches cut in tree-trunks to serve as a ladder, they stamped the ground in the narrow space, their red and black figures interweaving, while in the street the widow with bare breasts and uplifted arms, chanted with streaming eyes:

The column of ants has got up on the roof!
The column of ants has destroyed the house!
Has got up on the roof!
It is the ants which have destroyed the father's house!

The chant recalled, in veiled allusion, the dance of the jackal son of God, dressed in the fibres he had taken from his mother, the Earth, transformed into an ant, when he traced on the mythical terrace the first divination table.

The scene on the main square depicted, according to Ogotemmêli, the order of the universe in colour and in movement. On the terrace the masked dancers, like the jackal, had traced the future of the world.

But these movements and colours were ephemeral; some more lasting representation was needed to depict the universe in operation.

'On the front of the Binu sanctuaries,' said Ogotemmêli, 'you find white paintings of the sun and the moon, the stars, men and animals and material objects. These pictures last. They serve to keep the world in being continually. For these pictures also portray the structure of the life of man. White and motionless, they correspond to the movement and colour which enliven the main square and the terrace of the dead man's house.'

The Cult of Fire

THE cult of the dead was not the only occasion on which the Dogon celebrated mythical events symbolically. There was a mysterious cult, in which masks played a part, which the European had never been able to explain.

Here and there in the fields of the plateau or in the scree, may be seen, planted on suitable sites at ground level or on rocks overlooking areas of cultivation, blackened logs of wood roughly hewn into the likeness of animals' heads with wide open jaws. Some look like monstrous cocks buried up to their necks, their beaks open above the corn; others are like long, distorted dogs, baring their teeth in a menacing fashion.

According to popular belief anyone who steals from a field or a tree protected by one of these black logs will sooner or later be struck by lightning. These objects originated more particularly in a sanctuary in a cave in Dyamini, served by a priest of whom nothing was known.

Ogotemmêli had mentioned these logs when he was describing the descent of the celestial granary through space; as punishment for the theft by the smith of a fragment of the sun, the Great Nummo Pair had hurled thunderbolts at the granary.

'During the descent,' said Ogotemmêli, 'the Nummo hurled two thunderbolts from heaven, the female Nummo first and then the male, and this accelerated the fall of the granary so that the sudden shock of its impact with the earth broke the smith's arms and legs.'

The bolts fell one after the other beside the bellows in which was the fragment of the sun. The smith extinguished the fire with water from his leather bottle, and found two blackened logs shaped like open jaws. The male log was called *Anakyê*, and the female log *Badu*.

But there was another reason for the thunderbolts. As the descent to earth had been organized by the eight Nummo ancestors, the two Great Nummo sons of God wanted to be present at the cults which were going to be established.

'*Anakyê* and *Badu* are symbols of the two Spirits. The smith entrusted the cult to the family of the fourth ancestor. Other families joined in afterwards.'

'But why the logs shaped like jaws?'

'The *Badu's* mouth recalls that of the robber's crook in which the smith had picked up the fragment of the sun.'

Ogotemmêli paused in his account.

'You should ask Aninyou,' he said, 'grandfather of the priest of *Anakyê*. He knows all about these things.'

The European had already questioned Aninyou, a reticent old man of Upper Ogol, and it was after that enquiry that he had decided to get Ogotemmêli to talk about it. He made no reply to the suggestion, and the old man continued as if talking to himself:

'The smith went stealing with his robber's crook. It was in the mouth of this stick that fire began. That was the smith's gift to the world. That,' he added, 'is why the institution of ritual theft was started.'

Ritual thieves were to be found all over the scree and on the plateau. In Sanga every family head was a ritual thief, and a ritual crook was to be seen hung up in a smoky corner of the big house. It was a piece of wood curved into a crook and ending in a wide open mouth; in the curved part was a pair of pointed ears. Along the length of the stick like a mane ran a line of chevrons. It suggested a graceful stylized horse's head.

This object was a reproduction of the stick with which the smith effected his theft; and a family head who was too old to visit the villages on the occasion of ritual expeditions, delegated his powers to a younger man. The latter, with his colleagues, was instructed to conduct raids on small livestock, which were then eaten in common according to prescribed conditions.

The striking thing about this institution was that it operated only on the death of a member of this sort of council. The party of delegates at once went into action and set out for the neighbouring villages in search of unguarded or imperfectly guarded beasts. When a goat was captured, it was brought to the funerary hut, and its throat was cut there on the roof, in which a hole was made opening on to the room in which the dead body lay. A millet-stalk placed on the breast of the corpse led up to the opening and directed the blood which flowed from the victim's cut throat. By this channel part of the life-force of the deceased family-head went back again into the robber's crook, which had been placed against the hole. The stick was then brought to the big family house near the altars of the ancestors, and became the property of the dead man's successor.

This seemed in the nature of a ritual of restoration; in fact, as Ogotemmêli said:

'When anyone becomes a family-head, he receives, among other things, a portion of the life-force derived from the robber's crook near the altars. This crook recalls the one with which the celestial fire was stolen; but that which is of greatest worth is, ultimately, the smith himself, whom the crook represents.'

In all family altars the smith, seventh Nummo and eldest of the eight sons of the first human pair, is present. He gives his force to the new family-head who, at his death, gives it back through the intermediary of the crook. The family-head, during his tenure of office, is therefore, among other things, a representative of the Nummo smith, the thief of fire.

In every village the band of ritual thieves should strictly consist of five, the number of fingers on the thief's hand; but in practice this number is always exceeded, and there are as many thieves as there are families.

The reason for this institution, according to Ogotemmêli, was to commemorate the smith's action in stealing fire at the risk of his life in order to give it to men. Instead of fire we now steal sheep and poultry.

'The robber's crook,' he said, 'is like a hyena, which eats the meat all raw and red. This meat recalls the stolen embers of the sun.' Crooks with red jaws are sometimes painted on the façades of sanctuaries to represent the burning and the taking of bleeding meat. The line of chevrons along the handle of the crook is the path by which the smith fled from heaven.

From this institution there developed a method of suppressing thieving based on the two avenging claps of thunder, by which the first thief was assailed. The thunderbolts materialized in the form of two logs of wood shaped like the robber's crook; they were indeed of the very same shape as the guilty object. They were put in the care of two priests, who made a number of replicas, which they distributed to their relatives, to keep pilferers from the fields and trees. For there was no longer any need to steal embers from hearths, as the celestial smith had done.

The logs were like dead fires, but were still capable of drawing down thunder on guilty persons. The same function was performed by red masks made of bark of the *Lannea acida*, which also represented the dead fires of the thunderbolts which the smith had parried.

In his oblong hood into which his head fitted as a stalk of maize fits into its case of leaves, the masked man passing through the orchards spread terror among the women and children.

There were two sanctuaries in Sanga for these extinct fires, one for the *Badu* fire to the west of Dyamini, and one for the male fire *Anakyé* on the eastern edge of the Guendoumman quarter of Upper Ogol.

The *Badu* sanctuary was built at the entrance to a large cave, much of which was occupied by Binu buildings. It was surrounded by a small enclosure of dry stones, in which was a pile of blackened logs. The building itself was a cube of dried mud too small to hold a man, and on its walls were displayed lines of red and white chevrons.

Anakyé's temple, on the other hand, was in the open air flush with the shining rock sloping to the dip between the two Ogols. It consisted of a cylinder three cubits in diameter and as many in height covered by a flat roof. The door, hermetically sealed, was never opened in the presence of the European: nor was that of the *Badu* sanctuary.

He had, however, learnt from a reliable source that the altar inside each of these buildings had two small cups on it sunk in the earthen mortar, and it was on these that the priest poured offerings to the thundering pair of celestial Nummo.

It was there too that all the protecting logs were brought each year after the harvest to receive new force from a rite, the essential part of which was a representation of the theft of fire.

In Dyamini, as in the Ogols, two masks represented the male and female fires; a man played the part of the smith and brandished a torch, pursued by the two fires. In Dyamini the action took place among the rocks between the cave and a small hollow of earth covered with dry grass, which the man set on fire as he fled, to recall how the fire of the celestial granary, after its descent, spread over the earth.

In the Ogols, a race was arranged between the *Anakyê* sanctuary and a point on the border of Lower Ogol. The route thus ran through the field between the two villages in the hollow where the baobabs were.

The man with the torch started from the sanctuary, and ran down the slope through the stubble-fields, shaking his brand and scattering a shower of sparks and embers. For the smith in heaven dropped some of his fire as he ran, picked it up with his crook, and continued to run, losing it and picking it up again.

On reaching the border of Lower Ogol the runner turned and ran back to the sanctuary, from which he at once started out again. This performance was repeated three times, and all the time the two masks pursued the fugitive brandishing a knife. They symbolized the two thunderbolts launched by the Nummo against the guilty smith, and they never caught up with the torch-bearer till, at the end of the third course, he regained the sanctuary. He had by then made the complete circuit three times brandishing his torch all the while.

'These three courses,' said Ogotemmêli, 'recall the flight of the smith and his search for a way into the celestial granary, where he could hide the embers.' For in this ritual the circular *Anakyê* sanctuary represented the celestial granary.

The pursuit ended when a smith scanned the rock and beat upon it with the iron of his anvil. And the live fire, pursued by the two dead fires, gave life again to the hearths of this world as well as to the blackened logs which protect the crops and the fruit of the trees.

Twins and Trade

'I GOT nothing,' said Apourali with a broad smile. 'I haven't been out of the village; I hadn't the time. And you?'

'I got thirty francs,' said Ambara. 'From my mother's family in Mendêli—thirty francs!'

'*I* went to Dyamini,' said Koguem, 'to my mother's family, she is a Dandoulou. As soon as I got there, I said: "The cow has had two calves!" I got 400 cowries and 110 francs.'

For the last three months a considerable number of Dogon had been in a state of excitement on account of the twin calves of Mendêli. The event had taken place in September, and the news had spread rapidly from village to village all over the plateau and the scree. The prodigy was of deep concern to everybody, old and young, all who could talk or simply say: 'The cow has had two calves!'

For this birth had started an extraordinary movement of the population. Everyone able to walk and speak went to visit his mother's family to bring the news and receive a present in cash. In the past only women were asked for a gift, and they gave it in cowries. Today all the members of a family combine for the purpose, and usually give money. Old men, who could not get about, contented themselves with visiting their married women relatives in the village or waylaying them on their way to market.

But, by being related to a uterine lineage, one is equally a uterine relative of someone else, so that, ultimately, the money received after long toiling along the roads, is given back to others who come to bring the same news.

'One gives what one has received,' it is said, 'and, as one has had expenses on the way, the net result is a loss. As for those who do not stir themselves, they lose because they have to give without receiving. However it all makes money circulate.'

Accordingly because of the twin calves crowds thronged the

roads, getting and spending, not so much in honour of the calves as to celebrate the fact of a twin-birth, the cult of which extends all over Africa.

Most of the conversations with Ogotemmêli had indeed turned largely on twins and on the need for duality and the doubling of individual lives. The eight original ancestors were really eight pairs.

'The four men and four women,' said the old man, 'in their lower, that is, their sexual parts, were eight pairs. The four males were man and woman, but with the man dominant; in the four females the woman was dominant. They mated with themselves: each female part of each pair became pregnant and produced children.'

But after this generation, human beings were usually born single. Dogon religion and Dogon philosophy both expressed a haunting sense of the original loss of twin-ness. The heavenly Powers themselves were dual, and in their earthly manifestations they constantly intervened in pairs. Lébé and the seventh Nummo were a living couple; the ancestors of the Great Mask and of the mask-seat were a dead couple. It might even be supposed—though no Dogon had ever uttered such a blasphemy—that the first misfortune in the universal course of things was the oneness of God.

Actually the birth of twins is a notable event. It recalls the fabulous past, when all beings came into existence in twos, symbols of the balance between the human and the divine. It repeats the child-birth of the first woman and the transformation of her clitoris into a scorpion. The scorpion with his eight feet is a symbol of two new-born infants with their sum of eight arms and legs. He is also their protector: no one dares touch them for fear of his sting.

A twin-birth initiates a series of practices and rites of an exceptional character. It is not till eight weeks after the event— eight is the number of twins—that the mother emerges from her seclusion. At the first-fruits festival which follows, the children are shaved by adult twins, and the relatives put special jars on the family altar; for from their earliest days, these children will be the objects of a cult forming part of the cult of the family's ancestors.

This cult seemed to show that some special quality was attributed to the ancestry of twins. It was a popular belief that their mother had been 'touched' during pregnancy by a Spirit—it would never be called a Nummo, for that was too dangerous a name, too much for a human mouth to utter. The children of such a mother would therefore be essentially different from other children.

But all this was common knowledge, and the European had no desire to discuss all the different forms of ritual celebrated in such cases. Earlier enquiries had established all the details that could be desired, and he was anxious to find out what Ogotemmêli had to say about something which seemed to him to be highly significant—namely the special earthenware reserved for twins. These objects have a peculiar shape: each consists of two shallow round cups, five to six centimetres in diameter, joined together at the edge like a wide open oyster-shell. There was something of this sort in the celestial granary, at the top of the pyramid of superimposed jars placed at the point of intersection of the lower interior partitions. It covered the small container which held toilet perfumes and which formed the lid of the pot of oil, symbol of the foetus, which itself was set on top of the large jar symbolizing the womb. In this position it was placed in a context of generation: it was an invocation to creation by pairs, of which it was also a symbol.

'The two cups joined side by side,' said Ogotemmêli, 'are, like twins, of the same shape and size.'

On the day when the children are shaved, the father procures four double cups, which he places on the family altar, and two small trapezium-shaped pieces of leather, on each of which eight cowries are sewn. These objects are consecrated by a blood sacrifice of eight fowls, and are then made into pendants, which the children wear round their necks as a sign of their quality. The earthenware cups receive regular offerings from the relatives, and later from the twins themselves.

'The double cup,' said Ogotemmêli, 'is the symbol of twins—the same shape, same size, same words; and, just as the cups are equal to one another, so the twins are interchangeable, and therefore,' he added, 'trade began with twins.'

He dwelt on the notion of equality, from which (he said) the idea of exchange was derived. Twins have the right, the identical word; they have the same value, they are the same thing. Likewise the man who sells and the man who buys are the same thing: they are twins. And from the action of exchange between persons he passed to a consideration of the things exchanged.

'Trade,' he said, 'selling and buying different kinds of things, is exchanging twins.'

He meant that the things exchanged must be of the same value and exactly equivalent to one another, whether the exchange took the form of barter or a cash transaction.

'The twins who invented trade,' he went on, 'belonged to the sixth family; they were the first to be born after the descent of the granary containing the world-order. It was their father who found in the grave of Lébé the cowries that were to be used in trading.'

The shells had been placed where the dead man's fingers had been.

'The seventh Nummo,' said the old man, 'put the cowries in the place of the hands because men count with their fingers. He put eight for each hand, because when men first began trading they counted in eights.'

Ogotemmêli had his own ideas about calculation. The Dogon in fact did use the decimal system, because from the beginning they had counted on their fingers, but the basis of their reckoning had been the number eight and this number recurred in what they called in French *la centaine*, which for them meant eighty. Eighty was the limit of reckoning, after which a new series began. Nowadays there could be ten such series, so that the European 1,000 corresponded to the Dogon 800.

But Ogotemmêli believed that in the beginning men counted by eights—the number of cowries on each hand, that they had used their ten fingers to arrive at eighty, but that the number eight appeared again in order to produce 640 ($8 \times 10 \times 8$). 'Six hundred and forty,' he said, 'is the end of the reckoning.'

According to him, 640 covenant-stones had been thrown up by the seventh Nummo to make the outline in the grave of Lébé. So the cowries that the father of the first twins found in the ground when harvesting millet after the second sowing, were a foreshadowing of commerce. But in the very earliest days cowries were not the medium of exchange; on the contrary men began by bartering strips of cloth for animals or objects. Cloth was their money. The unit was a span-long strip twice eighty threads wide. A sheep was worth eight cubits of three handsbreadths each; a small measure of millet was worth one cubit. Later the value of things was fixed in cowries by the seventh Nummo, the master of Speech: a fowl was worth three times eighty cowries, a goat or a sheep three times 800 cowries, an ass forty times 800, a horse eighty times 800, an ox a hundred and twenty times 800.

At first, however, there was a shortage of cowries; the thirty-two shells found in the place of Lébé's hands and feet had been given to the twins born soon after the discovery. Of these, eight had been used by each twin as decoration for the leather pendants which showed their quality. That left eight for each of them.

According to a different account these cowries had first been exchanged with other men for poultry at the rate of four cowries for a bird. Then the fowls multiplied and the cowries, which were living things, also multiplied in the hands of their owners.

For the first exchange the twins took up their position on an anthill. One sold and the other bought. They took the ant as witness of the transaction. It is said also that the first exchange was between cowries and strips of cloth.

It was, therefore, in the presence of the earth's genitalia and of the ant, avatar of the earth, that the first commercial transaction took place. But the objects traded were alive: the cowries were live shells, and the cloth was full of words.

'The seventh Nummo,' said Ogotemmêli, 'had stipulated that the objects to be exchanged should be placed facing one another and the words effecting the exchange spoken before them. It was as if the objects spoke through the mouths of their owners and heard each other on the subject of their own exchange.'

The old man's voice was loud. He sat up straight in the embrasure, not sunk in on himself, as he usually was when the conversation turned on religious subjects.

'That was to make sure,' he said, 'that the objects agreed to it.'

Evidently an important point!

The chief factor, he explained, in an exchange or sale is the spoken word, the words exchanged between the two parties, the discussion of the price. It is as if the cloth and the cowries were speaking. The goods come to an agreement with one another through the mouths of men.

For there is a harmony between the life-force of the object and that of its owner. The life-force of cowries comes to them from Lébé, of whom they are an emanation, and the life-force of Lébé is bestowed on men; so also the weaver who sells a strip of cloth introduces his own life-force when he enfolds in it the Word of the ancestors. This is the case with any object made by man: a little of his life-force passes into the work of his hands and the mere fact of possession introduces into the material object forces that, in a sense, represent the owner.

If anyone has borrowed something which he cannot return, its force, which is the force of its owner, makes difficulties for the borrower.

In the case of purchase or exchange, the owner's force, having received compensation, can do nothing against the possessor. It would even seem that the two forces concerned change places, each taking the place of the other, which averts all danger from the new owner.

Ogotemmêli brought the conversation to a close with an enigmatic sentence:

'To have cowries,' he said, 'is to have words.'

Twins and Trade (continued)

IN the empty market-place where the Nazarene had gone in order to check some of his material, there was a tall stone fixed in a crack and bedded in with chips of sandstone. Before continuing his enquiry into trade, he had been getting information about this altar, known as the Market Lébé, whose custodian was one Allêguê of Barna. Conversations with this personage had not proceeded altogether smoothly, and one of his memoranda bore the note 'Allêguê is an arrant liar like all the Barna people'.

Allêguê wore the usual breeches fastened below the knee, a voluminous coat with sleeves, open at the sides, and a cap with two points hanging down over his cheeks. In the evening light the brown material was indistinguishable from the mud wall of the house where the conversation was taking place. Nothing could be seen of his face but a row of teeth, or of his body except the light-coloured palms of his hands when he opened them to emphasize his assertions.

Allêguê had at first maintained that the stone of the altar had risen of itself on the site 'without anyone knowing who had sent it there'. He thought this information would satisfy the European's curiosity. He added, however, that the same miracle had occurred at Bongo in Lower Sanga, but had not been a success.

'Bongo also had a market with an altar,' he said, 'but business there was bad, and in the end the two stones were joined together in the market near Barna.'

Allêguê would have liked to dilate at length on the obscure procedures, privileges, and organization attendant on the union of these two stones of mysterious origin. It was understood, of course, that the smaller of the two belonged to Bongo, that Barna's rights were much more extensive, and that the elders of Lower Sanga were not such fools as to suppose that they had the slightest chance of prevailing in the matter.

These orations, which sometimes led up to matters of importance, were interrupted by a single question on the part of the European:

'When a victim's throat is cut on the Market Lébé, who comes to drink the blood?'

This was enough to plunge Allêguê into profound reflection, and there the matter ended.

But the European had learnt enough to provide a clue to the observations of Ogotemmêli, which went on from the last phrase of the previous day: 'To have cowries is to have words.'

At the beginning cowries were exchanged for strips of woven fabric, that is to say, for the Word of the ancestors, and especially that of the seventh ancestor, the master of Speech. These cowries came from Lébé, himself offspring of the eighth ancestor, whose number was that of the Word.

The cowries then had made their appearance under the sign of the Word; they themselves were words in so far as they indicated figures, and were thus a form of language. They were means of expression, and perhaps in the first dawn of human relations, they served, on the same footing as spoken words, for exchanging ideas. There may perhaps have reached the Dogon, through those who introduced them, an echo of the use of cowries in distant lands.

Speaking of this obscure period, Ogotemmêli said: 'Originally cowries were used for exchanging words as well as for the exchange of goods. A man who had no cowries was unable to speak or could not speak as much as the others.'

It was not possible to enter more deeply into this ancient wisdom, which had grown threadbare and meaningless with the words in which it had been handed down, but was still real and living behind the blind eyes of Ogotemmêli.

Cowries, being the Word, had to circulate like speech among men, and Ogotemmêli repeated in this connection what he had already said about sacrifice:

'The Word is for all. Therefore it is necessary to exchange— to give and to receive.'

He took up once more the image of the strip of cotton taking shape on the loom, the warp representing the desert lands and the woof being the Word, the light, and the moisture that entered into them.

'The Nummo said that, when someone offers cowries for goods, the vendor dies if he refuses them. That was to compel him to exchange. Just as the strip of stuff gets longer and longer in the process of weaving, and cultivation spreads under the tool of the cultivator, so cowries ought to circulate.'

The force of this law is inherent in the cowries themselves, and it acts equally on the goods and on man. The whiteness of the cowries catches a man's eye and tempts him. Their force enters into him and stimulates his desire to trade.

The purpose of the pendants with the eight cowrie shells stitched on them, which twins wore on their chests, was, no doubt, to give visible expression to the constant appeal of commerce; and, conversely, this association of twins with trade and money makes them eminently successful traders.

They have in fact the reputation of being more successful than any others in whatever business they undertake, and people are often reluctant to trade with them owing to the belief that they have all the advantages on their side from the start.

'If you go to Mopti to sell your onions in company with a twin, you may be sure the purchasers will prefer his onions even if they are not so good as yours. His heap of money grows faster than yours does, and if your business is bad that is because your cowries have gone to him.'

Nobody doubted that the property of twins multiplied much faster than that of other people, and the reason was simple.

'They offer on their altar with its eight cups a sacrifice which ordinary people cannot offer. They say to the eight ancestors: "Here is your victim! Thank-you for yesterday! Do the same with the rest tomorrow!"'

As soon as twins are three or four years old, their parents buy them cattle with the cowries which have been given to their mother by their maternal aunts, and with these cattle oil of *Lannea acida* is obtained. With this oil drawn from the Nummo's tree they are anointed all over so as to display the permanent moisture required to ensure increase—so much so that the cattle which are associated with the oil, multiply themselves.

'No one takes any special care of these beasts; they fatten

themselves and reproduce their kind, while other beasts are exposed to danger.'

This tendency to succeed influences the neighbours. Before going to market the mother of twins presents herself at their altar and petitions the eight ancestors for protection and good fortune. 'Ancestor twins,' she says, 'come and guide me! Go before me!'

Being aware of this practice, very few women will run the risk of following such a mother along the roads leading to the market. Most women avoid her and take bypaths, being convinced that she will take advantage of all the good openings.

This privilege attaching to twin-births is also expressed by the free supplement which every vendor is expected to give to a purchaser who is a twin. This supplement is of little value nowadays; but originally it was much more: the vendor had to give double the amount of goods for the same price.

Similarly, when a twin is given a present, it has to be given in two equal parts, otherwise he would not accept it.

As a result of these customs and practices, a twin, so far as commercial matters are concerned, is regarded as exercising a dangerous power of attracting wealth. Nevertheless, no one would refuse to do business with him and, on the contrary, everyone is willing to give him presents.

'People give to twins,' said Ogotemmêli, 'in order to acquire something of their luck, and because they think that they will receive more than they gave.'

Thus, at the ceremony of the setting up of their altars, twins receive presents of cowries from all their relatives on the mother's and the father's side, who thereby secure for themselves some contact with good fortune. In the courtyard of the father's house the large family blanket, with its black and white squares, in which the dead are wrapped, is spread out on mats. The mother and the daughter who is helping her take their places on it, each holding one of the twins. To the tune known as the 'Chieftainship' played by a drummer all the relatives walk past and deposit their offerings in two heaps, the one on the right being for the mother and the one on the left for her husband.

Everyone gives something to both sides, but a larger portion to the blood relation.

The two heaps must be of equal size, because they symbolize

a buyer on the right and a vendor on the left. The pall for the dead, on which they are placed, is also the symbol of trade, for the twins who started the first exchanges sat on it, and it is made of black and white squares in equal numbers. A merchant who wears such a blanket will be prosperous in his business affairs.

But, though it is connected with trade, the blanket is not money. It is the most general form of wealth, and is not meant to circulate. The worst disgrace a family could suffer would be the sale of this treasured possession; and a man who did not own such an article would borrow one secretly for his departed ones, so as not to let it be thought that the family-group lacked one.

Unlike cowries, whose law is mobility, the covering is stable and immobile. It is, as it were, the end and object of family economy, the ultimate stage in the acquisition of wealth; and at funerals a family will proudly spread its coverlets over the façade of the house, thus displaying its inalienable possession.

The mother is therefore seated on the family's capital when she displays her two children and presides over the symbolic commercial transaction in which two heaps of money balance one another exactly.

She is seated on the symbol of cultivated land, with its multiple squares when, after her own exceptional act of fecundity, she presides at the proliferation of cowries. And the solemn ceremony proceeds in the same way even if one of the twins is not there. A twin is never said to be dead, but to have taken leave, to have flown.

In such a case the mother only is present with the surviving twin. If both die, the festival is celebrated for the child born next after them, who is held to be linked with the twins who came before him.

'He is as it were the remnant of the twins,' said Ogotem-mêli. 'He is called the "ashes of a man".'

For it is important to record the evidence of twin-ness restored, and to spread through the whole group the benefit, even if only ephemeral, of the primordial state.

After having been the centre of the multiplication of cowries, the children, thoroughly permeated by the atmosphere of trade and abundance, are carried to the market about midday, the hour when the market-place is full and the noise at its height.

'The confused noise of people's voices is the voice of the Water Spirits in human form come to do their shopping.'

This is the hour when beautiful girls, whom nobody knows, pass through the busy groups of buyers and sellers and disappear without trace. This is the hour when the Nummo cast their skins and, without anyone realizing what is happening, appear in the baskets of the merchants in the form of home-grown tomatoes.

At this auspicious moment the twins are exhibited to the crowd and to the invisible ones. In front of the market altar the family group halts for the consecration of the children to Lébé and the eight ancestors.

'To the Market Lébé we entrust these twins. May he protect and guide them on their way!'

The relatives then carry them three times round the market-place, thus enclosing groups of people from all over the country within the beneficent area where the circulation of money and goods is proceeding most vigorously.

The central point of this area is the stone altar set up to that Lébé, whose skeleton outline cast up by the Nummo is formed of the eight ancestors, the eight paired ancestors, the patrons of twins. It is they who drink the blood of sacrifices, and with them come the dead twins of all time, including the first twins, the inventors of trade. With them come also the supreme Nummo Pair, who never took fleshly form.

It is under the permanent sign of twin-ness that men have established their centres of trade and commerce.

The Signs of the Zodiac

In the course of those days occupied by conversations with Ogotemmêli and by a hundred other labours, and also during the nights when he considered and arranged his material, the European had been thinking, dimly at first but later more and more clearly, of certain cosmological details which, considered as a whole, caused him some surprise.

The role assigned to twins had not astonished him; he had already encountered several examples of the cult of twin-births in African countries. The ram with the calabash-sun on its head, alternating with a bull similarly equipped, had first excited his curiosity. Rams with spheres on their heads carved on the rocks of North Africa had already caused much ink to flow; some said they came from Egypt, others said it was the other way round. Many had identified the circle between the horns with the sun. All these speculations, which never got beyond the stage of hypotheses, were now suddenly illuminated by new light coming from regions whose contribution to the problem could not have been foreseen.

Up to now the Nazarene had been facing questions of long standing. The story of the scorpion, the result of excision, perplexed him: it was quite out of the ordinary. Twins! Ram! Bull! Scorpion! He thought of the Zodiac. But he kept this idea to himself. He hoped that the system might emerge naturally, of itself, from the conversations on the threshold where the Master sat.

Every day he wondered what revelations would come from the old man bowed down in the embrasure outlined against the dark background. Each day brought fresh food for thought, deeper satisfactions than he had ever known in all his career as an investigator. In the whole complex pattern the idea of the Zodiac was only one item among a thousand, but there was something exciting about it. Had the Africans their own coherent explanation of the symbol of the Zodiac, whereas the Mediterranean peoples had only the most childish notions about it? One could not seriously suppose that the peoples of antiquity actually saw in the sky a scorpion, twins and fishes, and that the position of the stars required twelve magical signs, in which a virgin was placed next to a pair of scales and a crab to a lion.

Twins! Ram! Bull! Scorpion! One day it occurred to the European to wonder whether the twelve signs were not to be found in the celestial granary which the smith had brought down along the rainbow. The granary was connected with the stellar system. It was itself composed of sky, moon and sun, and each of its stairways was associated with a cardinal point and a group of stars.

The twins appeared there, because the smith ancestor was dual, and because, moreover, he represented the male, and the granary the female element, with arms and legs raised supporting the sky.

The ram and the bull occupied the steps on the south side; the scorpion was underneath the floor, which represented the sun. As for the animal called *nay*, which means 'Sun', it was not a crab but a special sort of lizard. He had a place next to the scorpion.

The lion had a good place on the western stairway at the ninth step, which is the number of chieftainship. Ogotemmêli always insisted that the lion was gemelliparous, that is to say, it had not lost the primordial advantage: nor had the scorpion.

The virgin was there only in the form of the female-calabash on the head of the ram or the bull. It was also noteworthy that the unicorn, often included in this sign, had a curious counterpart in the ram, whose second sex organ grew between his horns and fertilized the virgin-calabash.

For a long time the scales seemed to the European to be lacking. According to all local reports, this article was a recent addition to Dogon economy; there was no trace of it in the granary. But the study of twins had provided a ray of light: the double cup with equal values, representing two interchangeable values, was a symbol of the scales. Its place was in the centre of the granary on the pile of jars.

FIG. 11. Signs of the Zodiac

The archer was clearly evident; the smith, who stole the sun, shot his arrows not only in self-defence, but also to provide for his descent. He shot one arrow into the vault of the sky and another at the roof of the granary.

Capricorn or the goat might possibly be represented by the goat of the southern stairway; but this was not very satisfactory, particularly as the goat of the Zodiac often has a fish's tail.

Aquarius, the water-carrier, was in the thread unrolled from the vast spindle formed by the granary. It unrolled itself in a spiral, which was compared by Ogotemmêli to a zigzag line.

As for the fishes, they were there, hanging from the navel of their twins, men and women on the northern stairway.

It seemed therefore to the European that, without presenting a considered system of the Zodiac, the cosmology and metaphysic of the Dogon provided at least a possible place for most of its signs. This place was certainly to be seen in the world-system brought down from heaven under the aegis of the smith, but it was more clearly visible in Dogon institutions.

On this last day with his instructor, when he was to give a general recapitulation, the European hoped to get a bearing on this question.

He had come to the conclusion that the symbolism of the Zodiac was an expression of two fundamental principles— the principle of water, the essence of all being, and the principle of twin-ness.

These two principles were linked to one another from the earliest times; the Nummo Pair, Water Spirits and the first successful children of God's work, were formed from water. God's seed, made of water, after a first failure resulting in a unique and consequently incomplete being, had produced this heavenly pair destined to be the directors of the world.

'Except the Nummo Pair,' said Ogotemmêli, 'no one can reorganize the world.'

The part played by twins had been a highly significant feature of the conversations, and had made possible the analysis of a number of institutions. But, to revert to the Zodiac, the European had tried to explain the square or rectangular figure by which the sign *Gemini* (the twins) is commonly represented. This quadrilateral figure, he thought, probably expressed the quadruple personality of the Pair, each of whose elements has from birth two souls. The number 4 is moreover the number of femininity, that is, of fertility. Ogotemmêli had often said that the ideal pair was composed of two females and consequently had the sign 8, the same as the creative Word.

But, if the twins were water, was water dual?

It was noteworthy that the emblem of *Aquarius* (the water-carrier of the Zodiac) was generally double, whereas the Dogon frequently represent water by a single zigzag line. On the façades of sanctuaries, on weavers' blocks, on wooden vessels, on masks, on robbers' crooks, on the doors of granaries, it was nearly always single. It is also single in the dance called 'chevron path', as also in the woof of fabrics, where it symbolizes the line of motion of water and the Word.

But its deeper meaning was shown on certain sanctuaries and on masks: it separated and at the same time united two areas often depicted in different colours; in it two rows of teeth fitted together. But it was above all in the primordial action of the weaver that its secret was revealed. It was the union of right and left perpetually balanced, perpetually moving forward on the warp.

The symbolism could be carried further; the zigzag line of the woof, symbolizing the movement of moisture in uncultivated regions, led up to the strip of equal black and white squares; eight strips went to form the covering for the dead; and it was on such a covering that the twins had inaugurated trade, in which merchandise is exchanged in equal quantities, as the black and white squares are equal in number and in size.

Twin-ness and water are therefore linked both in their nature and in their symbols, *Gemini* and *Aquarius*.

Enlightened by these last recapitulations, the European turned his attention to the various images and institutions which provided a key to the Mediterranean system of the Zodiac; and even though, oddly enough, the system as such was unknown to the Dogon, he found, in most of the signs, expressions of the two great principles on which Dogon thought was largely based.

The ram, avatar of the male great Nummo, has as head-dress a calabash-sun, avatar of the female great Nummo. The plume on his head is the (male) moon and, in virtue of his fleece of copper, he is also an emanation of the sun. He is therefore, in fact, a pair, and it might even be said that symbolically he displays his duality at least twice: he has two male sex-organs, and he is female twice over in respect of the solar sphere which forms his head-dress and the fleece which enfolds him.

He is also supremely the emitter of water and seed, inasmuch as he not only fertilizes the female principle between his horns, but also urinates rain on the world. His fleece is of copper, and therefore water; and beneath his tail, which ends in a serpent's head, projects an ear of millet; thus he is the moisture of vegetation.

Though he is no longer shown in full on the façades of sanctuaries, he is at least present on the pediments in the form of the double crook of his horns, on which the rain-clouds are caught.

The bull, his double, may be explained in the same way. As for the goat, she is an avatar of the Water Spirit in his ill-omened activities. The fish-tail of *Capricorn* is perhaps to be explained by the fact that the animal is always shown in water.

The counterpart of the crab is the lizard of the kind called 'Sun', avatar of the prepuce, seat of the female soul, which is the twin of the man whose birth, apparently, was single, whereas the lizard itself is dual. Its short tail is like its head and symbolizes the male penis, while its whole body is an avatar of the female prepuce. It may be pointed out in this connection that the Zodiac sign of *Cancer* (the crab) is a pair of figures shown head to tail, which would suit a lizard of the kind described. The lizard is moreover the associate of the scorpion, the male twin of the woman. The scorpion, who is believed to be dual, is the protector of twins, and his eight claws symbolize their eight arms and legs. He is connected with water in two ways: his sting absorbed the waters of the first woman's child-birth, and he is, like the lizard, an avatar of a moist sex-organ.

The lion, like the scorpion, is believed to be gemelliparous. His place is on the ninth step of the western stairway of the world-system, because he symbolizes chieftainship, the number of which is 9. Chieftainship is entrusted to Lébé, the dispenser of rain and director of vegetation.

The virgin is incorporated in the ram in the form of the calabash-sun. The emblem of the zodiacal *Virgo* (virgin) is a sort of letter 'm' with a stroke through the last leg of the letter, which may be compared with the emblem of the scorpion, whose last leg often ends in a point. The first of these emblems would represent the excised virgin, and the second the result of the excision, the animal armed with its sting representing the excised organ.

The double cup, which suggests the two pans of the scales, is the symbol of interchangeable twins; its purpose is to catch the blood and water of libations and sacrifices.

Sagittarius (the archer) is recalled by the smith armed with his bow and standing erect on the celestial granary, which is also his female twin with her four members lifted like a sort of framework supporting the sky. He is connected with water, because he is a Nummo, and because he extinguished the fires launched against him with water from his leather bottle.

The corresponding sign of the Zodiac, the arrow with a ball in the middle of the shaft, is no doubt the spindle piercing the spindle-whorl. The arrows shot by the smith into the sky and into the granary were spindles; to the one shot into the vault of heaven was attached the thread of the descent, which unrolled from the spindle planted in the roof of the granary. The granary itself was an enormous spindle-whorl, which had served as a targe for the arrow.

The *Pisces* (fishes) of the Zodiac, twins connected by a streamer or a duct coming out of their mouths, also symbolize water. They appear on the north stairway of the celestial granary, attached to the Bozo. Fish and men are twins, and the Bozo is himself of water, being the first fisherman of the Niger and the master of the river. The Bozo maintain what is called a 'joking relationship' with the Dogon who traditionally refer to them as 'fish that walk on land'.

It would seem, therefore, that the Zodiac of the Mediterranean peoples could be explained from the point of view of Dogon cosmology and metaphysic. But the European had no illusions about how such an argument was likely to be received by recognized specialists in academic circles. True, there were encouraging exceptions, brilliant minds which, though concerned mainly with classical studies, would regard remote civilizations with sympathy and surprise; enlightened amateurs, drawn to the African because of his art, and bold thinkers interested in speculations of an unusual character, seized eagerly on these problems. But they were lost in the crowd.

Has it not been established once for all that the African has nothing to give, no contribution to make, that he cannot even reflect ancient forms of the world's thought? Has he not always been relegated to the level of a slave? 'Consider the carvings of the great civilizations of antiquity! Where do the Negroes figure in these? Why, in their proper place, among the lesser races! What influence do you attribute to them?'

To which the answer is:

'It is not a question for the moment of influence exercised, but of influence received and preserved.'

But the discussion is futile. One is lucky to meet nothing worse than sovereign contempt embracing alike the investigator and the object of his study. Unconscious hatred is a common phenomenon.

Thinking of this deliberate failure to understand, this refusal to recognize, the European, in the presence of the courteous blind man, whom he was to leave on the following day, experienced a feeling of shame. He would have liked to show his respect for this man who, deprived of sight, spoke words which, as he himself said, were light. He would have liked to apologize for all the contempt and all the ignorance of Europe and America.

But the serenity of Ogotemmêli in his courtyard, among the lengthening shadows of the granaries, was far removed from the world of Europe and from men's remorse.

He was already grieving for his friend's departure, for his journey into the air in what he called an 'alpilani'. He would have liked to know its dangers, so that in thought he might share them with the Nazarene who had passed the hours with him on the straw in his house. He urged him to be careful, as he would have done to one of his own people going out to work in the fields.

'When we go out to the fields,' he said, 'we meet with thorns and serpents and damaging winds.'

A young chicken clucked beside him; he pushed it away with a movement of his hand. Then he drew himself up to his full height in his rags, and gave the evening greeting.

Farewell to Ogotemmêli

THE sun rose on the last working day; at this hour tomorrow the camp would be deserted. The European did not pay his usual morning visit to Ogotemmêli; he was occupied with the final preparations for departure and his last contacts with the local people.

The results achieved by the research team had exceeded all their hopes. The linguistic documentation, patiently accumulated in the course of conversations, journeys on horseback, and lengthy interrogations, revealed a rich language, with innumerable subtleties of expression and a clearly defined structure. The minutest activities of the Water Spirits were described in clear and picturesque terms. Distinctive forms of speech could be recognized in different districts, and in each district villages could be classified according to flexibility of phrasing and subtlety of vocabulary. Within the villages each quarter made fun of the accent and dialectal peculiarities of its neighbour, and a family, or even one man in a family, would be regarded as the arbiter of correct speech.

The young European woman in charge of linguistic research, by-passing informants who were considered authoritative, had discovered that Ogotemmêli was recognized as having the purest speech of the people of Upper Sanga, compared with whom the men of Lower Sanga were regarded as boorish peasants.

Investigation into territorial and family organization, agricultural rituals and the cult of the ancestors, had shed new light on a number of problems.

Incidentally the study of the Bambara had brought to light unexpected cosmologies and metaphysics. There too Water and the Word were the foundation of spiritual and religious life. There too coherent myths provided a key to institutions and customs; and there were many indications that, beneath the various ritual forms and patterns of behaviour characteristic of the African peoples of these regions, lay hidden the main features of one religion and one conception of the organization of the world and the nature of man. In every respect the expedition marked a turning-point in African studies. The results it had achieved were the reward of fifteen years of research, doggedly pursued, each stage developing harmoniously from the last, till the keystone of the whole system now appeared after a delay of six years caused by the war.

The European went over this balance-sheet again as, in the late afternoon, he made his way by the usual route to Ogotemmêli's house.

On the previous day he had given him a cock, bought for a good price, for a concluding sacrifice, to which all the foreigners were invited. With a sad heart he presented himself for the last time before the little door, which banged like a gong. Crossing the threshold he found himself in the courtyard, which seemed to be in a state of alarm. Ogotemmêli was sitting on the hollow stone, where the fowls used to come to drink. He was rating someone offstage, but not violently. His wife was standing on a mortar and looking over the wall between the two granaries into the Hogon's courtyard. His brother was also looking out on the north side, watching the animals on their way to and from the main square.

'The cock has flown!' said a voice.

This serious development dominated the farewells. The European was not sorry; it gave a certain light relief to the painful occasion. When one leaves a Dogon, how can one tell when one will see him again? Men's lives in this country hang on such a slender thread.

Ogotemmêli was on his stone, hands on his knees and face looking down. In a low voice he told his brother to take another fowl. The Europeans were standing in a line along the wall beyond which was the street. No tactless person was looking through the embrasure or any other gap in the mud wall. It was known that there was a sacrifice at Ogotemmêli's, and the passers-by averted their gaze out of deference for their neighbour's religion.

On the woodwork of an old door lying flat on the ground

were placed bands of dark leather and two oblong black objects. They were no doubt part of the hunter's altar which Ogotemmêli had inherited from his father, and which derived, by successive additions of earth, from the primordial altar, which had been the grave of the ancestor who invented hunting.

Ogotemmêli had told the stranger all about this altar, but it was difficult to ask for further information about these objects, which he now saw for the first time. Already the old man was handing his brother the knife with which to cut the throat of the emaciated grey fowl that was taking the place of the fine cock.

That would not worry the invisible. Blood is always blood, and a life is a life, whether it is the blood and the life of a scraggy fowl or a man or a fat bull. It was vexatious only for the humans concerned, because the flight of the victim made it impossible to honour the stranger as he deserved.

Ogotemmêli offered prayer. He called the heavens to witness; he made resounding channels ready for the flow of grace. He paid his debt to the Powers of Water, of whom he had perhaps spoken too freely to the stranger from the northern lands. He asked for a happy issue to the long homeward journey that the stranger was about to undertake. He turned his face to the north, to the land where the Europeans were said to live. It was a propitious hour, the hour when the shadows move upwards in the courtyards and outline the smallest recesses of the roofs, and when the sun, its force abated, drinks the blood on the altars less quickly than the thirsty souls.

Now the sacrificer, having sprinkled the objects with blood, had thrown the victim on the ground. It agonized in the surrounding silence. It was the end. All were thinking of the death of the grey fowl sacrificed in lieu of a better victim, but valid as are all deaths.

Ogotemmêli's brother quietly opened the door of the big house. Over the familiar threshold, where the old man used to sit every morning, he stretched out his hand into the darkness to the cage from which the sacrificial cock had escaped. He remained there for a moment or two as though to perpetuate in the eyes of the Europeans, in that solemn hour, the first causes, the supreme reasons, for the inferior quality of the sacrifice. He pointed to the worm-eaten basket, the prototype of which had served in mythical antiquity as a model for the world-system.

September 1947

This book, finished in June 1947, presents the essential elements of Dogon doctrine. The author had intended it also to be a testimony to his first contact with Ogotemmêli; and it was to have been followed by a series of other works, the material for which would have been provided by further conversations. But it could not be.

At the beginning of this month the author received from Sanga a letter dated August 10th, of which the following are the essential passages:

'This will astonish, and will greatly grieve, you. . . . It is that he whom you found to be the most devoted, the frankest and the most sincere of men, as well as one of the most learned in Dogon customs, your old Ogotemmêli, has fallen into the eternal sleep.

'He died on Tuesday 29 July 1947 at about 2 p.m. It was market day in Sanga. Before his death our millet was beginning to suffer from a slight drought; but on that very day, before his funeral, there was a moderate shower, which saved the crops. You can imagine why. It was because he had a 'rain-stone,' which you must know well.

'Do not any longer expect to see him again! May his name be immortalized in your works!'

This death is a serious loss to humane studies. Not that the blind old man was the only one to know the doctrine of his people! Other Dogon notables possess its main principles, and other initiates continue to study them; but he was one of those who best understood the interest and the value of European research.

He has perhaps left behind him living words, which will enable others to renew the thread of revelations. His ascendancy was such that it may be others will wish to follow his example.

But, however that may be, there will never be anyone with the noble gait, the deep voice, the sad and luminous features of Ogotemmêli, the great hunter, of Lower Ogol.

Fig. 12 TABLE OF

Numbers / Quality	1 SMITH	2 LEATHER-WORKER	3 GRIOT
Sex	male	male	male
	odd	even	odd
Position	right	left	right
Bodies	below	below	above
	lower		upper
Limbs	above	above	above
Granary	below	below	below
	right	right	left
	in front	behind	behind
	N.W.	S.W.	S.E.
Living beings	men and wild animals, vegetation	wild animals, vegetation, domestic animals	animals, birds
Constellations	Pleiades and Long Tail	Long Tail and Orion	Orion and Venus
Organs	stomach	gizzard	heart
Grains	little millet	white millet	shadow millet
Colours	yellow	red and white	red
Drums	kounyou	armpit (small)	armpit
Form of drum	woman's breast	man and woman	man and woman
Language	Toro 1	Toro 2	Mendeli
Wind instruments	mirliton	kan-horn	kan tolo horn
Form of wind instruments	Spirits	ass	ox
Sex	penis (big)	penis (lizard's head)	penis (long)
Form of sex	clapper	spear-shaped	
Fingers	second	fore-finger	thumb
Council House (pillars)	N.W.	W.	S.W.
	left	left	left
	front	middle	back
Regions	Daga	Ende	Mendeli
Technical (crafts and arts, etc.)	smithy, pottery, joining	tanning	poetry, song

CORRESPONDENCES

4	5	6	7 Master of Speech	8 Word
male	female	female	female	female
even	odd	even	odd	even
left	right	left	right	left
above	below	below	above	above
upper	lower	lower	upper	
above	below	below	below	below
below	above	above	above	above
left	right	right	left	left
in front	in front	behind	behind	in front
N.E.	N.W.	S.W.	S.E.	N.E.
birds, men	men and wild animals, vegetation	wild animals, vegetation, domestic animals	domestic animals, birds	birds, men
Venus and Pleiades	Pleiades and Long Tail	Long Tail and Orion	Orion and Venus	Venus and Pleiades
little liver	spleen	intestines	great liver	bladder
female millet	bean	sorrel	rice	*Digitaria*
whitish	bronze	black	rose	green and white
small	medium	calabash	drum	big
little men	lion	parturient woman	iguana	cow
Sanga	Toro 3	Bamba	Ireli	lingua franca
kan koulou horn	?	?	?	?
gazelle	?	?	?	?
?	womb (Pobu)	womb (antelope's foot)	womb (split)	womb (breast)
	egg-shaped	triangular	shuttle	trapezoidal
third	little	thumb	fore-finger	second
S.E.	E.	N.E.	N.	S.
right	right	right	centre	centre
back	middle	front	front	back
Sanga	Yanda	Bamba	Ireli	all regions
dance?	sculpture, painting, death	trade	weaving, music, dress, language	agriculture

SELECT BIBLIOGRAPHY

Calame-Griaule, Geneviève. 'Le vêtement dogon confection et usage.' *J. Soc. Africanistes*, *21*, 2, 1951, 151–162.

Calame-Griaule, Geneviève. 'Esotérisme et fabulation au Soudan.' *Bull Inst. franç. d'Afrique noire*, série B, *16*, 3–4, juil.–oct. 1954, 307–321.

Calame-Griaule, Geneviève. 'Notes sur l'habitation du plateau central nigérien.' *Bull. Inst. franç. d'Afrique noire*, série B, *17*, 3–4, juil.–oct. 1955, 477–499.

Calame-Griaule, Geneviève, *et* Calame, B. 'Introduction à l'étude de la musique africaine.' *Revue musicale*, numéro spécial 238, 1957, 1–24.

Calame-Griaule, Geneviève. 'Culture et humanisme chez les Dogon.' *Rech. et débats du Centre catholique des Intellectuels franç.*, 24, sépt. 1958, 9–21.

Calame-Griaule, G. *et* Ligers, Z. 'L'homme hyène dans la tradition soudanaise.' *L'Homme*, *1*, 2, mai–août 1961, 89–118

Calame-Griaule, Geneviève. 'Le rôle spirituel et social de la femme dans la société soudanaise traditionnelle.' *Diogène*, 37, janv.–mars 1962, 81–92.

Champion, P. 'Marcel Griaule.' *J. Soc. Africanistes*, *26*, 1–2, 1956, 267–271.

Champion, P. 'Bibliographie de Marcel Griaule.' *J. Soc. Africanistes*, *26*, 1–2, 1956, 279–290.

De Ganay, Solange, 'Notes sur le culte du Lébé chez les Dogon du Soudan français.' *J. Soc. Africanistes*, 7, 2, 1937, 203–211.

De Ganay, Solange. 1941. *Les Devises des Dogons*. Paris: Institut d'Ethnologie (Travaux et mémoires, 41).

De Ganay, Solange. 1942. *Le Binou Yébéné*. Geuthner (Miscellanea africana Lebaudy, 2).

Dieterlen, Germaine. 1941. *Les Ames des Dogon*. Paris: Institut d'Ethnologie (Travaux et mémoires, 40).

Dieterlen, Germaine, *et* De Ganay, Solange. 1942. *Le Génie des Eaux chez les Dogons*. Paris: Geuthner (Miscellanea africana Lebaudy, 5).

Dieterlen, Germaine. 'Mécanisme de l'impureté chez les Dogon.' *J. Soc. Africanistes*, *17*, 1947, 81–90.

Dieterlen, Germaine. 'Textes des allocations prononcées au cours des funérailles de Marcel Griaule à Sanga, présentés par G. Dieterlen.' *J. Soc. Africanistes*, *26*. 1–2, 1956, 273–277.

Dieterlen, Germaine. 'Parenté et mariage chez les Dogon.' *Africa*, *26*, 2, Apr. 1956, 107–148.

Dieterlen, Germaine. 'Marcel Griaule.' *Cahiers int. Sociologie*, *21*, juil.–déc. 1956, 177.

Dieterlen, Germaine. 'Résultats des missions Griaule au Soudan français (1931–1956).' *Arch. Sociologie des Religions*, 3, janv.–juin 1957, 137–142.

Dieterlen, Germaine. 'Notes sur les migrations soudanaises au Ghana.' *Africa*, *27*, 3, July 1957, 286–287.

Dieterlen, Germaine. 'Le rire chez les noirs d'Afrique.' 1958.

Dieterlen, Germaine. 'Symbolisme des masques en Afrique Occidentale.' 1959.

Dieterlen, Germaine. 'Mythe et organisation sociale en Afrique Occidentale.' *J. Soc. Africanistes*, *29*, 1, 1959, 119–138.

Dieterlen, Germaine, *et* Calame-Griaule, Geneviève. 'L'alimentation dogon.' *Cahiers d'études africaines*, 3, oct. 1960, 46–89.

Dieterlen, Germaine. 'Note sur le totémisme dogon.' *L'Homme*, *2*, 1, janv.–avr. 1962, 106–110.

Dieterlen, Germaine. *Le Renard Pâle*. Paris, 1963.

Griaule, Marcel. 'L'Afrique.' (In Huyghue, R. *L'Art et l'Homme*.)

Griaule, Marcel. 1938. *Jeux Dogons*. Paris: Institut d'Ethnologie (Travaux et mémoires, 32).

Griaule, Marcel. 1938. *Masques Dogons*. Paris: Institut d'Ethnologie (Travaux et mémoires, 33).

Griaule, Marcel. 'La personnalité chez les Dogons' (Soudan français). *J. psychologie normale et pathologique*, *37*, 9–12, oct.–déc. 1940, 468–475.

Griaule, Marcel. 'Nouvelles recherches sur la notation de personne chez les Dogon (Soudan français).' *J. psychologie normale et pathologique*, *40*, 4, oct.–déc. 1947, 425–431.

Griaule, Marcel. 'Descente du troisième verbe chez les Dogon du Soudan.' *Psyche*, 13–14, nov.–déc. 1947, 16.

Griaule, Marcel. 'L'arche du monde chez les populations nigériennes.' *J. Soc. Africanistes*, *18*, 1, 1948, 117–126.

Griaule, Marcel. 'L'alliance cathartique.' *Africa*, *18*, 4, Oct. 1948, 242–258.

Griaule, Marcel, *et* Dieterlen, Germaine. 'Un système soudanais de Sirius.' *J. Soc. Africanistes*, *20*, 2, 1950, 273–294.

Griaule, Marcel. 'Réflexions sur les symboles soudanais.' *Cahiers int. Sociologie, 13*, 1952, 8–30.

Griaule, Marcel. 'Le savoir des Dogon.' *J. Soc. Africanistes, 22*, 1–2, 1952, 27–42.

Griaule, Marcel. 'The Dogon.' (In Forde, D. (ed.). 1954. *African Worlds*. London, Oxford Univ. Press, pp. 83–110.

Griaule, Marcel. 'Remarques sur l'oncle utérin au Soudan.' *Cahiers int. Sociologie, 16*, n.s. 1, 1954, 35–49.

Griaule, Marcel. 'Symbolisme d'un temple totémique soudanais.' 1957.

Griaule, Marcel. 'Classification des insectes chez les Dogon. Introduction de G. Calame-Griaule.' *J. Soc. Africanistes, 31*, 1, 1961, 7–71.

Leiris, Michel. 1948. *La Langue Secrète des Dogons de Sanga (Soudan Français)*. Paris: Institut d'Ethnologie (Travaux et mémoires, 50).

Paulme, Denise. 1940. *Organisation Sociale des Dogon (Soudan Français)*. Paris: Ed. Domat-Monchrestien.

Tait, David. 'An analytical commentary on the social structure of the Dogon.' *Africa, 20*, 3, July 1950, 175–199.

Zahan, D. 'Aperçu sur la pensée théogonique des Dogon.' *Cahiers int. Sociologie, 6*, 1949, 113–133.

INDEX

Abortion, 144
Agriculture, origin of, 48
Altars, 131-2, 175-6
— ancestral, 93, 101, 102, 136-7, 160, 181
— of Lébé, 116-17, 133, 135
— personal, 162-8
— *see also* Sacrifice
Amma, *see* God
Ancestors, and animals, 127-8
— birth of, 22
— and clothing, 79
— and construction of world, 41-6, 50, 51, 60
— cult of, 174, 179-85
— eight original, 24-8, 30-1, 103, 104, 111, 128
— 'home' of, in family house, 93
— *see also* Binu, Lébé, Nummo
Animals, 35, 36, 37, 124, 126, 144
— and ancestors, 127-8
— 'prohibited', 124-9
— ritual, 110-11
— in sacrifice, 130
— and twins, 127-8, 144
Anthill, 17, 25, 26, 28, 29, 123, 138
Art, African, xii-xiii
Aru people, 175-6

Bambara people, xiii, 8, 217-18
Baobab trees, 56-7, 89, 196
Basket, in plan of world-system, 31-4, 41
Beer, 174, 176, 177
— and the cult of the dead, 179-85 *passim*
Binu (ancestor) cult, 99-103, 123-9, 134, 166, 167, 191
Birds, in world-system, 35-6
Blood, 40, 130, 131, 132, 158, 159, 164-5, 180
— menstrual, 21, 146-7, 169
— *see also* Sacrifice
Bozo people, 3, 36, 215
Burial, 49, 96

Calabash, 106-7, 110
Cap, Dogon, 7, 20-1, 70, 79; ill. p. 126
Cattle, 130
Chequer-board, symbolism of, 111-12
Childbirth, 95, 144, 156, 198-9
Children, 144, 156
Circumcision, 22, 23, 126, 128, 146
— and the dual soul, 155-61
Classes, nominal, 145
Clay, 17, 19, 89
Cloth, 28, 73
Colours, symbolism of, 79-80, 108, 109, 146
Copper, and drums, 65, 67
— and the Hogon, 120-22
— ornaments, 81
— and the sun, 16, 19, 26, 106, 109
Corn, ears of, 103
Correspondences, table of, 222-3
Cosmology, African, xiii-xiv
Cotton, 28, 29, 71, 157
Cowries, 109, 200-2, 204-5
— in world-system, 51-3, 55
Crook, robbers', 42, 193, 194
Cult objects, 101, 102, 110-11, 124
Cults, ancestral, 174, 179-85
— Binu, 123-9
— of fire, 192-6
— Lébé, 115-22
Cup, double, 199, 211, 215

Dances, Dancing, 170, 171, 180, 186-91
Dead, cult of the, 179-85
— pall of the, 73, 74, 79, 89, 111, 207, 213
Death, 123, 169-78, 179-5 *passim*
— of twin, 208
de Ganay, S., 3
Dialects, 7
Dieterlen, G., 3
Digitaria exilis, 31, 38, 145, 148, 149
— and menstruation, 150-4
— threshing of, 152-3
Divination, 135, 183

Dogon people, xiii, xv-xvii, 1–3 and *passim*
— genealogy of, 167
Dress, Dogon, 62–3, 78–80, 83
Drums, 64–7, 187, 189
Drunkenness, 179–80, 183

Ear, sexual significance of, 81, 139
Earth, mother of jackal, 16–23, 146, 169, 170, 186
Eight, as symbolic number, 22, 24, 26, 31, 44, 103, 109, 111, 200–1
— *see also* Ancestors, eight original
Excision, 16–18, 23, 126, 128

Family head, 111
— and ritual theft, 193–4
Fingers, numerical value of, 54–5
Fire, 107, 134
Fish, in world-system, 36, 215
— cult of, 192–6
Fleece, 106, 109
Funeral rites, 180–1, 186

Genealogy of the Dogon people, 167
God (Amma), and creation of universe, 16–23, 31, 138, 140, 159
— as father of jackal, 186–7
— *see also* Nummo
Gold, 106, 109
Grain, 31, 38
— *see also* Digitaria exilis
Granary, 11–12; ill. p. 110
— as pattern of world-system, 30–4, 37–40, 41, 42, 71, 72, 127, 142, 211
Griaule, Marcel, expeditions of, xi
— funeral of, xiii *n.*
— methods of study of, xiii
— publications of, xii

Hair, 81–2
Hearth, 92, 94
Hogon (religious chief), 8, 60, 63, 79, 116–20, 133, 135, 149, 166
Hook, iron, 102–3, 110
House, Dogon, 28, 69, 91–6; ill. p. 126
Hunting, 14–15

'Impure', the, 87, 133–5, 149, 180
— and death, 181–5
Incest, of jackal and earth mother, 21, 23, 146, 169, 170, 186

Intercourse, sexual, 17, 22–3, 25, 95–6, 107, 140
Iron-workers, of the Niger, 3

Jackal (*Thos aureus*), son of God, 17, 21, 22, 27, 44, 140, 169
— and dancing, 186–7, 191
— source of all disorders, 156
— *see also* Incest
Joking relationship, 215

Killing, ritual, 131
Knowledge, 'deep', xiv-xv
— 'simple', xv-xvi
Kourumba people, 3

Land, cultivation of, 77; ill. p. 110
— division of, 76
Language, 26, 145
— of drums, 66
— origin of, 20
Lannea acida, 25, 75, 97, 105, 106, 205
Lébé, oldest man, 48–9, 57, 60–1, 94, 109, 116, 202
— cult of, 115–22, 134, 135, 165, 166, 203, 204
— eaten by Nummo, 50, 58, 59, 102, 116, 135, 166
— grave of, 57, 72, 96, 101, 133, 200–1
Life-force, 19, 87, 88, 107–8, 131, 138, 202
Lines, zigzag, 110, 111, 189
Lion, 35, 211, 214–15
Liver, eating of, 132, 133–5, 138, 147
Lizard, 126, 160, 161, 214
Logs, ritual, 192–5 *passim*

Market, Dogon, 62, 63
Mask ¦ Great, 137, 174–5, 178, 184
Masks, 94, 110, 111, 180, 188, 189, 190
Menstruation, 97, 146–7
Moisture, importance of, 169–71
Moon, 16, 17, 110
— and pottery, 90

Niger, 36
Noise, prohibition of, 68, 87–8, 141, 153
Nummo twins, 96, 109, 110, 131, 132, 157, 187, 192, 193, 196, 198, 200, 201, 205
— and circumcision, 22
— and copper, 122
— created by God, 18
— and dancing, 188–9

Threshing, of *digitaria*, 152–3
Tortoise, 35, 111; ill. p. 127
'Totemism', 99, 125–6
Trade, and twins, 197–209
Transubstantiation, 136
Trees, in world system, 35
Twin-ness, concept of, 127–9, 156–8, 198
Twins, 18, 19, 20, 22, 23, 24, 42, 60, 61, 211–13
— and animals, 127–8
— death of, 208
— and trade, 197–209
— and water, 18, 213
— *see also* Nummo; souls, dual

Unicorn, 210

Village, Dogon, 11, 95–8
— diagram of, 95

Water, 18–19, 50, 108, 138–43 *passim* 171

— god, 100
— lilies, 106, 108
— and Nummo, 18–19, 86, 109, 212
— Spirit, 103, 105, 106, 109, 113, 138, 150
— and twins, 213
— *see also* Moisture
Weaving, 27, 28, 29, 70–4, 138
— as a form of cultivation, 77
Week, Dogon, 62
Wombs, classification of, 144–5
Women, 141–54 *passim*
— work of, 71, 75, 88–90, 149–50
Word, 26–83 *passim*, 49, 135, 136
— and cowries, 202, 204
— and fertilization, 138–43, 147
— and weaving, 73
World-system, construction of, 31–3, 35–40, 41–6
— in paintings, 112

Zodiac, signs of the, 210–17